CA
AN
Edi

Aw   arnered
pra   tional
auc   )e of her
wo   *ties of*
Fic   lernism.
As   ze–
wii   he
grc

T   Shields
her   ›board,'
per   n aims
as a   nd, the
Un   of
Shi   the
nov   her
pla   nking.
An   auto-
bio   )lism.
Wł   uage,
anc   ourselves, the contributors argue that Shields has taken a step
beyond postmodernism by suggesting that we can transcend
the limitations of its epistemology.

Containing several essays on *Swann* and *The Stone Diaries*,
Shields's most popular works, and the most extensive annotated bibliography available of works by and about Shields,
this collection will appeal widely to scholars, students, and
readers of Carol Shields and Canadian fiction.

EDWARD EDEN is an associate professor of English at Hanover
College.

DEE GOERTZ is a professor of English at Hanove

Carol Shields, Narrative Hunger, and the Possibilities of Fiction

Edited by
Edward Eden and Dee Goertz

UNIVERSITY OF TORONTO PRESS
Toronto Buffalo London

ISBN 0-8020-3660-0 (cloth)
ISBN 0-8020-8489-3 (paper)

Printed on acid-free paper

National Library of Canada Cataloguing in Publication

Carol Shields, narrative hunger, and the possibilities of fiction /
edited by Edward Eden and Dee Goertz

Includes bibliographical references and index.
ISBN 0-8020-3660-0 (bound)   ISBN 0-8020-8489-3 (pbk.)

1. Shields, Carol, 1935– – Criticism and interpretation.
2. Narration (Rhetoric)   I. Goertz, Dee   II. Eden, Edward,
1964–   III. Title.

PS8587.H46Z615 2003   C813'.54   C2002-904927-X
PR9199.3.S514Z615 2003

University of Toronto Press acknowledges the financial assistance
to its publishing program of the Canada Council for the Arts
and the Ontario Arts Council.

University of Toronto Press acknowledges the financial support for
its publishing activities of the Government of Canada through
the Book Publishing Industry Development Program (BPIDP).

for Carol

Contents

Acknowledgments

We would like to thank President Russell Nichols of Hanover College for providing funds from the Academic Entrepreneurship Fund to support this book, and also for sending us an essay by Carol Shields that he discovered. We would also like to thank our colleagues in the English Department at Hanover for their suggestions on the project. Judith Nagata of the Hanover College Library was helpful with bibliographical and editing advice; our student researcher, Miranda Bailey, did excellent work in finding obscure literary criticism and interviews. Student assistants Jess Andres and Amanda Wischmeier aided in the preparation of the index. Janet E. McIntosh sent helpful newspaper clippings from Toronto, and Pat Schuring provided timely and accurate typing and manuscript preparation for several chapters. We would especially like to thank our contributors for generously offering advice to us and to each other, for meeting all their deadlines, and for their patience in the long process of vision and revision, writing and rewriting. The anonymous readers of the manuscript and the University of Toronto's Manuscript Review Committee made many suggestions that dramatically improved the quality of our final product. Our editors at University of Toronto Press, Jill McConkey and Siobhan McMenemy, made many helpful suggestions and provided essential support and hand-holding. We also thank copy editor Ken Lewis and editor Frances Mundy for their help in the final stages of preparing the manuscript. Gianna and Olivia Goertz Bennett and Fiona Eden have patiently ignored this project for a long time; Silas Eden has had less to endure only by virtue of being born during the process. And Rick and Melissa are still married to us, which is a testament to their love and patience, for which we are grateful. Finally, we would like to thank Carol Shields herself not simply for her gracious help in the publishing process, but for the inspiration that led us to pursue this project.

CAROL SHIELDS, NARRATIVE HUNGER, AND THE POSSIBILITIES OF FICTION

Introduction

EDWARD EDEN

The morning after Carol Shields delivered her address 'Narrative Hunger and the Overflowing Cupboard' at her alma mater, Hanover College, I ran into a student who had heard her speak. I asked Gwen what had struck her most about Carol's speech. 'She has such a beautiful voice,' Gwen replied.[1] This response reveals much about the issues Shields raises in the essay that begins this volume. Literary critics might interpret Gwen's response as a comment on Shields's distinctive narrative tone, her ability to combine trenchant satire with an appreciation for mystical or transcendent moments embedded in the quotidian. Of course, these critics would be correctly identifying an important component of what makes Shields such a remarkable writer, but they would also have been led astray by what Shields calls 'the crippling limitations that language imposes.'[2] Gwen was responding to Shields's physical presence, and, in particular, to the *sound* of Shields's voice, her rich, mellifluous, meditative, playful, indescribable tones. This slipperiness of language – a deconstructionist would say this inevitable *misprision*, this disconnection between the signifier and the signified – is at the heart of Shields's essay and her literary *oeuvre*. As she once noted in reference to the stories in *Various Miracles* (1985), 'every story turned on some variable of language – its excess, its preciosity, its precision or distortion, its gaps and silences, its blustering and sometimes accidental ability to arrive at clarity or at least to disturb the air with its rhythms and colours.'[3] Shields's sophisticated and self-conscious awareness of the opportunities and limitations language imposes on literary artists is a central theme of her writing, and an important source of inspiration for this book.

The scholarly essays collected in this volume devote extensive attention to these issues of language, particularly in light of contemporary debates over postmodernism and its relation to feminist cultural critique. But in addition to its focus on language, Shields's work continually alerts us to the pleasures and perils of biography – much of her work focuses on the nature of the self, and how that self gets reflected or represented in literary works. While Shields has a sophisticated understanding of the self as postmodern construct or linguistic cipher, she also insists that 'we need to know the connection between the words and the person who makes them up.'[4] Her novels explore the domestic lives of women in twentieth-century North America, finding the mystery and otherness embedded in what in many ways is a narrow, conventional, and restricted cultural space.

Shields herself had ample experience of the narrowness and constriction of unimaginative, prudent, suburban American life. She was born and raised in the leafy, protected suburb of Oak Park, Illinois. Shields recalls the simplicity and sheltered nature of her childhood nostalgically in a number of interviews and essays, yet this nostalgia is always tinged with a critical awareness of that world's limitations.[5] In an interview with Joan Thomas, she describes the world of her childhood as 'prudent ... Prudent parents, careful, conventional. A prudent school system, too.'[6] Aside from the occasional 'bohemian' family and the 'wonderfully liberating shock' she experienced when her 'utterly familiar neighborhood' revealed the surprise and mystery of a family speaking another language, Shields writes mostly about the rigidity and conventionality of her childhood.[7]

Going away to Hanover College in small-town southern

Indiana was not a movement out into the great wide world. On a visit to Hanover in May 1996, Shields told me that in the 1950s 'Hanover was a very repressive place. Everyone had to wear pleated skirts and bobby socks. What I remember best are the saddle shoes. One couldn't wear just any saddle shoes, they had to be Spaulding saddle shoes. People could see you coming down the street, and if you weren't wearing Spauldings, they wouldn't speak to you.' Despite the repressive social atmosphere, Shields remembered many of her professors fondly, impressed by their force of personality and their learning. While Shields was an outstanding student in the English Department, conservative social standards intruded even into the academic life of the College. By virtue of her high grades and excellent writing, Shields had earned the John Livingston Lowes Award as the outstanding English major at the College. Nevertheless, the English Department told her, they decided to give the award to the next-highest ranking student because he was a man and the award would help him in his career.[8] Graduation from Hanover was a liberating experience; the night before graduation, Shields and several of her sorority sisters held a ritual bonfire in which they burned their saddle shoes. 'We were so ready for the sixties when they finally came,' she told me.[9]

Shields spent her junior year of college studying at Exeter University in England, where she met Canadian engineer Donald Shields, whom she married in the summer after graduation. While Shields speaks of the sixties as a breath of fresh air, a liberating time to live through, most radicals would not have recognized her as a kindred spirit. She followed her husband as his academic career took him to universities in Toronto, Ottawa, and Winnipeg, while she spent most of the decade raising her son and four daughters. As her daughter Anne Giardini writes, 'She raised five children, managed a large house and always worked or studied (or both) part time. She made all the meals, did all the laundry, painted the walls and sanded and refinished old furniture. She made Halloween costumes, cookies, pies, and birthday cakes.'[10] Despite this typical vision of a 1950s housewife, Anne remembers recognizing her mother's care to understand and record their domestic lives. Even as a teenager, she perceived Shields's 'focus on the interior, the hidden, the unsaid, the unknown' (9).

While Shields won her first literary award for poetry in 1965, her career began in earnest with her M.A. studies at the University of Ottawa and the success of her first novel, *Small Ceremonies* (1976). From this point onward, Shields has been recognized as a distinctive voice in Canadian fiction. *Small Ceremonies* won the Canadian Authors' Association Award in 1976. While this novel and *The Box Garden* (1977) have fairly traditional plots, in these early novels Shields focused on subjects that seemed stubbornly 'untellable,' especially the complexities of women's experience of work, family, and marriage.[11]

Shields's career took a significant turn in the 1980s. Suffering from writer's block while working on *Swann*, Shields liberated herself from traditional realist conventions by adopting a wide variety of narrative stances in the stories collected in *Various Miracles* (1985).[12] Since then, Shields has published her best and most critically acclaimed work, especially *Swann* (1987) and *The Stone Diaries* (1993), which was a finalist for the Booker Prize and winner of the 1995 Pulitzer. Shields garnered much praise from contemporary theorists when she began to construct these sophisticated metafictional experiments that heighten the reader's awareness of the tenuousness of knowledge of the other – or of the self, for that matter. The gruesomely playful approach to the Death of the Author in *Swann* and the complex narrative structure of *The Stone Diaries* have been labelled 'postmodern' by many writers.[13] The writers in this collection, however, argue that Shields has taken a step beyond postmodernism by suggesting that we can transcend the limitations of its epistemology, rejecting Wittgenstein's and Lyotard's rather cynical suspicion that the world is nothing but narrative.[14]

'Narrative Hunger and the Overflowing Cupboard' effectively articulates the intellectual background of Shields's fiction. This presentation, published for the first time as Section One of this volume, is the organizing principle behind the nine critical explorations of Shields's work collected here. 'Narrative Hunger and the Overflowing Cupboard' seeks to explain the failures of both traditional and contemporary narratives; the essays in this book argue that Shields's own creative work is a series of attempts to address the problems she articulates in this essay. Shields's term 'narrative hunger' is a theory of both reading and writing. The term 'hunger' implies that the reader suffers an incompleteness that can only be fulfilled through ingesting a narrative. The writer's responsibility, then, is to help readers realize their incomplete selves, to help them relate to a world that is incomprehensible, alienating, exhilarating, and strange. Thus reading should provide 'an angle of vision that renews our image of where we are in the world' (21). This theory of reading implies a bond between reader and writer, world and text. Shields's sense of the flimsiness of language as a vehicle of human connection owes much to contemporary literary theory as articulated by both deconstructionists and scholars of cultural studies. With admirable brevity, she is able to explain why language so often seems 'emptied out or else suspiciously charged' (24). As Dianne Osland and Lisa Johnson point out in their essays, however, Shields's narratives do not suggest that language is so fractured and distorted that communication, real human connection, is impossible. Despite a cupboard overflowing with stories, narrative hunger persists because of the failures of writers, readers, and especially literary critics. Shields notes that 'enormous quantities of stories – perhaps the finest stories of our culture – have been lost to illiteracy or lack of permission ... most often: "Woman, hold thy tongue!"' (26). In the essay, Shields identifies forces and practices, some political, some aesthetic, and some historical, that have combined to limit the kinds of stories that make it from the narrative cupboard to the reader's table. In her own fiction, Shields has consciously worked against these forces, exploring the domestic, the quotidian, and the transcendent.

The essays in Section Three emphasize that Shields sees her experiments with language, narrative stance, collage, or metafictional commentary as more than simply a language game. In 'Narrative Hunger,' Shields clearly articulates the idea that it is impossible to know the Other, or even to know the self; it is also clear from her novels that the concept of a unified self is fundamentally in question. Chiara Briganti highlights the elasticity of Shields's representation of the self, contending that by the end of *The Stone Diaries*, Daisy has 'ceased to reinvent herself and has petrified around the edges of her mother's absence – thus both embracing and containing maternal chaos' (195), yet she also insists on Daisy's tie to her mother. The title of Section Three, 'To "Shorten the Distance between What Is Privately Felt and Universally Known,"' stresses that connections like that between Daisy and her mother *do* exist, even if they cannot be proven in any formal sense. These connections take a variety forms. Pursuing Shields's concept of narrative hunger as a theory of reading, for example, Lisa Johnson shows how each reader creates her or his own version of *The Stone Diaries* in collaboration with the author. Dee Goertz shows that the randomness and irony of the maze references in *Larry's Party* create a cosmic authorial joke that highlights the notion that symbolism – and, by extension, language itself – is by its nature arbitrary, even though it is an essential tool for constructing meaning out of our fragmentary perceptions. Kathy Barbour turns an ironic eye on the hubris of literary-critical analysis itself, arguing that despite epistemological uncertainty, 'shared meaning *can* be felt, understood non-verbally, through a gradual build-up of shared experience, and through goodwill and willing perception' (275). It is through these essentially human relations that readers and writers can help to assuage the world's narrative hunger.

The essays in this collection begin a critical conversation on several works by Shields that have been given short shrift in the literature, especially *Small Ceremonies*, *The Republic of Love*, and *Larry's Party*. However, the essays in this collection also make an important contribution to scholarship on Shields in emphasizing her creative formal experiments and her transcendence of contemporary suspicions about narrative. Much of the best recent scholarship, especially that of Winifred Mellor, David Williams, and Simone Vauthier, focuses on Shields's use of postmodernist strategies such as 'disruptions,' metafictional games, collage, and shifts in narrative stance that undermine the stability of the speaking subject.[15] Other writers emphasize Shields's focus on the lives of ordinary women, on the realities of work, and on the intricacies of daily rituals – in short, they identify her with the realist tradition.[16] Scholars interested in these approaches will find nearly all of the extant scholarship on Shields summarized in Faye Hammill's annotated bibliography, which forms Section Four of this volume. Collectively, the essays in this book synthesize previous scholarship, showing how Shields uses the techniques of experimental fiction to tell stories that lie at the heart of our culture, rather than in its margins. In the process, Shields finds a way past what Patricia Waugh calls 'the generally apocalyptic vision of much postmodern thought'[17] by affirming the ties that bind reader and writer, world and text, language and the real world.

While much of the argument of this book, then, places Shields's work in the context of current ideas about literature, we also seek to establish Shields's place in the broader sweep of literary history. James Atlas's claim that 'she *is* our Jane Austen' seems trite, but it helps us begin to locate Shields in the canon of world literature in English.[18] Like Austen, Charlotte Brontë, George Eliot, and Henry James, Shields places a high priority on the interior life, especially the subtleties of how language both separates and unites people in their everyday experience. In addition, Shields represents the real lives of everyday people, not neglecting the realities of work, home, and social relations. Contemporary North American writers such as Anne Tyler, Alice Munro, and John Updike have created similar fictional worlds. While these affinities place Shields squarely in the tradition of the realist novel, her best work –

Swann, Various Miracles, and *The Stone Diaries* – draws also upon a tradition of metafictional experimentation that runs from Sterne through Woolf and Joyce to contemporary writers such as Kundera, Barthelme, and Pynchon. Like Margaret Atwood, Louise Erdrich, Jeanette Winterson, or Toni Morrison, however, Shields does not practise this formal experimentation simply for its own sake. By combining the concerns of the traditional realist novel with the formal experimentation currently associated with postmodernism, Shields makes a distinctive contribution to contemporary world literature, freeing the realist novel from 'the rigidities of genre,' opening it up to new forms of narrative play and new opportunities to construct stories of moral consequence.

The voice of Tom Avery, in *The Republic of Love*, is 'a slidy tenor with pliant honeyed bands of laughter'; it is 'the voice of a healthy and optimistic human being who if he has dark visions keeps them to himself.'[19] We cannot accuse Carol Shields of keeping her visions to herself; she has millions of readers in places ranging from Norway to Australia. Nonetheless, it seems to me that her voice is fundamentally healthy. She is certainly aware of the dark visions that beset all people at one time or another, but she is also aware of, and insistent that we not forget, the beautiful, the miraculous, the transcendent moments embedded in everyday experience. The essays in this volume seek to explain both the complexity and the beauty of Shields's accomplishment; collectively, we look forward to an extended conversation with future critics on the nature and meaning of narrative art, and the contribution Shields in particular has made to the genre.

Notes

1 I'd like to thank Gwen Amman, Hanover College class of 2000, for permission to quote her. Shields's presentation, given while she was a visiting scholar at Hanover, was delivered in the Fitzgibbon Recital Hall of the Lynn Center for Fine Arts on

26 September 1996. A transcript of the talk, which differs in some respects from the essay published in this volume, is available in the Hanover College archives. Shields was awarded an honorary Doctor of Humane Letters degree from Hanover College in May 1996.

2 Carol Shields, 'Narrative Hunger and the Overflowing Cupboard,' p. 24 (in this volume). Further references will be made parenthetically.

3 Carol Shields, 'Arriving Late: Starting Over,' in *How Stories Mean*, ed. John Metcalf and J.R. Struthers (Erin, ON: Porcupine's Quill, 1993), 250.

4 Carol Shields, 'A Likely Story: A Conversation with Carol Shields,' interview by Katie Bolick, *Atlantic Unbound* 283.1 (Jan. 1999), http://www.theatlantic.com/unbound/factfict/ff9901.htm (consulted 3 Sept. 2000).

5 For biographical information on Shields's childhood, see Carol Shields, 'Thinking Back through Our Mothers: Tradition in Canadian Women's Writing,' in *Re(dis)covering Our Foremothers*, ed. Lorraine McMullen (Ottawa: U of Ottawa P, 1990): 9–13; Bolick, 'A Likely Story'; Abby Werlock, *Carol Shields's 'The Stone Diaries'* (New York: Continuum, 2001), chapter 1; Mel Gussow, 'A Celebrator of the Little Things,' *New York Times*, 10 May 1995, p. B2; Giles Smith, '"When I Read Books, I Certainly Don't Read for the Plot": An Interview with Carol Shields,' *The Independent*, 3 July 1995, Supplement, pp. 4–5; Joan Thomas, '"Writing Must Come Out of What Passionately Interests Us. Nothing Else Will Do": An Epistolary Interview with Carol Shields,' *Prairie Fire* 16.1 (Spring 1995): 121–30; Shields's untitled essay in *For the Love of Books: 115 Celebrated Writers on the Books They Love Most*, ed. Ronald Schwartz (New York: Grosset, 1999), 243–5; and Andrew Marshall, 'Eight Hundred Women Heard My Voice,' *The Independent*, 9 Sept. 1997, Tabloid, p. 10.

6 Thomas, 122.

7 Thomas, 126.

8 Shields told this story to the English Department at Hanover during a dinner in September 1996. More information about Shields's college career is available in Kent Thompson, 'Reti-

cence in Carol Shields,' *Room of One's Own* 13.1/2 (1989): 69–76. Thompson was Shields's classmate at Hanover and is also a Canadian novelist and academic.

9 A rather quirky example of Hanover's patriarchal atmosphere in the 1950s later becomes significant in *The Stone Diaries*. Technically, Shields did not graduate from Hanover College, but from the Long College for Women. Early in the twentieth century, a Hanover trustee objected to college education of women and led an effort to return the College to an all-male institution. As a result of conflict within the board of trustees, Hanover established the Long College for Women, named after Henry C. Long, a major donor to the College who *did* support women's education. Long College for Women was a fictional construct; female students lived on the same campus and attended the same classes as men throughout the period of its existence. The only public manifestation of the Long College for Women was that female graduates of the College between the 1930s and the early 1960s received diplomas from the Long College for Women. In *The Stone Diaries*, Daisy Goodwill attends Long College for Women, making her a fictional graduate of the same fictional college from which Shields herself graduated. A similar kind of association arises in the incident in which Warren Flett reads one of Daisy's college essays on Camillo Cavour – an essay very similar to one Shields recalls writing in an interview.

10 Anne Giardini, 'Reading My Mother,' *Prairie Fire* 16.1 (Spring 1995): 9. Further references will be made parenthetically.

11 The term 'tellability' comes from Mary Louise Pratt, *Toward a Speech Act Theory of Literary Discourse* (Bloomington: Indiana UP, 1977). Pratt explains that writers do not see events as stories – potential narratives – unless they contain something 'unusual, contrary to expectations, or otherwise problematic' (136). As Shields notes in 'Narrative Hunger and the Overflowing Cupboard,' happily married lives are the most 'untellable' of all in our culture: 'Couples who have good sense, who discuss and resolve their differences and care deeply about their bonds of loyalty, are clearly as simple-minded and unimaginative as their creator. There they sit with their hobbies and their wallpaper

and their cups of filtered coffee, finishing each other's sentences and nodding agreement. She sends his winter coat to the cleaners and worries about his asthma. He continues to find her ageing body erotic, and he is also extremely fond of her way with grilled peppers. This is all very well, but what can be done with folks so narratively unpromising?' (33).

12   Shields describes this in an interview with Harvey De Roo, 'A Little like Flying: An Interview with Carol Shields,' *West Coast Review* 23.3 (Winter 1988): 40–1.

13   For analysis of *The Stone Diaries* as a postmodernist text, see Winifred M. Mellor, '"The Simple Container of Our Existence": Narrative Ambiguity in Carol Shields's *The Stone Diaries*,' *Studies in Canadian Literature* 20 (Summer 1995): 96–110; Gordon E. Slethaug, '"The Coded Dots of Life": Carol Shields's Diaries and Stones,' *Canadian Literature* 156 (Spring 1998): 59–81; Simone Vauthier, 'Ruptures in Carol Shields's *The Stone Diaries*,' *Anglophonia: French Journal of English Studies* 1 (1997): 177–92; and David Williams, 'Re-imagining a Stone Angel: The Absent Autobiographer of *The Stone Diaries*,' in *O Canada: Essays on Canadian Literature and Culture*, ed. Jørn Carlsen (Aarhus, Denmark: Aarhus UP, 1995), 126–41.

14   In *The Postmodern Condition* (Minneapolis: U of Minnesota P, 1984), Jean-François Lyotard identifies the 'crisis of narratives' (xxiii) as the constitutive element of postmodernism. Lyotard does not *deny* the existence of reality, but he certainly does not believe in it either: 'there is no reality unless testified by a consensus between partners over a certain knowledge and certain commitments' (77), he writes, implying that there is no reality except for a reality constituted by narrative. Lyotard also argues that 'science and industry are no more free of the suspicion which concerns reality than are art and writing' (76). Lyotard is only one of many postmodernists who suggest that language might be the only reality.

15   See note 13 above. See also Simone Vauthier's several articles on short stories from *Various Miracles*, and a number of articles on *Swann*, including Brian Johnson, 'Necessary Illusions: Foucault's Author Function in Carol Shields's *Swann*,' *Prairie Fire* 16.1

(Spring 1995): 56–70, and Barbara Godard, 'Sleuthing: Feminists Re/writing the Detective Novel,' *Signature: Journal of Theory and Canadian Literature* 1 (Summer 1989): 45–70.

16 For readings of Shields as a domestic or realist writer, see Laura Groening, 'Still in the Kitchen: The Art of Carol Shields,' *Canadian Forum*, Jan./Feb. 1991, pp. 14–17; Abby Werlock, 'Canadian Identity and Women's Voices: The Fiction of Sandra Birdsell and Carol Shields,' in *Canadian Women Writing Fiction*, ed. Mickey Pearlman (Jackson: UP of Mississippi, 1993), 126–41; and David Williamson, 'Seven Steps to Point-of-View Perfection,' *Prairie Fire* 16.1 (Spring 1995): 105–14.

17 Patricia Waugh, 'Stalemates? Feminists, Postmodernists and Unfinished Issues in Modern Aesthetics,' in *The Politics of Pleasure: Aesthetics and Cultural Theory*, ed. Stephan Regan (Buckingham: Open UP, 1992), 178.

18 Quoted in Claire Whitcomb, 'Plainly Jane,' *Victoria*, June 2001, p. 32.

19 Carol Shields, *The Republic of Love* (New York: Penguin, 1994), 267, 138.

SECTION ONE

Narrative Hunger and the Overflowing Cupboard

CAROL SHIELDS

Narrative Hunger and the Overflowing Cupboard[1]

CAROL SHIELDS

Someone asked me not long ago what I did when I was not writing or reading. A good question, I thought, and naturally I pondered it. Of course, much that I do can be filed under the title of what Isak Dinesen calls 'this business of being a woman.' I cook, shop, write notes, keep in contact with my family. Other than that, I mostly walk around and think about narrative, about the telling of stories, what they mean, these stories – and why we need them.

Tonight I want to talk about the stories that sustain our culture and how they correspond or fail to correspond with our lives, about our narrative hunger and the overflowing cupboard, the whole world, that is.

I remember some years ago, when I was in France, walking past a street person sitting on his patch of pavement with a sign around his neck, which said 'J'ai faim' (I am hungry). When I saw him again, an hour later, he was eating an enormous ham sandwich, and it occurred to me that the sign around his neck should have been corrected to read 'J'ai eu faim' (I was hungry). Here, to be sure, was a man momentarily satisfied but conscious of further hunger to come, and gesturing also, perhaps, toward an enlarged or existential hunger, toward a coded message, a threaded notation, an orderly account or story that would serve as a witness to his place in the world.

For if literature is not about the world, what is it about? Luckily all the world is up for sale. Unluckily, a good part of the world falls through the narrative sieve, washing through the fingers of the recorders' hands and becoming lost. It is this simultaneous abundance and loss that I want to think about: how, while the narrative cupboard is bursting, the reader is often left fed, but still hungry. There is so much that lies out of reach, so much that touches only tangentially on our lives, or confronts us with incomprehensible images.

Everyone recognizes that narrative hunger is part of the human personality. Why else are our newspapers filled with advice columns? It's not, I think, for the solutions that we devour this daily stream of print, but for the glimpse of the human dilemma, the inaccessible stories of others.

Even the smallest narrative fragments have the power to seduce. School children learn in their arithmetic books about Mary Brown who buys three pounds of turnips at twenty cents a pound and four pounds of cheese at five dollars each. How much change will she get back from a fifty-dollar bill? The answer arrives easily, or not so easily, but leaves us tugging after the narrative thread – who is this Mary Brown, and what will she do with all that cheese? And what of her wider life, her passions and disappointments?

The obituaries in our local newspaper speak of the late departed Elvira Martindale, who, besides being devoted wife to, beloved mother of, was also Manitoba Ladies Lacrosse Champion in the year 1937. Was that championship day the centre of her life story? (I used to be ashamed of reading the obituaries, and then I discovered that everyone else did too, and that they read them, not out of morbidity, but out of a natural, and I like to think healthy, longing to expand their own lives and their narrative possibilities.) John J. Trevor, we read in the same newspaper, has fought his affliction bravely, and in death, asks that in lieu of flowers, friends and family send contributions to the International Society of Button and Buttonhook Collectors. A little lower on the same page – this was a particularly rich day – Ross and Judy McGowan of

Calgary perish in a car accident after 'a great day of powder skiing.'

Telephone companies have learned to pitch their TV ads in emotional narrative contexts. You've all seen them: the tense lonely father anxious to hear whether his son has passed his bar exam. An elderly woman awaiting news of the birth of her granddaughter. These are weepies, little melodramas, bad art perhaps, but packed like appetizers, hors d'oeuvres, to appease our narrative hunger.

The manufacturers of Dewar's Whiskey know how much we need the seeds of stories, and how we need, too, to place our own stories beside those of others: to compare, weigh, judge, forgive, and to find an angle of vision that renews our image of where we are in the world. Their advertisements, usually on the back covers of slick magazines, profile the beautiful and rich, tell us when and how they made their first million dollars, what book they are currently reading, what is their favourite meal, their favourite restaurant, and, of course, favourite drink, their philosophy for success – the same life-bytes, in fact, that novelists seize upon.

Then there are family-video adventures, preserved and available to a tiny audience. And anecdotes swapped at lunch or overheard on a bus. The world tap-dances to the evanescent music of the half-heard story, and like all writers, I depend on eavesdropping to refill my narrative litter bag. Only last year I was rewarded while at a sidewalk café. We found ourselves sitting between two most interesting narratives, a narrative cross-draught, as it were. At one table, two thirtyish women had their heads together, and one said to the other, 'Do you honestly believe my two little itty-bitty affairs could have alienated my husband?' At the other table sat two business-men, suits, ties, haircuts. The older turned to the younger and boomed, 'We'll cross that bridge when we get to the bottom of the barrel!' Exactly the kind of narrative fragment I treasure. Like most writers, I suffer a sort of scavenger's guilt, and often feel the impulse to confess on the title pages of my books something like 'I'm sorry' or 'Forgive me.'

And then there are newspaper fillers: an item in the *Globe and Mail*, for instance, noting the fact that eleven people are killed annually in North America by overturned vending machines – a narrative nugget I was able to use in *The Stone Diaries*.

TV sitcoms. Song lyrics. Jokes. Urban myths. Comic strips. Such a wealth of material to draw on, but never ... quite ... enough. And never quite accurate either, glancing off the epic of human experience rather than reflecting it back to us. And provoking, at the same time, that puzzling contradiction: that narrative hunger is a perverse pleasure to the overfed.

It is also a yardstick, a time-keeper. You may recall Virginia Woolf in *The Waves* saying, 'If there are no stories, what end can there be, or what beginning?' How are we to measure and identify time's segmented scroll? Umberto Eco says, 'We are narrative animals. When we try to tell the story of what happened to us, we understand what happened to us.'

Roland Barthes, who often put things as ambiguously as possible, occasionally offered a cool, clean statement or question. 'Isn't storytelling always a way of searching for one's origin?' Of course, the storyteller, or novelist, may be answering questions that no one has posed, but that everyone recognizes.

We may not know exactly what a novel is, but there are certain characteristics of 'the novel as we know it,' and teach it – that is, the novel that went off like a firecracker in 1740 and which continues to be, in our society anyway, the literary form of choice. Some of these characteristics include: a texture that approximates the world as we know it; characters who in their struggle for the world resemble ourselves; dilemmas which remind us of our own predicaments; scenes that trigger our memories or tap into our yearnings; and conclusions that shorten the distance between what is privately felt and universally known, so that we look up from the printed page and say, 'Ah-hah.'

But how relevant are these definition points, and how close to our lives have our narratives ever come?

We can start, maybe, with the admission that both real events and their accompanying narratives are conveyed to us by words, and that words, words alone, will always fail in their attempt to express what we mean by reality. We cannot think without words – or so many believe – and thus the only defence against words is more words. But we need to remember that the labyrinth of language stands beside reality itself: a somewhat awkward, almost always distorted facsimile or matrix. Experience – reality, that is – possesses immediacy; language plods behind, a rational or irrational tortoise. It may take pages of print to reproduce a registered vision, a shooting star, an uplifted ocean wave, an uplifted eyebrow, even.

What if we were to estimate that half of felt experience falls away in our efforts to describe or contain or conserve a moment in time? Now here, I have a visual aid I have to show you. If you were to imagine that this disk, and I think you can all see it in its lovely green colour, represents the well-stocked narrative cupboard and that it is diminished by that estimate – one-half; it now looks like this [here Shields cuts the disk in half with scissors].

Think of the naïve tourist who recorded in his diary a description of a crier in his mosque, believing he would recall with his written artefact the notes of the call to prayer. Language, which is useful in the province of the intellect, is a relatively clumsy vehicle in the expression of emotion and of narrative movement. Even the finest brush strokes of Henry James or Marcel Proust or Alice Munro are dabs in the darkness. The weightiest, most detailed description of the storming of the Bastille – to take an instance – forms a papery, speculative rustle beside the actual event. 'Writing is mere writing,' Annie Dillard says, 'and literature is merely mere.' 'An ordinary reader opening up a book,' she says, 'can't yet hear a thing. It will take half an hour to pick up the writing's modulations, its ups and downs, loves and thoughts, and its unwinding story, a story that relies on language – its only assigned building material – to give it permanence and shape.' 'Reality,' which Nabokov tells us is the only word in the language that always needs a pair of quotation marks around it, smells better than words, tastes sharper, presses on the skin more compellingly.

Ironically, the real world is often shown as fragmentary, a sort of secondary lesion of the senses, interrogated on every side by technology, unwilling to stand still long enough to be captured by definition. And language, our prized system of signs and references, frequently appears emptied out or else suspiciously charged.

So I hope I can begin with this shared notion: that both 'reality' and literature are joined in a need for language and that they labour under the crippling limitations that language imposes. And I hope you'll agree with me, too, that language is not disinterested, that it flows from a bag of cultural references, both private and shared. It flows with purpose, with, shall we say, an agenda. The crier in the minaret has an agenda, too, no doubt, but the man jotting his notes into his travel journal, or perhaps relying on his video camera, is moved by completely other forces.

Narrative, which questions experience, repositions experience, expands or contracts experience, rearranges experience, dramatizes experience, and which brings, without apology, colour, interpretation, and political selection, has been with us since the earliest stirrings of the human tongue. The primal narratives are believed – though how can we be sure – to be accounts of fallen heroes or adventures of the hunt. Imagine a small colony of an early culture, then, seated around a fire and discussing the capture of, say, a male bison. Someone will begin the tale; but who is that someone and how has he been selected? Is it because he captures the details accurately or because he is able to speak vividly? (I'm using the 'he' pronoun deliberately since it was mainly male-narrated stories that entered the literature before the eighteenth century.) [Here Shields cuts the green semicircle in half.]

Even as late as 1967, Northrop Frye, that good and humane scholar, was able to announce authoritatively that there are precisely four forms of fiction; this, by the way, may have been the last time in our history that such definitive summations were possible. Frye's essay lists dozens of male fiction writers (and one woman named George and another named Jane), a disproportion of writers and women's experience that radically diminishes the narrative pool.

But I'd like to return for a moment to the primitive storyteller relating the story of the hunt. Does he know the value of a narrative pause? Does he know how to lead up to the bison's death, how to keep his audience waiting, how to bring a scene into focus by a telling detail or by the use of metaphor? Is he able to release himself from the tyranny of authenticity and, with the full complicity of his listeners, heighten his narrative with a small exaggeration ... perhaps even a gross exaggeration, perhaps even the break of an important sequence or the insertion of an inventive incident or character or the substitution of one event for another? Perhaps he'll turn the male bison into a female, give it an extra horn or a set of wings. What if the storyteller has never seen a bison, what if the hunting grounds had lost their promise and nothing remained but an old inherited narrative of the storyteller's forebears – will he be forced to relinquish his place around the fire, will he be silenced, mocked for his distortions and inventions and roughly dismissed? Or will he find a place of honour in his society, a society that admits, openly or tacitly, that our own lives are never quite enough for us, that a hunger for narrative, for storytelling, that is, is probably about 40,000 years old?

And yet we continue, even today, to be troubled by a perceived dichotomy between what is called 'reality' – those quotes again – and what is known as fiction. As biographer Richard Holmes says, 'Fiction married fact without benefit of clergy.' This sorting out of 'reality' and invention is not a new problem but a very old one, and it has to do, I think, with the inability of fiction to stare at itself. So many questions arise. Is there such a beast as truth? Can we set aside our attachment to truth-telling? Who makes the rules? Who is telling the story, and how does the teller relate the tale? Exactly how far can a teller take a tale? Can a fiction writer, for instance, write about a year that is 400 days long? About daisies that fall from the sky instead of rain – as in García Márquez's *One Hundred Years of Solitude*? Can a novelist rename a street in Winnipeg – I got into all sorts of trouble when I did – or make a cat fly? Do we accept the fact that fiction is not strictly mimetic – that we want it to spring out of the world, illuminate the world – not mirror it back to us?

Yes, you will say, or perhaps no, and your response will depend on the culture you live in, the era into which you were born, and the width or narrowness of your aesthetic or moral responses. Huge pieces of potential narrative have been sacrificed in the name of authenticity, of not telling the untrue, not risking deviance [snip]. Here I can only guess at the loss, and here I should also say that every healthy writer – and perhaps reader too – has a healthy respect for deviance.

Reality has generally held on to its authority, at least until recently, but fiction, it seems, has been defending itself forever. Either that or finding sly wink-of-the-eye ways to circumvent moral scepticism. The 'stories' that take their roots in mythology or in our scriptures establish their legitimacy by their divine origins or ethical purpose. The novels of Danielle Steele demand their way by promising a light diversion from the serious problems that trouble us. Narratives without a ticket don't always get on the train.

Enormous quantities of stories – perhaps the finest stories of our culture – have been lost to illiteracy or lack of permission, either a prohibition placed on the storyteller – most often: 'Woman, hold thy tongue!' – or the simple inability to write down one's experience on paper. Historian Theodore Zeldon, who has written with such thoroughness about the civilization of France, tells us that in the eighteenth century nine-tenths of the French were peasants. Yet, we possess only one personal eye-witness account of French peasant life in that century, and even that account must be looked at with scepticism since its author became literate eventually and left his peasant past behind, thereby skewing the sample. There are, however, dozens of novels set in rural France of that period – novels whose authors have leapt across the synapse of what is known and what is imagined, or deduced their historical narratives from artefacts, paintings or documents. Do at least some of them get it right? An unanswerable question – an unfair question, perhaps. Is conjecture better than nothing at all when it comes to reaching into the narrative cupboard for something to eat?

'Humankind cannot bear very much reality,' T.S. Eliot once said [snip]. 'Happy stories are doomed to extinction,' [snip] says American fiction writer Peter DeVries. 'We will never have a true account of war,' says U.S. novelist John Hersey; 'no one could bear to write it; no one could bear to read it' [snip]. 'The world would split in two if one woman told the truth,' said poet Muriel Rukeyser [snip].

Then, there are the stories that are excavated authentically enough from the past, but which lose their meaning to contemporary sensibility. Many readers are familiar with Robert Darnton's book *The Great Cat Massacre*, in which a famous eighteenth-century joke is examined in order to see what light it throws on French society at that time, on the way people thought during the Enlightenment. In the joke, we are introduced to a cat-loving master printer in Paris. His young and unruly apprentices kill his dozen or so cats one night, and string them up in the print shop for their master to discover in the morning. That is the joke, a joke that travelled across Europe and apparently cracked up the populace over a period of several years. This cat massacre joke has been carefully analysed for historical context, for language puns, looked at from every possible perspective. But its humour remains stubbornly opaque, even alarming. Something is askew here in the society that delighted in it, or could it possibly be with us?

Jokes are often the most opaque part of our cultural skin. I was recently leafing through a 1950 copy of *Collier's Magazine* and noticed a cartoon in which two men, night janitors, were cleaning an office. One of them is leaning over and reading a piece of paper stuck into a typewriter. 'Bad spelling,' he comments, 'erasures, poor spacing ... brother! She must be terrific.' It took about a minute for me to understand the joke, and I only understood it because I'm old enough to remember that dumb women, back in 1950, signified femininity and sexual excitement. I would like to think that twenty-year-olds would be as baffled at this cartoon as I am by the cat massacre joke.

Another problem: since the days of relating stories of the hunt around the fire, we've grown self-conscious about our fiction, inventing categories – tragedy and comedy, after all, are only a convenient and arbitrary shorthand, a crude approximation – and we've made rules about how stories must be shaped. Rules about unity of time and space, about conflict, rising action, and the nature of story conclusions. Our narratives, then, have had their hair cut and permed; they've been sent to the fat farm, where they've learned to take nano-bites out of their own flesh in order to maintain a sleek literary line, a line that will assign itself to one of those major genres, or else surrender to deconstructive surgery and disconnect, more and more, from the texture and rhythm of 'reality.'

For a life does not unfold in chapters – you may have noticed this. A life does not have an underlying theme, yet we seem to believe a novel must. A life does not build slowly but steadily to a climax. A life is rarely restricted to three main characters. In life a new character may enter the scheme in the final pages, but in fiction, we have declared this an offence against aesthetic order. And, ungainly or overweight stories fall out of the narrative record [snip]. They are too bulgy for theory, too untidy for analysis. Too hard to teach – and, in or out of the official canon, stories really are described as being teachable or not, and you can imagine what happens to those that are deemed unteachable [snip, snip].

All of us in recent years have been inhaling the pollen of contemporary literary theory. It tends to alter our thinking about which stories are admissible to our culture; it catches in the throat, and in the layers of the brain where the drifted texts and discourses and deliberate misreadings and discontinuities are privileged over the linear, the didactic, the epiphanic [snip].

Contemporary stories may be very different from the old tale of the bison hunt, but the long history of the teller and the tale does offer up a remarkably persistent pattern, what critics such as Robert Alter call 'deep structures.' You can go straight to Ulysses to see an early model: the tale of the wanderer, the homeless, the picaresque hero with an unsteady eye and an inability to effect change, a being helplessly adrift. Often orphaned spiritually or else psychologically, and often wounded, maimed in some way, either metaphorically or otherwise, the picaresque traveller announces to us the confession of non-belonging. Today, we might describe such a person as being incompletely socialized, someone who stands outside of events, who in fact chooses that position.

Contemporary literature is populated by similar witnesses, those beings who are, to use Georg Lukács's term, deprived of a transcendental shelter or abode. Or they are in transit, in a state of what George Steiner calls in-betweenness, and further confused by disappearing landmarks or by the absence of shared events or ceremonies.

And so, if the outsider is the most persistent of literary heroes in our tradition, we can conclude that those who elect themselves writers are also outsiders, those under-socialized beings. What, then, happens to the narratives that arise at the centre of our society – and to the point of view of those who choose to stay rooted at the centre? Are they lost? Are these narratives erased from the collective memory as well as the literary storehouse? If so, what an enormous gap between the nexus of life and the literature that grows around its margins. You can see the predicament this puts us in: society invites its outsiders to keep the narrative record, to select and shape those stories which will survive in the culture [snip].

John Barth writes in a recent book about the central question fiction poses, which is not 'What happens?' but 'Who am

I?' He is almost certainly, though he doesn't say so, writing about the fiction of contemporary white Europeans, which may indeed concentrate its gaze on the question of self and the nature of self-identity. He is, in his work and in his view of narrative, eliminating, cutting off [snip] an immense slice of the world's story hoard, those stories possessing the brevity and shape of a Zen koan, or stories such as we find in the Cree tradition that refuse to complete themselves according to the narrative arc our culture has sanctioned, stories from a more communally conscious culture that is more likely to say 'Who are we?' rather than 'Who am I?'

Certain narratives are lost because they are not in the right place at the right time. Particular works, according to Robert Alter, were 'admitted to the canon chiefly because of their consonance with the distribution of power in society, their effectiveness in reassuring or training or telling people so that they will better perform their given social role.' We can take it that works that did not reassure or train or reinforce were lost [snip].

Even within our own culture, certain narrative material leaks away for want of a catchment vessel. I'm told by a friend that English is poor in words that describe mystical or transcendental experiences, and there is a well-known and bitterly chilling story about a New England housewife who, when washing dishes one evening, happened to notice how the soap bubbles gathered in a wreath around her wrist, and how the fading light from the window picked up a thousand tiny rainbows. She found the moment beautiful and profound, and seemed to sense in the apparition something of the order and meaning of the universe. Excited, she called her husband and attempted to share the vision with him. He immediately sent for an ambulance and had her transferred to a mental hospital [snip, snip].

We speak, too, of the absent narratives, the negative element of a photographic record – the dark void or unbridgeable gap, shadows and mirages, the vivid dream that fades by morning, the missed bus, the man we didn't marry, the unconceived child, the confession murmured to a priest, or else *not* murmured to a priest. The pockets of time and light that are too transitory to be put into words or even catch the eye. This narrative lint refuses to collect itself and is lost to our memory and to the narrative record [snip].

I recently read a book called *Ruby: An Ordinary Woman*, made up of diary extracts of one Ruby Aliside, so ordinary a woman that you probably would not recognize her name. The diary spans the years between 1909 and 1969. They were rescued by a granddaughter and put into print. How many other such accounts go to the dump? Accounts that like Ruby's will change forever the way we think of women's lives during that period?

Assumption and presumption distort our stories. One summer, in north central Iceland, I was told Monica's story. The name Monica pulled on an underground wire, reminding me of that other Monica of the Oval Office. But, no, the Icelandic Monica was virtuous. She and her husband lived in a poor stone house by the side of a gorge which separated them from their village, which they and their seven daughters could only reach by descending the steep sides of the gorge and then climbing up the other side. The husband died, just as Monica's eighth child was to be delivered. She decided to move her house across the gorge. Slowly, painstakingly, she and the seven daughters dismantled the house and carried it stone by stone across the gorge, reassembling it on the other side, where she was greatly rewarded and honoured for her spirit. A charming folktale, I thought, but no, it is a true story: the stones, the gorge, the seven daughters – and the tale is not that old. I was shown photos of Monica, not paintings, photos of her and the grandkids. It was the president of Iceland who honoured her, not some ancient tribal chief.

Our stories distort and tease the past, then; probably no one ever thought otherwise. And futuristic stories have always, for some reason, been relatively few in number, tinged with the exotic and often politically weighted. What, then, of the stories of the moment; do they possess the midnight shine of verisimilitude, and can we trust them to give a portrait or a sense of meaning or even to tell us what people do and think when they are alone in a room?

In recent years, the spectre of political correctness has touched all of us, placing a fence around our available narrative field, restraining even the possibilities of observation, let alone development. Political correctness, of course, has suppressed great widths of narrative life in the past – almost all of gay society, the larger part of women's sexuality – and also Catholics, Protestants, disbelievers, each taking their turn on the absentee list [snip, snip].

There are curious deformations in our stories of the present day, too. Our forebears, those bison hunters already alluded to, were comfortable writing about bison hunting. Bison hunting was their work. It took up sufficient time in their lives to warrant narrative clothes. Many contemporary narratives, on the other hand, pretend that people don't work. You may have noticed that novelistic events tend to happen on weekends or during off-hours. We may be told that so-and-so is an architect, but we never see her at her drafting table designing shopping malls. And certain other work choices hardly ever make it to the fictional page: upholsterers, mechanical engineers, horticultural workers, those who work at home.

Domesticity has not flourished in contemporary fiction, either. A thousand years from now, readers will look back on the novels of the twentieth century and wonder whether or not we possessed a domestic life at all. A bed, a roof over our heads, toothbrushes, forks and knives, alarm clocks, birth control devices – these accoutrements have been curiously erased except in so-called 'marginal fiction,' often women's fiction.

Today's narratives have also radically reinvented marriage and divorce profiles in our society. One marriage in every two fails, but look into the other world of the contemporary novel, and we find the divorce curve running wildly out of a 50 percent range. We rely on Jane Austen to show us attitudes toward marriage in her society, the search for a life partner, the developing notion of a marriage of friendship. But ask yourself when you last read a contemporary novel about happily married people. For one reason or another, enduring marriages, that other half of the statistical pattern, find little space on the printed page. Is it simply that our novels have become photo opportunities for people in crisis? Or is the task too demanding? How is a novelist to pump the necessary tension into the lives of the happily committed? Even the suggestion of a sound marital relationship posits the suspicion of what is being hidden and about to be revealed in the forthcoming chapter. Couples who have good sense, who discuss and resolve their differences and care deeply about their bonds of loyalty, are clearly as simple-minded and unimaginative as their creator. There they sit with their hobbies and their wallpaper and their cups of filtered coffee, finishing each other's sentences and nodding agreement. She sends his winter coat to the cleaners and worries about his asthma. He continues to find her ageing body erotic, and he is also extremely fond of her way with grilled peppers. This is all very well, but what can be done with folks so narratively unpromising? Coupledom, especially when seen in an unsparing light, should not necessarily equal boredom. And it might be interesting to see novels look inside their own human packaging and admit that a long relationship – the union of two souls, the merging of contraries forever – can be as complex, as potentially dynamic, and as open to catharsis as the most shattering divorce.

The notion of conflict in fictional narrative may also need reassessment. We may find that conflict is centred not in the fibre of human arrangements but in the interstices of human thought. How well or how poorly can we connect with another human consciousness? 'Only connect,' E.M. Forster said, but did he mean in life or in literature? It might be a project for the narratives of the next millennium, asking why the rub of disunity strikes larger sparks than the reward of accommodation, and how we've come to record what separates us rather than what brings us together.

If postmodernism has proved a synthetic discourse, un-animated by personal concerns, it has at least given writers a breath of that precious oxygen of permission and, more important, time to see in what ways the old realism – the mirror of the world – has failed us.

It was, perhaps, not real enough. It focused too compulsively on phantom inventions, categories, genres. It trafficked too freely in moments of crisis, searched too diligently for large themes and too preciously for graceful epiphanies. It banished certain parts of our language to certain emotional parts of the house. The people who appeared in 'realistic' fiction were seldom allowed the full exercise of their reality, their daydreams, their sneezes, their offended appetites, their birthday parties, their toothaches, their alternating fits of grotesque wickedness and godly virtue. Their meditative life was neglected. Realistic fiction passed too quickly through the territory of the quotidian and dismissed as though they didn't exist those currents of sensation that leak around the boundaries of vocabulary. The realistic tradition stressed the divisiveness of human society and shrugged at that rich, potent, endlessly replenished cement that binds us together.

Our narrative cupboard is far from being bare, but it seems it needs restocking. We need perhaps to turn back to that twilight of the gods where our stories were born. And ahead to narrative's full potential, that bountiful human impulse that says, 'Once upon a time ...,' which opens every question, every possibility.

There has been much serious thinking these last thirty years or so about just why we need narrative so desperately. The remarkable Wendy Steiner, in her book *The Scandal of Pleasure*, tells us that art – and I'm thinking of narrative art here – lures us into a dreamlike world of radical freedom where the rules and habits of our consciously regulated lives are suspended, and where we remain capable of reflection and judgement and from which we return with heightened awareness of the tastes and choices that ordinarily define and confine us.' And so, she continues, 'art allows us to understand without assenting – to go over to the other side and still stay home, to be violated, and yet in control.' Art, the writing of novels, for instance, is part of the 'realm of thought-experiment that quickens and sharpens and sweetens our being in the world.'

Since getting inside reality rather than getting reality right is the task of narrative fiction, it is inevitable that our stories will never mirror back to us a perfect image. But fiction has the power, dangerous or useful, to normalize the marginal – and we are hearing more and more these days of those voices from the margin; this is the good news. These previously unheard narratives bring with them their different rhythms and their alternative expectations.

Women's writing has already begun to dismantle the rigidities of genre, those four basic types of fiction referred to earlier, and to replace that oppressive narrative arc we've lived with so long, the line of rising action – tumescence, detumescence – what some feminists call the ejaculatory mode of storytelling.

There is much talk, too, these days of the failure of psychotherapy, that it may never have cured anyone. It has, however, allowed people the possibility of narrative strategy, opening their lives to the kind of digressions that build to narrative form. Canadian critic Martin Levin advises that we think of analysis less as therapy and more as art, of gently teasing the meaning out of an unfinished novel. 'Think,' he says, 'of its value deriving from its view of the mind's infinite imaginative facility, and not from its largely imaginary curative powers.'

At this point, I wish I had the power to glue back together this representation of our shattered story hoard, because it does seem true that more is permitted in our narrative today; more can be said. The writer Russell Hoban reminds us that the bricks are falling out of the tower, letting the craziness in, expanding what we think of as reality. Film, which conveys narratives of action superbly, has left the written word, by default perhaps, what many of us value most in narrative: the interior voice. Reflecting, thinking, connecting, ticking, bring-

SECTION TWO

The 'Precious Oxygen of Permission': Shields's Experiments with Narrative Form

SARAH GAMBLE

FAYE HAMMILL

DIANNE OSLAND

WENDY ROY

MELISSA POPE EDEN

Filling the Creative Void: Narrative Dilemmas in *Small Ceremonies*, the *Happenstance* Novels, and *Swann*

SARAH GAMBLE

In 'Narrative Hunger and the Overflowing Cupboard,' Carol Shields describes herself as a writer preoccupied with 'narrative ... the telling of stories, what they mean, these stories – and why we need them' (19). It is a statement that functions as an apt description of the content of this essay, which aims to explore how Shields uses her narratives to reflect on narrative. Her belief that 'narrative hunger is part of the human personality' (20) echoes the view expressed in an essay by Barbara Hardy that 'we dream in narrative, day-dream in narrative, remember, anticipate, hope, learn, hate and love by narrative.'[1] The implication of this statement is that storytelling is much more than mere entertainment: instead, it is an activity which is essential in enabling us to conceptualize the world around us and explain us to ourselves. The extent to which narrative functions as a medium of perception is one of Shields's central concerns in her fiction, which poses a number of questions regarding the nature and function of narrativity. What are the means by which narratives are created? Is true originality possible? Where does narrative end and 'real life' begin? Do some forms of storytelling have a more privileged relationship to reality than others?

Many of these questions are ones that have been posed in a postmodern context: in *A Poetics of Postmodernism*, for example, Linda Hutcheon argues that the postmodern condition is defined by a preoccupation with 'the process of narrativization,' which 'has come to be seen as a central form of human comprehension, of imposition of meaning and formal coherence on the chaos of events ... Narrative is what translates knowing into telling.'[2] This, I would argue, is a fair description of Shields's approach in her fiction, although she herself has dismissed any notion that her writing is influenced by postmodern ideas, saying that, although her experience of teaching in universities has 'made me more self-conscious about the act of writing, especially postmodern theories about writing,' she finds such ideas 'fascinating' rather than 'useful.' 'You would think that all this critical thinking would inhibit the writing itself, but it seems that, when sitting down to work on a novel, I undergo a shifting of gears, dismissing it completely.'[3] Nevertheless, the innate self-reflexiveness of Shields's fiction certainly opens her work up to postmodern interpretation, particularly because of her awareness of the problems inherent in the adoption of a naïve narratological position. As Peter Lamarque says, narrative does not just constitute a window on reality, but also, to a large extent, determines what that reality will be, since 'narration of any kind involves the shaping and recounting of events ... [which] must be shaped and ordered. Narrative imposes structure; it connects as well as records.'[4] A narratological world-view enables us to impose a pattern on randomness, and thus make sense of it, but it is also a process that entails the omission of anything that does not fit into that conceptual framework. As Shields herself puts it, 'Unluckily, a good part of the world falls through the narrative sieve, washing through the fingers of the recorders' hands and becoming lost' (20).

The feature that links the novels which will be discussed in this essay is their exploration of this struggle to create narratives – a struggle which is not confined to the thematic level of the text but also influences its formal pattern. Shields's first novel, *Small Ceremonies* (1976), is relatively conventional in form, but her two *Happenstance* novels (1980/2) and *Swann* (1987) play much more daring games with narrative construction, presenting the reader with multiple, frequently contradictory, points of view, and a variety of different styles and techniques. Shields is particularly concerned with exploring the limitations of narrative, and the experimentation in her texts tends to push toward the point where the conventions of storytelling falter, and language falls silent.

Shields's dramatization of the process whereby narratives are created directs her attention to the figure of the writer. All four novels discussed here have writers as their main characters – in fact, both *Small Ceremonies* and *Swann* feature several writers, who practise in competing or contrasting genres. *Small Ceremonies* features a biographer, an academic researcher, and two novelists (one established, one struggling), while *Swann* is narrated from various points of view, including that of an academic, a biographer, and a journalist.

The task of the writer, however, is never presented as an easy one. In a prose-poem entitled 'The Page,' Margaret Atwood speaks of the 'horror' of the blank page, which 'has no dimensions and no directions. There's no up or down except what you yourself mark, there's no thickness and weight but those you've put there.'[5] Theoretically, the blank page is full of potential, but both Atwood and Shields imply that the writer frequently freezes in the face of its implicit creative challenge to 'say something new.' While all of Shields's writers strive to be creative, most are despondently aware that even their best efforts consist of not much more than creative recycling. Nor does Shields exclude herself from this process, since her own narratives exhibit a self-conscious preoccupation with striving for new ways of both seeing and telling.

Accordingly, patterns of repetition, doubling, and exchange are central to all the novels discussed here. *Small Ceremonies* begins with the Gill family – Judith, Martin, and their two children – gathered around the table for their Sunday ritual of high tea, 'brought back from England where we spent Martin's sabbatical year.'[6] This is an act of double replication, for it not only recapitulates an event which took place in the past, but also appropriates part of one culture and reproduces it, slightly awkwardly, in the context of another. Judith Gill, the novel's narrator, is only too well aware of this, critiquing the custom even as she defends it:

> [W]e carry on the high tea ritual. But we've never managed to capture that essential shut-in coziness, that safe-from-the-storm solidarity. We fly off in midair. Our house, perhaps, is too open, too airy, and then again, we are not the same people we were then; but still we persist. (2)

Following high tea, the family settle down in front of the television to watch a wildlife documentary on the mating habits of birds: the next morning, Judith hears local women on the radio announcing a 'glass blitz,' which will organize the recycling of old bottles.

What these events have in common is the fact that they all describe closed circuits – re-enactment, coupling, and recycling. Moreover, immediately after she hears about the glass recycling drive on the radio, Judith settles down to work on her current biography. This creates an immediate association between writing and recycling which traps the writer herself within such self-replicating loops. This correlation is reinforced by the way in which Judith conceptualizes the life of her subject, the Canadian writer Susanna Moodie, itself as a piece of glass, 'glazed over with a neat edge-to-edge surface,' and her task as biographer as one which entails looking for 'the cracks in the surface' (7):

> Already I've found, with even the most casual sleuthing, small passages in her novels and backwoods recollections of unconscious self-betrayal, isolated words and phrases ... I am gluing them together ... into a delicate design which *may just possibly be* the real Susanna. (7, my emphasis)

The qualification in the above passage is telling, indicating

Judith's awareness that her search for 'the real Susanna' is bound to fail. For all her attempts to unearth a hidden, more 'authentic' persona from the books, letters, and journals Moodie left behind, Judith knows that 'characters from the past ... lie coldly on the page. They are inert, having no details of person to make them fidget or scratch; they are toneless, simplified, stylized, myths distilled from letters; they are bloodless' (53). 'Susanna Moodie' is thus not a person but a linguistic cipher which points to nothing but more words, more manuscripts, and all Judith as a biographer can do is rearrange those words a little.

Small Ceremonies, therefore, presents biography as a kind of borderline genre, not quite history, not quite fiction; yet it is this very transitional status that provides Shields with a standpoint from which to critique both history and fiction. In *A Poetics of Postmodernism*, Linda Hutcheon coins the term 'historiographic metafiction,' which she defines as a mode which 'always asserts that its world is both resolutely fictive and yet undeniably historical ... what both realms share is their constitution in and as discourse' (142). This is almost exactly the function fulfilled by biography in Shields's work, for in presenting a life as a story, the biographer also exposes history itself as a narrative construct, 'unavoidably figurative, allegorical, fictive ... always already textualised.' (143). Shields's writing, therefore, echoes what Hutcheon identifies as postmodernism's deliberate confusion of 'the notion that history's problem is verification, while fiction's is veracity ... Both forms of narrative are signifying systems in our culture; both are what Doctorow once called modes of "mediating the world for the purpose of introducing meaning"' (112).

The implication of Hutcheon's statement is that history and fiction do not exist in dialectical opposition, as is popularly supposed, but side by side – a view which is echoed in the dismantling in *Small Ceremonies* of Judith's highly conventional distinction between the two modes. Whereas biography, she says, relies on 'a profusion of material,' fiction 'has to be spun out of simple air ... it all had to be made up' (66).

However, her discovery that her friend Furlong Eberhardt's highly successful new novel plagiarizes the unpublished manuscript of her own doomed attempt at fiction reminds her of what she actually already knew, but had conveniently forgotten – the creative process is considerably less reliant on pure inspiration than is popularly supposed. The plot structure appropriated by Furlong was not, in fact, Judith's invention, but was itself copied from the notebooks of another aspiring writer, John Spalding, the owner of the flat in which the Gill family lodged during their year in England:

> So simply, so transparently, and so unapologetically had he stolen the plot for *Graven Images* – stolen it from me who had in turn stolen it from John Spalding who – it occurred to me for the first time – might have stolen it from someone else. The chain of indictment might stretch back indefinitely, crime within crime within crime. (106)

Judith's notion that the act of plagiarism of which both she and Furlong are guilty is only the latest manifestation of an endless replication of the same material brings us back to the concept of recycling with which the book began, for the implication here is that fiction may consist of nothing more than the art of creative rearrangement. Indeed, Furlong justifies his actions by aligning himself with Shakespeare, who 'stole his plots ... Borrowed them from the literature of the past, and no one damn well calls it theft' (132).

Rather like a game of Chinese whispers, in which a word is repeated so many times it becomes meaningless, the result of conceptualizing the act of writing as a self-replicating loop is to rob the act of plagiarism of its significance. If recycling is something even iconic writers like Shakespeare do, in the end, Furlong's offence is not that he has copied his material, but that he has recalled Judith's guilt regarding her own plagiarism, which she has tried to edit from her personal life-story. The act of plagiarism is central to this novel because it highlights both the necessity of thinking in narrative forms and the perpetual provisionality of doing so. Judith's view that 'breathing, waking and sleeping; our lives are streamed and shaped into stories' (51) is one which the book upholds in its dismantling of the distinctions between history and fiction, but it also shows the way in which often the most important details and significant events are ones which remain hidden, unspoken and unrecorded.

Accordingly, while Shields goes along with the postmodern view that history, like fiction, is a discourse, she also follows up on the implications of such an assumption. After all, narrative is not an infinitely flexible medium, but one which necessarily has to function according to certain conventions; moreover, it is inextricably dependent on language, a notoriously slippery medium of communication. Shields has spoken of the way in which she uses her fiction to pinpoint 'the failure of language, the abuse of language, the gaps in language,'[7] a statement which indicates her fascination with the notion of using her narrative to convey the unsaid or (even more radically) the unsayable.

Small Ceremonies reflects this preoccupation in the way in which it revolves around points of rupture or silence: events or artefacts which cannot be encoded in language or be contained within conventional narrative patterns. There are points where Shields deliberately leaves blank spots within the text, indicative of experiences or concepts incapable of ever being contained within a conventional narrative framework. One such blank spot is provided by Judith's husband, Martin, a Milton specialist, who tires of producing 'derivative' (82) pieces of conventional literary criticism. Instead, he decides to create a graphic diagram in the form of a tapestry of the themes of *Paradise Lost*, using different colours for each theme: 'red for God's omnipotence, blue for man's disobedience, green for arrogance, and, let's see, yellow for pride and so on' (83).

Martin's production – half academic analysis, half work of art – can be viewed as a significant event within the novel. For a brief moment, inspiration erupts from the confines of language and the artificial distinctions of genres and creative forms, becoming something which is genuinely inventive. However, it is in the nature of epiphany to be ephemeral – the force of Martin's creative vision is not sustained for long, nor will he attempt to reproduce it. As he wryly remarks to reporters, 'I wouldn't trust my luck twice' (143). In the end, his inspiration becomes commodified when he sells his tapestries to the highest bidder, an achievement rendered mundane by the fact that he uses the money to pay off part of his mortgage.

Shields's avoidance of any attempt to describe the tapestries directly in her text indicates an authorial refusal to lock them up in the very prison-house of language from which they have escaped. Because the narrative point of view never strays from Judith's perspective, and her one glimpse of Martin's work is confined to a bad newspaper photo, 'smeary and porous and not very effective' (143), the resulting blank space in the text can only be filled by the reader's imagination, not with words.

However, this is not the only blank spot in the novel, for, intriguingly, Shields plays the same game with John Spalding's literary plot unearthed by Judith. Although Judith tells us that it is 'not only clever ... [but] astonishingly original' (71), she never elaborates on that initial statement; hence, it remains undescribed within the novel. Could it be that, in spite of Furlong's cynical assertions that plagiarism is intrinsic to the act of writing, there might still be genuinely new ways of expressing oneself within narrative structures? As Shields herself asserts in 'Narrative Hunger and the Overflowing Cupboard,' 'we've made rules about how stories must be shaped' (28) and discard anything that doesn't fit into that rigid pattern – but what if a writer could devise more innovative, flexible forms capable of catching that 'narrative material [which] leaks away for want of a catchment vessel' (30)?

The fact that Spalding's plot becomes, like Martin's tapestry, a potential opening in Shields's text teases us with the possibility that it was indeed original, although by the time it has reached Furlong Eberhardt via Judith Gill it is a copy of a copy. It is also abandoned by its originator, who finally attains his goal of being published with a book which draws on the correspondence between his daughter and Judith's son in order to tell the story of a Canadian family living in England. At the end of the novel, therefore, the cycle of replication is complete, for if it opened with Canadian re-enactment of English ritual, it ends with English appropriation of Canadian experience.

Small Ceremonies compares particularly well with Shields's two *Happenstance* novels, which reproduce the same marital dynamic as *Small Ceremonies* in an inverted form. This time, it is the wife, Brenda Bowman, who is the craftsperson, and her husband, Jack, the struggling and stubbornly uninspired writer. However, Shields's use of narrative point of view is rather different here, and far more expansive. *Small Ceremonies* is focalized exclusively through Judith, and this narrowed-down perspective enables Martin's work to function as the focal point of meaningful silence in the text. In *Happenstance*, however, Shield adopts the rather more complex tactic of pluralizing the dominant narrative perspective, telling the same story twice from contrasting, frequently competing, viewpoints – those of the husband and of the wife.

The novel covers a week in the life of Brenda and Jack, during which time Brenda, a semi-professional quilter, attends a craft exhibition in Philadelphia, leaving Jack to take care of their children and continue working on his book on Indian trade practices. Such an oppositional structure positively invites the reader to set Brenda and Jack against each other: Jack the historian, who works with words and abstract concepts divorced from real life, against Brenda the craftsperson, whose quilts possess a functionality which links them to the realm of material reality. Each, in different ways, wishes to create, but, as in *Small Ceremonies*, only the one who forsakes words is successful.

Happenstance: The Husband's Story opens with Jack's rather grandiose opinions concerning the nature of history, which, he has concluded, 'is eschatological ... not the mere unrolling of the story. And ... not the story itself. It's the end of the story.'[8] Jack's analysis, however, presumes rather too easily that history is a linear narrative that *has* an ending. Shields treats Jack very much the same way she treats Judith in her subtle undermining of his ideas via her manipulation of the very narrative structure in which they are expressed, for he is a character in a book (or books) in which the whole notion of 'ending' is problematized. Indeed, there are two different ways of approaching the concept of 'the end' in this pair of linked texts. One is that there are *two* endings, the wife's and the husband's; and although the action of the narrative concludes at more or less the same point for both of them – Jack's meeting of Brenda at the airport on her return from Philadelphia – their separate points of view on the same event are entirely different, with the result that the text as a whole refuses to coalesce into a neat and tidy conclusion. Alternatively, it's possible to take the view that the narrative as a whole has *no* ending, an idea reinforced in recent editions of the novel. Although originally published two years apart under different titles,[9] the wife's and the husband's stories are now printed together back-to-back, thus placing the dual endings squarely in the middle of the book. Once one story has been concluded, this structure draws the reader into the next and back again, creating a never-ending Möbius strip of a narrative.

Moreover, throughout *Happenstance: The Husband's Story*, Shields is constantly evoking the traces of other stories and texts, which adds to the sense of narrative plurality. For example, Jack's failure to complete his book is ironically underlined by his belief that he has been pre-empted by another work that reproduces his research exactly. The author, Harriet Post, is a former lover of Jack's, although he has had no contact with her for years, and no idea that she was working in the same historical area. Although we later learn that Jack has jumped to the wrong conclusion through a semantic misunderstanding – his subject is the trade practices of North American Indians, whilst Harriet's is the trade practices of the Indian subcontinent – this part of the plot nevertheless recalls the double literary theft in *Small Ceremonies*, and Harriet Post herself is recognizable as another of Shields's absent writers, like Spalding, Mary Swann, and Susanna Moodie, who appear in the text through the traces of their literary activity rather than as characters. Jack's narrative is haunted by the shadow of Harriet Post – his memories of their sexual encounters, the publisher's note of her book's imminent release – but she is never fully embodied within it. Instead, she hovers on the margins of the story, an echo of Jack's former life which is never explored in any detail, and which thus resists being tied off in order to form the narrative into a cohesive whole – a fact only underlined by Jack's tentative attempt to renew communication with her at the end of the book, which ends in failure. In the final analysis, Harriet represents the contingency of endings, which impose an artificial sense of finality on an ever-proliferating pool of narratives.

This sense of narrative overspill is also conveyed in the way in which the two companion novels relate to each other. Brenda's story, although it inevitably overlaps with Jack's in places, offers a completely different perspective on events, and their contrasting points of view become identified with their different creative practices. While Jack wrestles with language and syntax, spending whole afternoons writing and rewriting a single paragraph, Brenda finds her work with fabric and thread 'ridiculously easy' (17). She has long since given up trying to rationalize the means by which she devises her patterns and colour schemes, deciding that they 'come from some more simplified root of memory' (16). And although she gives her quilts titles, she does not agonize over the process, attaching signifier to signified quite at random:

> She was thankful no one asked her any more what such-and-such a quilt was 'about.' She wouldn't have known. And she was thankful, too, that she was seldom pressed about the reasons behind the naming of her quilts. Even Jack no longer cocked an eyebrow and asked: Why *Spruce Forest*? Why *Bud-*

dha's Chant? Why *Rock Splinter*? It was assumed that she must have her reasons, that along with her gift for stitchery went a body of belief, an artist's right to interpret and name. (17)

If in *Happenstance: The Husband's Story*, Shields points to the limitations of narrative by signalling the existence of things which cannot be contained by a single authoritative account, in Brenda's text she achieves the same objective by returning to a modified version of the 'blank spot' technique she employed in *Small Ceremonies*. Brenda's quilts, because they have not been formulated through recourse to narrative processes, are resistant to linguistic means of description, and thus form points of hesitation in the text. Unlike Martin Gill's tapestries, however, which are never glimpsed directly within the narrative, Brenda's quilts are described in some detail – but in a way that makes clear that language can do no more than skim over their densely patterned surfaces. For example, the centrepiece of Brenda's exhibit at the craft symposium is a quilt entitled *The Second Coming*, which is described as 'a blocked bed of colour – greens and yellows mostly – with a kind of frenetic heat rising from one end. And, like a footnote or an inscription, dark-purple stains printed the edges with shapes that resembled mouths' (18). Language's failure to transmit anything like an adequate picture of the quilt is inscribed through the use of analogy – 'kind of,' 'like,' 'resembled' – which is employed, not as a device to heighten the description, but to convey a sense of approximation.

Moreover, Brenda's art is shown to be becoming increasingly radical in its form. Her latest work-in-progress has abandoned convention almost completely, and thus is even more linguistically elusive: it appears in the text only as a piece 'three-quarters finished' with 'no real pattern to it, only a cauldron of colour, yellow mostly' (44). It provides the only direct description of a quilt to appear in Jack's account, too, for he contemplates it in the final chapter of his narrative, seeing 'a whirl of colour, mostly yellows with a few slashes of violent green. The yellows churned from a boiling centre ... a strange and complex explosion of light' (191–2). But although Jack's description is slightly more verbose than that which appears in Brenda's story, it adds nothing concrete in the way of detail: the stress laid upon light and movement has a blurring effect which avoids exactitude, creating an impression rather than a picture.

The title of this piece, *The Unfinished Quilt*, also emphasizes the way in which it functions as a link between Jack's and Brenda's stories, for it is another way in which the concept of 'the end' is critiqued. To label something 'unfinished' is to imply that it will never be completed; otherwise, the title would no longer make sense. Thus, this quilt remains a piece forever in suspension between language and form: it will either remain unfinished, in which case it will not really be a quilt, or it will be finished, and thus exceed the linguistic parameters set by its designation. In a sense, *The Unfinished Quilt* functions as an ironic counterpoint to Jack's unfinished book, highlighting the very different ways in which Brenda and Jack apprehend the world around them. While Jack may strike the right postmodern attitudes, the knowledge that narrative will only ever be an approximation of experience torments him. His final admission, that 'some connection between perception and the moment itself would fail, would always fail' (193), is not so much a revelation as an admission of defeat. Brenda, however, perceives stories in much the same way as she does the patterns of her quilts. Narrative for her is multiple and fluid, defined not by endings, but by continuity:

> History was no more than a chain of stories, the stories that happened to everyone and that, in time, came to form the patterns of entire lives, her own included ... These stories rose out of mystery, took shapes of their own, and gave way in good time to newer and different stories. (127–8)

So while Jack's manuscript, unfinished, is nothing, Brenda's unfinished quilt is already something, because it participates in a creative continuum greater than the sum of its individual parts.

What *Small Ceremonies* and the *Happenstance* novels have in common, therefore, is their treatment of the concept of narrative, which is simultaneously celebrated and critiqued; a double-edged agenda which is echoed in the distinction all three texts make between the writer and the craftsperson. While the writer is portrayed in the process of agonized struggle, attempting to break out of a closed cycle of replication but failing every time, those characters who express themselves through craft transcend the limitations of narrative convention and linguistic structures. The provisionality of narrative is also asserted in these novels' evocation of other stories and lives that hover on the boundaries of the text, creating points of rupture at its very edges.

All of these themes reach their fullest measure of development in *Swann*, one of Shields's most widely read and discussed novels, which is centred wholly upon the question of literary origins and textual authority. While in *Happenstance* Shields split the narrative point of view between two people and two novels, *Swann* is even more fragmented. It is divided into five separate sections, four of which are narrated from the point of view of different characters. The final section is written as a film script, and adopts (for the only time in any of the four novels discussed here) an objective perspective on events.

What links all these pieces of narrative together is another of Shields's absent writers, a dead Canadian poet named Mary Swann. Fifteen years before the story opens, she was murdered by her husband on their farm at the edge of the remote town of Nadeau, Ontario – all that survives is a small volume of sparse, cryptic poetry published after her death. All four of the novel's narrators are in some way preoccupied with her: Sarah Maloney, an academic studying Swann's work; Morton Jimroy, who is writing a biography of Swann; Rose Hindmarch, the librarian at Nadeau and an acquaintance of Swann's; and Frederic Cruzzi, the publisher of Swann's verse.

The final section of the novel brings them all together at the first academic symposium on Swann's work, an event that is intended to mark her integration within the canon of Canadian literature.

Mary Swann thus functions as this novel's *idée fixe*, yet the obsessive interest that all four narrators display in her life and her work only serves to make her absence all the more glaring. Sarah Maloney's comment '[I]n a sense I invented Mary Swann and am responsible for her'[10] is absolutely correct, for what the reader is presented with is four different versions of a figure who ultimately evades explanation or categorization. What particularly perplexes both those who met Swann while she was alive (Rose Hindmarch and Frederic Cruzzi), and those who study her work (Sarah Maloney and Morton Jimroy), is the glaring disjunction between the life and the poetry. This, as Sarah Maloney puts it, is 'the central mystery: how did she do it? Where in those bleak Ontario acres, that littered farmyard, did she find the sparks that converted emblematic substance into rolling poetry?' (31). It is a conundrum that Morton Jimroy finds particularly frustrating, for his whole biography depends on making such a connection, finding 'the one central cathartic event' (111) that inspired creativity in a farmer's wife. All he can find, however, is a life in which 'each year ... seems a paroxysm of renewed anonymity' (110).

Mary Swann, therefore, fulfils the same role in this text as Susanna Moodie in *Small Ceremonies* because, like Susanna, she is simply not recuperable. All 'Mary Swann' really consists of is a collection of artefacts – her collection of poetry, two blurred photographs, the Parker pen with which she wrote, her notebook, her rhyming dictionary – and the novel traces the dissemination of these objects among the characters. Rose Hindmarch gives the notebook and rhyming dictionary to Sarah Maloney; Morton Jimroy has Mary Swann's pen and a photograph. The other photograph is in the museum at Nadeau, and the few surviving copies of *Swann's Songs* are in the hands of Sarah Maloney, Morton Jimroy,

Frederic Cruzzi, and a handful of other Swann scholars. The issue of ownership thus becomes crucial, since if Mary Swann is the sum of the things she left behind, to own those things is the only way in which the woman herself can be laid claim to.

One of the main themes of this text is the different, often highly dubious, ways in which these objects are gained, and the reasons behind such acts of acquisition, a process which comes to represent the characters' various attempts to fill the narrative vacuum left by Mary Swann's essentially ordinary life and endow it with meaning. Yet the circulation of artefacts which takes place in the novel does not, in fact, achieve anything beyond the formation of yet another closed circle marked by endless repetition. Acts of theft, which recall Shields's earlier preoccupation with plagiarism, are commonplace – Morton Jimroy steals Mary Swann's pen from her daughter and one of the two photographs kept in the museum at Nadeau, and it is evident that Sarah Maloney appropriated her copy of *Swann's Songs* from the holiday cabin in Wisconsin where she first found it. The novel's most audacious act of robbery, however, is perpetrated by a book dealer, Brownie, who systematically steals all surviving copies of Swann's collection of poems in order to enhance its commercial value.

However, the twist in this particular text is that there may, in fact, be nothing to steal. Frederic Cruzzi's narrative reveals that the poems left with him by Mary Swann on the night she died were accidentally destroyed, and had to be reconstituted from memory and surviving fragments by Cruzzi and his wife:

> They struggled and conferred over every blot, then guessed, then invented. The late hour, the river of black coffee, and the intense dry heat in the room bestowed a kind of reckless permission. At one point, Hildë, supplying missing lines and even the greater part of a missing stanza, said she could feel what the inside of Mary Swann's head must look like. (222–3)

With this revelation, the authenticity of these verses is thrown into doubt, since their connection with the legitimating authority of the author has been severed. Moreover, such a dubious 'recreation' of Mary Swann's poems also renders essentially meaningless the activities of those who are attempting to develop academic careers through the promotion of Mary Swann's literary reputation.

However, there's yet another ironic turn of the narrative screw to come, which Shields leaves to the very end of the book, when Brownie, in a struggle to escape apprehension, throws a pillowcase containing all existing material by Mary Swann out of a hotel window. Its contents are irretrievably scattered, 'mixing with the snow and carried by the wind into the street' (309). Left, literally, with nothing, the members of the Swann symposium unite in order to yet again reconstruct her poetry. Whereas in *Small Ceremonies* it is John Spalding's plot which is transmitted from one teller to another, in *Swann* Mary Swann's poems become copies of copies only dimly related to their originator. *Swann* is also reminiscent of *Small Ceremonies* in its refusal to condemn the act of plagiarism. Indeed, in this novel it is the 'ceremonial act of reconstitution' (311) which forms what is probably the only truly creative achievement in the novel.

What makes *Swann* different from the other novels discussed in this essay is the lack of a craftsperson: a figure capable of staging a breakout from the closed circulation of stories and manuscripts saying the same things over and over again in the same old ways. Yet this is not to say that the cycle isn't broken again here, for it could be argued that it is in Mary Swann herself that the two figures unite. Peter Lamarque's comment that 'the etymology of "fiction" reveals its roots in the idea of making and fabricating'[11] has important implications in this context, since it can be used to break down the distinction upheld in both *Small Ceremonies* and the *Happenstance* novels between those who create with language and ideas and those who don't. All readers of Swann's work note its rootedness in the minutiae of everyday life, although many, such as Sarah Maloney, cannot accept it at face value and constantly try to endow it with 'deeper' meaning: 'Take "Lilacs," her first published poem. It pretends to be an idle, passive description of a tree in blossom, but is really a piercing statement of a woman severed from her roots, one of the most affecting I've ever read' (50).

But Sarah is surely over-intellectualizing here. Perhaps Mary Swann is a unique figure within Shields's fiction – a writer for whom language is absolutely sufficient to delineate her experience. Sarah suppresses the journal given to her by Rose Hindmarch because of her '[p]rofound disappointment' that instead of 'elucidation and grace and a glimpse of the woman Mary Swann as she drifted in and out of her poems,' what she gets is 'the ups-and-downs accounting of a farmer's wife, of *any* farmer's wife' (49). But that, surely, is the point – Mary Swann is no romantic genius, but a woman who used words like tools to describe an existence which, until its bloody and dramatic ending, was essentially representative of the absolutely ordinary. What the critics cannot grasp is that her spare, elliptic poetry is sufficient unto itself: it is not intended to be metaphorical or allusive or deeply meaningful, but a direct expression of concrete experience. Ironically, however, this is precisely what makes Mary Swann extraordinary, for she occupies a most privileged position in Shields's work: a writer whose work has the tangibility of craft, since it arises spontaneously from the limited conditions of her life.

In the end, though, what legitimates Mary Swann's work is not really the work itself, particularly as by the end of the novel, it is only an echo or approximation of the original anyway. This essay began with a discussion of the significance of images of replication within Shields's work, and argued that they symbolize the writer's entrapment in well-worn narrative patterns and modes. What *Swann*, in particular, stresses is that this motif can be approached another way, if the notion of replication is replaced with the concept of exchange. Replicated narratives may be poor copies of an original, but narratives that are *exchanged* become vibrant and alive, and the act of retelling creative in itself.

Such moments can be found in *Small Ceremonies* and the *Happenstance* novels as well, but they still tend to centre on forms of communication that escape the confines of the printed page. At the end of *Small Ceremonies*, Judith is transfixed by a group of deaf people dining in a restaurant, their 'flying fingers ... shaping a private alphabet of air,' and linking them together 'in a unique festival of silence' (178). For Judith, this experience becomes emblematic of the necessity of 'embracing others along with their mysteries' (179), and reminds her that the vision of the biographer will only ever be imperfect. Throughout *Happenstance: The Wife's Story*, quilts become the focus of acts of community and storytelling, from the women who regularly gather in Brenda's work-room, to the recollections of her fellow delegates explaining how they sew their memories into patchwork patterns.

In *Swann*, however, the act of narrative exchange which closes the book is purely linguistic. The Swann symposium has been defined by the competitive jostling amongst the assembled academics, all ambitious to make their names as pioneering theorists of Swann's works. But the book ends with them briefly united in the task of reassembling a single poem, each line being contributed by a different voice in what becomes an almost ritual sharing of knowledge:

SARAH: And becoming part of larger loss
CRUZZI: Without a name
WOMAN WITH TURBAN: Or definition or form
JIMROY: Not unlike what touches us
CRUZZI: In moments of shame. (312)

As these closing lines of the novel make clear, this act of unity remains fragile, underscored with a haunting sense of lack. The words themselves are 'part of a larger loss / without a name,' for they will still always fall short of experience. Within the world of the text, the origin of this creative force is dead and gone, and Swann's words are only an approximation of whatever it was she meant to say. Moreover, Shields's reproduction of the completed poem on the following page has the effect of drawing the reader out of the text, and even further away from Mary Swann, who becomes doubly distanced – not just by death, but by her fictionality. That her name continues to be cited as the poem's author only emphasizes her absence, for it has become a floating signifier unattached to any concrete referent. Nevertheless, the attempt to recreate her is important, not because it has any hope of succeeding, but because it forges a connection, however fleetingly, among a disparate group of individuals. The reader is required to take this moment of epiphany at face value here, even though it's shot through with a certain amount of irony: Shields's use of a film-script format in this final section, which refers to the characters throughout as actors, ultimately draws attention to their fictional status as well, thus adding yet another layer to the interlocked levels of narrative operating within the text.

Swann is, on one level, a literary crime story, centrally concerned with tracking down the mystery behind the disappearance of the poet's manuscripts. However, Shields has said that 'the real mystery, and the one that interests me, is the mystery of human personality and the creation of art,'[12] a comment that links this text with the others under discussion in this essay – all of which, firstly, assert the fundamental separateness of human beings, and, secondly, trace the creative struggle entailed in the attempt to bridge that gap. In this context, Shields implies, narrative structures allow us to know, but never quite enough. Instead, these novels feature brief moments of epiphany – Martin Gill's tapestries, Brenda Bowman's quilts – in which narrative itself is transcended and seen anew. Such moments do not last, however, leaving the writer all too frequently stranded within a closed cycle of stories which have all been told before. But *Swann* makes an important point, which is that to tie a story down to a single author is to isolate it and deprive it of that connection to other narratives that would give it meaning.

Plagiarism is a crime only when the law of copyright is invoked, whereby the solitary artist 'owns' his or her work, and builds a reputation upon that ownership, jealously guarded. *Swann*, however, ends with a ringing endorsement of the benefits of creative recycling, in which narratives are shared and enriched by the inspiration of many. In the course of this text, the poems of Mary Swann are systematically cut loose from the defining signifier of the author and pass into common ownership, for by the end of the novel, they owe more to communal endeavour than to a single, isolated act of creativity. It is a conclusion which affects Shields's own authorial status, reiterating her belief that, published writers or not, all individuals share a collective hunger for narrative. This, therefore, is the true significance of the blank space left by the absent author in Shields's works, a space which is waiting to be filled with a multitude of voices exchanging stories, and through them building communities, families, and lives.

Notes

1 Barbara Hardy, 'Towards a Poetics of Fiction: 3) An Approach through Narrative,' *Novel* 2 (Fall 1968): 6.
2 Linda Hutcheon, *A Poetics of Postmodernism: History, Theory, Fiction* (London and New York: Routledge, 1988), 121. All further references are to this edition.
3 Donna Krolik Hollenberg, 'An Interview with Carol Shields,' *Contemporary Literature* 39.3 (1988): 345.
4 Peter Lamarque, 'Narrative and Invention: The Limits of Fictionality,' in *Narrative in Culture*, ed. Christopher Nash (London and New York: Routledge, 1995), 131.
5 Margaret Atwood, 'The Page,' in *Murder in the Dark* (London: Jonathan Cape, 1984), 44.
6 Carol Shields, *Small Ceremonies* (London: Fourth Estate, 1995), 2. All further references are to this edition.
7 Harvey De Roo, 'A Little like Flying: An Interview with Carol Shields,' *West Coast Review* 23.3 (1989): 45.
8 Carol Shields, *Happenstance: The Wife's Story / Happenstance: The*

novel, incorporating gentle parody of the genre as well as self-reflexive commentary on the language of love and the plots of love stories. Sarah Gamble's essay in this volume discusses three of Shields's novels from the 1970s and 1980s which explore the 'struggle to create narratives' (40), and this exploration is continued in *The Republic of Love*, which is as much preoccupied with the stories we tell about love as with the subject of love itself. My essay will examine the balance Shields strikes among paying homage to the romance, reflecting upon its structures, and subverting it.

The title of *The Republic of Love* provides the first indication of its links with paperback romances, many of which have the word 'love' in their titles. The original working title was the more enigmatic 'Bodies of Water,'[2] and the substitution of *The Republic of Love* gives much more emphasis to the romantic aspect of the story. The novel consists of the interwoven stories of two lonely people, Tom Avery, a radio disc jockey, and Fay McLeod, a folklorist. They do not meet until half way through the book, but the alternation between their two perspectives sets up an immediate reader expectation that they will end up together. They fall in love at first sight, they encounter problems which are later resolved, and the novel ends with their marriage and a glimpse into their happy future. This satisfying, if predictable, pattern is continually disrupted, however, by the less traditional elements of the plot, characterization, and narrative structure. For example, Shields begins the story of her female protagonist: 'It's Good Friday, a cold spring morning, and Fay McLeod, a woman of thirty-five, is lying in bed beside a man she no longer loves' (4). Immediately we are alerted to Fay's age and sexual experience, and these characteristics set her apart from the young, innocent heroines typical of fictional romance from the eighteenth century to the twentieth.[3] Shields may end her novel with a marriage, but she begins with a break-up. In fact, separations and divorces are scattered liberally throughout the book, and the debris of failed relationships provides the primary context for the development of the central partnership. Tom has three divorces behind him, and Fay has lived with three different men. It is no surprise, therefore, that Fay is extremely sceptical about romantic love, but the quotation which opens this essay reveals the shift which takes place in her outlook as a result of meeting Tom. It is her movement from irony to wonder, rather than the story of her falling in love, which forms the central narrative of *The Republic of Love*. The progression from a fear of commitment to an attitude of complete trust is, in fact, not untypical of the romantic heroine. According to Scott McCracken's analysis of the popular romance, 'each narrative charts the heroine as she goes through a period of personal transformation.'[4] What is *not* typical is Fay's tendency to analyse romance intellectually rather than allowing her emotions to guide her.

Fay's attitudes to love are often influenced by, and expressed through, her research in folklore. The narrator refers back to a period when Fay, at twenty-two, studied the conjugal arrangements in five different countries for her M.A. thesis: 'She concluded that the marriage ceremony itself constituted a mere rubber-stamping of a more significant, though far less codified, premarriage agreement – which was the exchange of sentiments between a woman and a man that declared their hearts to be open to one another. (Not that she used the word "heart" in her thesis, and not that she risked, except within the boundaries of crisply set quotation marks, the word "love.")' (220). The narrator paraphrases Fay's conclusions, reintroducing the word 'heart' which she had refused. There is an edge of irony in the bracketed comment which alerts us to the fact that Fay's thesis inadvertently reveals her romantic beliefs about love, even as she attempts to conceal them using scholarly circumlocutions.

At the time when she meets Tom, Fay is working on a book about mermaids, and her comments about them demonstrate her tendency to place love in opposition to rationality and intellect. After several weeks travelling in Europe and carrying out research, she feels that

the mermaids have affected her equilibrium ... She's sick of mermaids. Their writhing bodies. Their empty, unblinking faces shrieking for love ... Not one of the mermaids she's seen has had a whit of intelligence about her ... Love, love, love is all they can dream up down there in their underwater homes. They're starved and vapid and stupid as fish. They're impoverished by love, maddened by love, they're crazy as ... as crazy as Fay is herself. (222, last ellipsis in text)

Here Fay considers her desire for Tom as a form of insanity which deprives her of her balanced, detached perspective on life. Tom is influenced by the same conventional belief in the opposition between passion and rationality, and is worried because he has sent Fay a letter to tell her that he loves her: 'he was a fool. He was a nut case ... he was a loony because he'd gone and written that foaming-at-the-mouth letter to Fay McLeod' (213–14). In more cheerful moods, however, he knows that 'when he sat down twelve days ago at his kitchen table, pen in hand, scattering words over the pale blue paper – foolish words, crazy words – that he was as deeply, rationally sane as he'd ever been in his life' (215). Tom's vacillation between these opinions points toward the ambiguities in modern attitudes toward reason, emotion, and love, but the novel as a whole endorses the more optimistic of Tom's assessments of his own mental state. The narrative constructs love as a crucially important and serious aspect of human life, and Shields ultimately rejects the idea that being in love represents an aberration from normal behaviour.

Tom's reflections on his letter also raise the issue of the language of love, which is further explored through comments on Fay's research. Part of her thesis on marriage (the most important part, according to her supervisor) discusses the forms of words used to declare affection, and she says of the phrase 'I love you' and its equivalents in various languages: 'It is so deeply embedded in the culture that it is not easily dislodged by fashion, and generally it holds on to its potency despite the corruption of popular songs, cheap slogans, greeting-card verses, and the like' (221). This statement points to one of Shields's central concerns in *The Republic of*

Love: the need to reclaim the language of love from the realm of cliché. The narrator repeatedly draws attention to instances when the characters have bravely uttered something which sounded like cliché but which in fact expressed their genuine feeling: 'For anniversaries [Fay's parents] do not exchange gifts. They are each other's gift. Fay's mother actually said this once. Out loud. Each other's gift' (16). Another example which Fay particularly recalls concerns Strom, the husband of her godmother, Onion: 'Once, years ago, he had turned to Fay in a restaurant and said, "Without Onion there is nothing of value in this world for me, nothing"' (72).

Fay's slightly incredulous response to these statements is consistent with her refusal (in the period before meeting Tom) to take love seriously or to acknowledge its centrality in human lives. This is an attitude which Carol Shields evidently wishes to discredit. In a 1993 interview, she said of *The Republic of Love*:

> I felt ... that I wanted to rescue [the love story], hold it up against other major themes ... Love is the basis of our lives. I don't think of it as a minor theme and yet we all know it's been relegated to Harlequin romance novels. Serious, reflective people do not fall in love; it's embarrassing even to say so. I don't believe that for a minute, so I want to write about love.[5]

Her comment about Harlequin romance novels implies that she views them as a lesser genre, and considers that the theme of love is diminished by being confined to this type of literature. But *The Republic of Love* pays a certain tribute to the popular romance by borrowing its plot patterns and upholding the importance of love as a life experience and a subject for fiction. The romantic novel celebrates the primary human desire for love, rather than dismissing it as embarrassing, and Carol Shields repeats this gesture. She draws attention to the fact that no cultural capital has accrued to the romantic novel, and that no 'serious' writers have experimented with it as a form, and she thereby indicts social attitudes to love, rather than romantic fiction itself:

> Fay's noticed something she's never noticed before. That love is
> not, anywhere, taken seriously. It's not respected. It's the one
> thing in the world everyone wants – she's convinced of that –
> but for some reason people are obliged to pretend that love is
> trifling and foolish.
>
> Work is important. Living arrangements are important. Wars
> and good sex and race relations and the environment are impor-
> tant, and so are health and illness. Even minor shifts of faith or
> political intention are given a weight that is not accorded love ...
> It's womanish, it's embarrassing, something to jeer at, some-
> thing for jerks. Just a love story, people say about a book they
> happen to be reading, to be caught reading. (248)

This shows that, since meeting Tom, Fay has rejected her
earlier belief that falling in love is inconsistent with her intellectual seriousness; and the reference to love stories in this
passage indicates Shields's interest in re-evaluating the literary status of fiction about love. The mention of being 'caught
reading' a love story raises an issue which Dianne Osland, in
her essay in this collection, discusses in relation to *The Stone
Diaries* (1993) – the sense of guilt experienced by romance
readers because they are perceived to be wasting time and
money on repeated versions of the same wish-fulfilling fantasy. Also, Shields's phrase 'Just a love story' contains a faint
echo of Jane Austen's famous attack in *Northanger Abbey* (1818)
on those who denigrate novels: '"And what are you reading,
Miss –?" "Oh! it is only a novel!" replies the young lady; while
she lays down her book with affected indifference, or momen-
tary shame.'[6]

If popular romances have provided one model or intertext
for *The Republic of Love*, Jane Austen has surely provided
another. Shields's ongoing interest in Austen has culminated
in a biography, analysed by Melissa Eden in this volume.
Shields has said that she feels a particular affinity with Austen
and other nineteenth-century women writers because 'they

did understand the love story. They understood the importance of finding the other and weren't ashamed of it.'[7] In her contribution to the present collection, Shields identifies Austen's books as models for her own fictional explorations of enduring relationships and 'the search for a life partner' (32). As Jay Dixon points out:

> One of the main criticisms of Mills & Boon books is that their plots are all the same: girl meets boy, they encounter problems, girl runs away, girl returns, all is miraculously explained away, and marriage ensues. This, of course, is the plot of Charlotte Brontë's *Jane Eyre*, Jane Austen's *Pride and Prejudice*, Samuel Richardson's *Pamela, Cinderella* and *Beauty and the Beast*.[8]

This is also the plot of *The Republic of Love*, but its relation to Austen's novels goes beyond plot and theme, because Austen modifies the conventions of the popular fiction of her era just as Shields does, and in similar ways. Although the distinction between popular and 'literary' fiction had not been articulated in the eighteenth century, there were already two rather formulaic genres which attracted readers in substantial numbers but also attracted a certain measure of contempt: the sentimental novel and the gothic romance. These were the models most readily available to Austen, and her earliest responses to them are expressed through overt and sustained parody. Gothic fiction is parodied, of course, in *Northanger Abbey*, which was begun in 1797 when the gothic novel was at the height of its popularity, and Austen's early piece *Love and Friendship*, written in 1790, mocks the literature of sentiment, which was extremely popular in the 1770s and 1780s.[9] In her major novels, by contrast, Austen salvaged what she found to be usable from the established forms of romantic and sentimental fiction, and discarded the rest. Her mature work (with the exception of her final, unfinished book, *Sanditon*) only occasionally refers to the literary tradition which stands behind it. She sometimes includes parodic elements, such as the mild parody of Fanny Burney and Sir Samuel Egerton Brydges

in *Pride and Prejudice*,[10] but these are very subtle in comparison with the open ironic imitation which characterizes
Northanger Abbey.

Although Austen's major novels do not tend to signal their
differences from earlier fiction explicitly, those differences are
very clear when her writing is compared with that of Samuel
Richardson and of the female writers who emulated him. For
example, these fictions inevitably centred on the courtship of
a young, virtuous, beautiful, and submissive girl, and the
same kind of heroine was to be found in the gothic novels.
Austen, while retaining the focus on courtship, created far
more complex, individual heroines, whose intellectual and
emotional responses and perceptions are not – as with Pamela
or Clarissa – entirely governed by strict codes of feminine
conduct. Austen's heroines deviate from the sentimental stere-
otype in a variety of ways – by being intelligent and mature
(Elinor), wilful and prone to error (Emma, Marianne), less
than beautiful (Catherine), past the first flush of youth (Anne),
insignificant (Fanny), or spirited and confident (Elizabeth).
Shields's response to popular fiction in *The Republic of Love* is
broadly comparable to Austen's response in her major novels,
because the divergence between Shields's text and its popular
model emerges primarily through implicit comparison, with
just a touch of mild parody.

As Austen does in *Persuasion*, Shields creates a rather untypical female protagonist, who is more experienced and intellectual than the average romantic heroine. (I say 'intellectual'
rather than 'intelligent' because the heroines of many popular
romances are represented as particularly intelligent.)[11] A more
striking deviation from the pattern of romantic fiction is the
equal attention which she gives to her male protagonist. Popular romances, as Janice Radway comments in her important
study *Reading the Romance*, almost always focus on female
experience: 'On first discussing romances with [a sample of]
readers, I was struck by the fact that individual books were
inevitably registered in their memories as the stories of particular *women*.'[12] In these and other ways, Shields's novel

modifies the conventions of the romance without direct parody, but it is possible to argue that in some parts of the narrative there is a dimension of parody, in the sense described by Linda Hutcheon as 'a playful, genial mockery of codifiable forms.'[13] Popular romance is certainly a codifiable form, and there is frequently a note of gentle mockery in Shields's attitude toward it, even though she relies on romance for the basic structure and value system of her story. The comic tone of Shields's narrative immediately distances it from the vast majority of popular romances, and she subjects some of the staple elements of the genre to a humorous reworking. For example, the scene in which the protagonists fall in love at first sight begins with a beautiful image of Tom's first glimpse of Fay, running through the rain with a bunch of balloons, but their subsequent conversation takes place in the unromantic setting of a children's party. It is so noisy that they can barely hear each other, and their conversation is stilted and awkward. Tom offers Fay a lift home, only to remember a few minutes later that he has not brought his car. Their wedding and honeymoon are also most unconventional – the original church wedding and large party have been cancelled, and they are married in a courtroom, with no guests, and an officiant 'reading from a rather worn photocopied sheet' (358). The honeymoon consists of two days spent in Tom's apartment, eating canned soup and sardines, during 'the coldest twenty-four hour period ever recorded in the region' (360). These scenes repeat the basic plot events of the traditional romance but defy reader expectations about the presentation of those events; and this strategy fits Hutcheon's definition: 'parody is repetition, but repetition that includes difference.'[14] Shields's purpose in introducing critical difference into her romantic novel is to offer alternative versions of the love story, releasing it from conventional, idealized fictional patterns and incorporating into it elements of unpredictability, complexity, provisionality, and comedy.

Hutcheon argues, further, that in the background of a parodic text 'will stand another text against which the new creation is implicitly to be both measured and understood.'[15] In the quotation which opens this essay, Fay mentions 'romance fiction' and also uses the term 'romance' to describe her relationship with Tom. This explicitly invites the reader to compare Shields's account of a love affair with those offered in paperback romances; and other self-conscious references to love stories within *The Republic of Love* have a similar effect. Whilst I would not argue that *The Republic of Love* is a full-blown parody, its orientation toward popular romance is aptly described by Hutcheon's statements. There is a parodic dimension in its response to romantic fiction, just as there is a parodic dimension in Austen's response to eighteenth-century sentimental fiction.

In Jane Austen's era, fiction of all varieties was widely read but was at the bottom of the hierarchy of literature. The heroine of *Northanger Abbey* perceives the novel as a feminine – and therefore inferior – species of writing. 'You never read novels, I dare say,' Catherine comments to Henry Tilney, adding: 'they are not clever enough for you – gentlemen read better books.'[16] Tilney disagrees with Catherine, and through him Austen voices her objections to this evaluation of fiction. However, the contention that the audience for eighteenth-century novels was predominantly female is tentatively supported by J. Paul Hunter: 'the plots of novels suggest that authors envisioned many women readers among their audience, perhaps even *predominantly* women readers. Fewer women than men were literate, but a larger proportion of women probably (though we cannot be sure) read novels.'[17] We can be very sure that the readers of today's popular romances are almost all women, and that many of them come from lower socio-economic groups.[18] Inevitably, the association of the romance with an audience of this description lowers the literary status of the genre. The status of romances is also damaged by the fact that they are sold at airports and railway stations and are therefore much more readily perceived as commodities to be exhausted and replaced than are novels bought at bookshops or borrowed from libraries. There is a tendency for Carol Shields's books – particularly her early ones – to be seen as women's novels because of their domestic settings.[19] By the time she wrote *The Republic of Love*, she had escaped this classification to a certain extent, yet some of the reviews suggest that the book has been viewed as popular women's fiction. Antonia Bremner's review in the London *Times*, for example, is placed in the Saturday edition and is extremely short. Bremner compares Shields to Mary Wesley and reviews *The Republic of Love* alongside a book called *The Last Honeymoon*, by Shelley Weiner.[20] All this suggests a new women's paperback rather than a 'literary' novel, although Bremner does mention that half of the story is told from the male protagonist's viewpoint.

Despite Shields's exploration of male as well as female experience, and despite the complexity and intellectual sophistication of her narrative, *The Republic of Love* has attracted remarkably little critical attention, and did not receive nearly as many reviews as her other novels.[21] Only two short articles have been published about it: one which focuses entirely on the Winnipeg setting, and another which devotes half its space to *The Stone Diaries*.[22] In fact, the response to *The Republic of Love* among reviewers and critics provides a striking justification of Shields's contention that love and love stories are not taken seriously; and it is also possible that her use of a popular genre has reduced the interest of this novel for academic readers. Yet the same is not true of her 1987 novel *Swann*, which is modelled on another popular fictional genre – the detective story. Interestingly, *Swann* and *The Republic of Love* are the only two of Shields's books which have so far interested film producers,[23] and this may be due to the popular appeal of romance and mystery respectively. *Swann*, however, has also inspired a substantial amount of academic discussion, most of which has focused on Shields's subversion of the conventions of the detective novel.[24] The key point here is that the element of subversion is much greater in *Swann* than in *The Republic of Love*, and the parody far more obvious. *Swann* entirely displaces the mystery from the centre of the novel, since the identity of the criminal can be guessed at a fairly early stage; and the crime (stealing books) is not exactly sensational. The importance of the murder within the plot is also minimal, and, as Barbara Godard points out, 'What is mysterious in this novel is not the death of Mary Swann but her life, which defies reconstruction.'[25] The pleasure of this book is therefore very different from the pleasure of reading a traditional detective story: it inheres mainly in such things as the reader's recognition of Shields's parodic strategies and literary jokes, and in the comedy surrounding the machinations of the literary scholars. These features have made the novel attractive to real-life scholars. The pleasure of *The Republic of Love*, by contrast, derives in part from the characteristic feature of formula romance, described by Janet Batsleer as 'knowing that the happy ending is coming, but not knowing exactly how.'[26] Its story is 'the one story' which, as Dianne Osland comments, romance addicts need to read over and over again (88).

The basic romance pattern of *The Republic of Love* is familiar and intelligible to all readers of fiction. However, although the novel exploits the appeal of this popular genre, it is more than 'just a love story.' It is certainly not directed at the Mills & Boon / Harlequin readership: it aspires to a much higher literary-intellectual status. These aspirations are particularly visible in the sophisticated and sometimes self-reflexive construction of the narrative. The first chapter of *The Republic of Love* uses a technique which reappears at the beginning of *The Stone Diaries*: it gives an account of events which happened to the protagonist as a baby. The story recounted in the opening chapter of *The Stone Diaries* is presented from Daisy's point of view, but could not possibly have been remembered by her since it concerns her own birth. Likewise, Tom's account of being nurtured as an infant by twenty-seven home economics students is an amalgam of second-hand accounts and fantasy. The fantasy results from Tom's adult longing for love: 'The twenty-seven mothers pressed him close to their tender sweater fronts. They would have given him anything, their own breast milk had there been any to offer. With the softest of brushes they smoothed his half dozen silken hairs. Such love, such love – ah God, he'd never know love like that again' (3). This rather overcoloured, sexualized language gestures toward the popular romance, but the rhetoric is deflated by the comic touch of the six hairs, not to mention the absurdity of Tom's status as a home-economics demonstration baby. Also, the impossibility of separating the factual from the imagined details in Tom's account of his infancy destabilizes the reader's relationship to the world of the text. According to Scott McCracken, 'Whereas the solution to the murder mystery suggests that the world is knowable ... in the romance text, desire and fantasy disrupt the reader's perception of a knowable world.'[27]

Tom's fantasy fills in the gaps in the story of his life with narrative. Through Tom, Shields emphasizes 'that narrative hunger is a part of the human personality'[28] and thereby draws attention to her own methods of narrating. This self-reflexivity is evident from the first paragraph of the novel:

> As a baby, Tom Avery had twenty-seven mothers. So he says. That was almost forty years ago.
>
> Ask me more, his eyes beg, ask me for details.
>
> Well, then. At three weeks of age, there he was, this little stringy wailing thing ... His mother ... was hospitalized for six months. Where was his father in all this? What father? Ha! That's another story. (1)

This passage arouses the reader's curiosity, but only partially satisfies it, since the reference to the father is not explained until much later. This is an effective strategy for drawing the readers into the story, whilst also alerting them to the fact that they are being drawn in. The phrase 'another story' also points toward the intersections between the story that is about to be told and hundreds of other stories, concerning people who play a minor role in the tale of Tom Avery. The novel contains many of these other narratives alongside the story of Fay and

Tom, which is itself two stories, since most of the events involving them both are narrated twice, once from her point of view and once from his. The different narrative strands in the novel are interdependent, the most obvious example of this interconnectedness being the comic 'merry-go-round' of partner swapping which links Fay to Tom via a string of ex-lovers (Tom was married to Sheila, who then married Sammy, who then married Fritzi, who had been married to Peter Knightly, who subsequently became Fay's partner).

There are two primary purposes to the inclusion of all the additional stories and minor characters. First, they emphasize the way Fay and Tom are enmeshed in a complex network of human connections, and this is a modification of the conventions of traditional romance. Shields explicitly signals this in a metafictional passage:

> The problem with stories of romance is that lovers are always shown in isolation: two individuals made suddenly mythic by the size of their ardour ... Fay has noticed how love in old-fashioned novels ... tends to be shown as a rarefied blessing, accompanied usually by perfect health, full employment, closets full of clothes, and, most particularly, a conspicuous absence of other people ... Their families, their friends, even their work and their separate histories pale beside their rapture. (333)

In *The Republic of Love* itself, by contrast, all these factors loom large. Family, friends, work, and separate histories are accorded quite as much space in the narrative as Tom and Fay's relationship itself, and they have an immense effect on that relationship. The impact of family is particularly emphasized through the separation of Fay's parents, which precipitates the breaking of her engagement to Tom. The fact that both couples reunite does not erase the meaning of these separations – as Fay observes afterwards: 'Love restored is not precisely love redeemed' (364).

As for work, the love songs which Tom plays on the radio and the comments made by callers to his phone-in show frequently affect his view of his relationships with women; and, likewise, Fay's research on mermaids shapes her understanding of romance and desire. There is a substantial amount of detail about both their careers, and this results from a conscious effort on Shields's part. She remarks in her essay in this volume that 'many contemporary narratives ... pretend that people don't work,' adding that 'certain other work choices hardly ever make it to the fictional page' (32). In *The Republic of Love*, she chooses very unusual careers for both her protagonists, and she commented in a 1996 interview:

> It was when I was writing *The Republic of Love* that I made it a project to write about work in a serious way ... I've always noticed that there wasn't much work in novels ... But someone pointed out to me that this isn't true, for example, if you go a little further down in literature. You find that vocation is very important – in Doctor/Nurse novels, for example.[29]

This last observation could suggest a further continuity between Shields's novel and popular fiction, but she qualifies the connection by adding: 'I'm not sure how much actual work goes on there,' which implies that her consideration of vocation is to be more serious and sustained than that which is found in hospital romances.[30] Janice Radway points to the ultimate conservatism of formula romance on this point: 'all romances ... eventually recommend the usual sexual division of labour that dictates that women take charge of the domestic and purely personal spheres of human endeavour.'[31]

The second purpose of the many minor characters in the novel is to offer a range of viewpoints on love, marriage and romance. The novel mediates between them without offering a final judgment, although some of the opinions are privileged while others are presented ironically. For example, Tom's first wife Sheila asks, 'Love ... Who needs it?' (49). She says this fairly seriously, but it comes to seem ironic because the entire novel demonstrates how much people need to love and be loved. The minor characters tend to espouse one particular view, whereas the protagonists try out several before they make up their minds:

> 'It's a kind of perversion,' Fay said, 'the whole love business.'
>
> She doesn't really think anything of the kind, but she likes to toss her half-formed thoughts at Beverly, who has a talent for weighing all conjectures evenly, taking them into the neat drum of her head and abstracting the outrageous along with the rational.
>
> 'Perversion?' she said. 'Pu-lease. You'd better explain that.' (108)

This is an apt description of the way in which the narrative is constructed, with its many voices and testing of ideas, a strategy which – as Sarah Gamble points out – Shields had already used in *Happenstance* and *Swann*. In *The Republic of Love* traditional conceptions of love are weighed and questioned. For example, one of Fay's insights – 'Love is not necessarily patient. She knows that. Nor kind' (224) – exists in implicit dialogue with Saint Paul's formulation: 'Love is patient; love is kind' (1 Corinthians 13:4). One chapter begins by listing a series of folk-wisdom utterances on the subject of love, each beginning 'They say.' These statements cannot all be reconciled with one another and represent a spectrum of possible ways in which one can be affected by being in love. Over the course of the novel, Tom and Fay receive a myriad of incompatible advice, and this gradually reveals to them that they cannot take the experience of any other couple as a guide for their own relationship, and that fictional love stories are equally unhelpful. This forces them to evolve their own definitions of love. Thus *The Republic of Love* refuses a unitary or objective interpretation of its subject matter: it deconstructs the term 'love' by demonstrating its differing signification for different characters, but without finally rejecting the possibility that two people can discover a meaning in it for themselves. The ultimate success of Tom and Fay's relationship affirms the human potential for permanent attachments, but the multiple perspectives on love articulated by the various characters in *The Republic of Love* qualify and amplify this central narrative. As Shields said of the novel at the time when she was writing it: 'It's about ways of looking at love.'[32]

The views expressed on love and romance are inevitably skewed by the general outlook and the current mood of the character concerned. As her relationship with Peter is ending, Fay thinks of romance in rather jaded terms. 'Romance, Fay knows, grabs onto people like a prize deformity; it keeps them on edge, taunts them, then slitheringly changes shape and withdraws ... Recently she has begun to understand it for the teasing malady it is' (37). The image of romance as taunting and then metamorphosing and withdrawing clearly emerges from her research on mermaids, and this further illustrates the way in which Fay's thinking about love is coloured by insights derived from her professional research as well as by her own direct knowledge. Conversely, her interpretations of mermaids are influenced by her own life experiences, as in this passage:

> She has taken the Metro to Trocadero ... and found ... the extraordinary Belle Epoque building whose ornate front door is surrounded by two ecstatic double-tailed sirens ... their faces masked by sexual desire and numbed by their enforced solitude. This, Fay decides ... is the mer-condition: solitary longing that is always being thwarted. No, not thwarted – denied. (202–3)

At this point, Fay has been travelling alone for several weeks. She is filled with sexual longing for Tom, and has been wondering whether she has denied her own desires and needs. Clearly, her vision of the mermaids' hunger and frustration is partly produced by her own feelings. As Shields remarked in an interview: 'The mermaid is one of the most interesting parts of our iconography because the mermaid doesn't reproduce; she has no reproductive organs, and is always alone.'[33] Fay's interpretations of the mermaids reveal her own fears about future loneliness and her frustrated longing for a child, as well as her intense sexual desire for Tom.

The foregrounding of Fay's sexuality distances her from the heroines of eighteenth- and nineteenth-century fiction, and also from the popular romances of the pre-1970 period, whose heroines were usually far less sexualiy experienced than the heroes. Many romance writers, in recent years, have responded to feminism by creating independent, sexually active heroines, but Fay's somewhat colourful sexual past is unconventional even when measured against these more liberal paperback romances. In terms of marriage, on the other hand, Shields's text converges to a certain extent with the popular romance. Radway comments:

> I have ... been struck by the urgency ... with which romance authors assert that the newly active, more insistent female sexuality displayed in the genre is still most adequately fulfilled in an intimate, monogamous relationship characterized by love and permanence ... [I]n every case, these romances refuse finally to unravel the connection between female sexual desire and monogamous marriage.[34]

The ending of *The Republic of Love* also endorses the idea that a successful monogamous marriage can be the ideal context for sexual love. But while Radway refers only to the fulfilment of female desire in marriage, Shields includes male sexuality also. Both Fay and Tom are sexually active before they meet, but Shields represents the physical relationship developed between them as far more satisfying than those they engage in with partners whom they do not love. Fay's desire for Peter Knightley retreats when she realizes that she is not in love with him and that their partnership cannot become permanent. A few weeks later, in bed with a man she has only just met, Fay 'found herself floating between waves of appetite and a stern minor-key voice, her own, that said: You must not let this happen again.' The narrator adds: 'There are certain moments in her life of which she is deeply ashamed, and this, she knew ... was going to be one of them. There was too much carelessness here.' The last sentence of the chapter is: 'No, it must not happen again' (60). This rejection of casual sex is not couched in moral terms, yet it is very clear-cut. It is repeated in Tom's encounter with Charlotte Downey, who gives him precise instructions for bringing her to quality orgasm. The chapter concludes with a clear echo of the earlier one: 'Never again, he said to himself. Never again' (146). The near-identical representation of casual sex as unfulfilling and demeaning for both hero and heroine shows that, even as Shields reasserts the importance of marriage and monogamy, she refuses to reproduce the conventional gender economy of the popular romance.

Carol Shields repeatedly interrogates the traditional assumptions of the romantic novel. Romantic fiction generally assumes that love is the highest good to which an individual can aspire, that a person in love is in a state of grace, and that marriage is the natural fulfilment of love. Shields questions and tests these assumptions, yet ultimately she upholds them all, though with certain qualifications. This illustrates her strategy of rescuing the basic plots, values, and ideals from traditional love stories, and embedding them in a more complex and self-reflexive kind of fiction. She said on BBC Radio 4 in March 2000: 'I love structure and I love usurping traditional structures. I don't know how I came to be so rebellious because I'm not in my everyday life. But if the novel is going to continue, I think it has to be subverted, and I'm interested in trying to make some new shapes that fit our life.'[35] This is precisely what she does in *The Republic of Love*: she takes a traditional structure, the romantic novel, and reshapes it to fit the lives of modern people. *The Republic of Love* replicates the ideology of the popular romance, both through its emphasis on the centrality of love in human lives and through its ultimate privileging of marriage over other forms of relationship. But these traditional features coexist in Shields's novel with unconventional elements: the detailed exploration of the heroine's sexual past; the emphasis on the professional, community, and family aspects of the protagonists' lives; the equal attention paid to male and female perspectives; the destabilizing of the term 'love' itself; and – most strikingly – the preoccupation with the nature of stories about love.

'Narrative hunger' is explored in *The Republic of Love* in relation to the specific attractions of romantic fiction (a theme which is examined from a different angle in *The Stone Diaries* and discussed by Dianne Osland in this collection). More generally, the novel emphasizes the characters' hunger for 'real-life' narratives of romance: Tom and Fay are fascinated by the stories of each other's past relationships as well as by the ongoing story of their own love affair. The larger pattern of their story matches that of countless other novels about love, and the last paragraph of the novel – which actually describes Fay's mermaid book – could equally well describe *The Republic of Love*:

> Fay ... is on the whole happy with the book ... The cover (in shiny reds, blues, and greens) shows a mermaid surfacing from a wavy stretch of sea water. Her face is blurred. Her abundant hair gestures toward sexual potential. In one of her hands is a comb, representing love and entanglement.
>
> The other hand, which is uplifted (waving or perhaps beckoning), symbolizes a deep longing for completion, the wish for rapturous union, a hunger for the food of love. (366)

Sexual potential and entanglement form the substance of the story, but almost all the characters are motivated by 'a hunger for the food of love,' and the closure supplied by Shields's traditional happy ending implies that this hunger has finally been satisfied. Tom and Fay find 'completion' in each other; the novel is also complete – and yet there is an acknowledgment of the artificiality of such endings. The marriage of Tom and Fay is not really an ending but a new beginning. Their story is not complete (though we shall never know how it goes on), for desire and curiosity are still present. Shields's final sentence emphasizes, not actual completion or rapture, but the *longing* for completion, the *wish* for union, and the *hunger* for love.

Notes

I would like to thank the editors of this volume for their helpful comments on an earlier version of my essay.

1 Carol Shields, *The Republic of Love* (London: Flamingo, 1993), 250. All further references are to this edition.
2 Carol Shields, 'Interview with Carol Shields,' interview by Eleanor Wachtel, *Room of One's Own* 13.1/2 (1989): 45. Shields comments that the title had to be changed because another book called *Bodies of Water* had lately been published.
3 This essay necessarily includes some generalizations about popular romance. These are possible because romantic fiction is fairly formulaic, but it should be noted that there are many variations within the genre. There are, for example, divorced Mills & Boon heroines, but they are the exception rather than the rule. For details, see Jay Dixon, *The Romance Fiction of Mills & Boon 1909–1990s* (London: U College London P, 1999), 1–11.
4 Scott McCracken, *Pulp: Reading Popular Fiction* (Manchester: Manchester UP, 1998), 80.
5 Carol Shields, 'Interview with Carol Shields,' interview by Marjorie Anderson in May 1993, *Prairie Fire* 16.1 (1995): 143.
6 Jane Austen, *Northanger Abbey*, ed. Claire Grogan (Peterborough, ON: Broadview, 1996), 60.
7 Shields, interview by Marjorie Anderson, 146. Further evidence for Shields's interest in Austen is that she is a member of the Jane Austen Society of North America, and in 1991 she wrote an article, 'Jane Austen Images of the Body: No Fingers, No Toes,' for their journal, *Persuasions*. Her biography, *Jane Austen*, is published by Weidenfeld and Nicholson (London, 2001).
8 Dixon, 1.
9 For a discussion of the popularity of sentimental fiction in the late eighteenth and early nineteenth century, see John Mullan,

'Sentimental Novels,' in *The Cambridge Companion to the Eight-eenth-Century Novel*, ed. John Richetti (Cambridge: Cambridge UP, 1996), 236–54.

10 See Sandra M. Gilbert and Susan Gubar, *The Madwoman in the Attic: The Woman Writer and the Nineteenth-Century Literary Imagination* (New Haven, CT: Yale UP, 1979), 120.

11 Janice A. Radway found that her sample of romance readers rated this as the most important quality in a heroine. See Rad-way, *Reading the Romance: Women, Patriarchy, and Popular Litera-ture* (1984; rev. ed., London: Verso, 1987), 77.

12 Radway, 77.

13 Linda Hutcheon, *A Theory of Parody: The Teachings of Twentieth-Century Art Forms* (New York: Methuen, 1985), 15.

14 Hutcheon, 37.

15 Hutcheon, 31.

16 Austen, 120.

17 J. Paul Hunter, 'The Novel and Social/Cultural History,' in Richetti, 22.

18 See Dixon, 29, 182; Radway, 11.

19 See Shields, interview by Anderson, 141.

20 Antonia Bremner, 'Raising Wedded Blisters,' review of *The Republic of Love* and *The Last Honeymoon, Times Saturday Review*, 4 April 1992, p. R37.

21 This fact reflects a survey of British, rather than the North American, newspapers. The difference is particularly noticeable in comparison with *Swann: A Mystery* (Shields's first novel to be published in Britain), *The Stone Diaries*, and *Larry's Party*.

22 See the essays by Nodelman and Thomas in the Bibliography in Section Four of this volume.

23 The film version of *Swann* (dir. Anna Benson Gyles; screenplay David Young) was released at the 1996 Toronto Film Festival. Shields was asked by a Winnipeg producer to write a screenplay for *The Republic of Love*, which she did in 1993, but the film has not been produced.

24 See the Bibliography in this volume for details of articles on *Swann* by Begley, Buss, Godard, Hammill (two articles),

Johnson, Smyth, Sweeney, and Thomas (two articles). See also
Barbour's essay in this volume.

25 Barbara Godard, 'Sleuthing: Feminists Re/writing the Detective
Novel,' *Signature: Journal of Theory and Canadian Literature* 1
(Summer 1989): 57. See also the essay by Barbour in this volume
for further discussion of this point.

26 Janet Batsleer, 'Pulp in the Pink,' *Spare Rib* 109 (1981); reprinted
(excerpt) in *Reading Popular Narrative: A Source Book*, ed. Bob
Ashley (1989; rev. ed., Leicester: Leicester UP, 1997), 219.

27 McCracken, 79.

28 Carol Shields, 'Narrative Hunger and the Overflowing Cupboard,' p. 20 (in this volume).

29 Carol Shields, interview by Sima Rabinowitz, *Hungry Mind
Review* (Feb./March 1996), http://www.bookwire.com/hmr/
hotp/interviews/96–02/sima.html (consulted 17 May 2000).

30 Note also Jay Dixon's contention that the rights of single and
married women to find fulfilment and financial independence
through work have been championed by many Mills & Boon
authors (113–14). Radway found that her sample of romance
readers admired the heroine of Elsie Lee's *The Diplomatic Lover*
(1971), who works in the diplomatic corps (79), and Radway
lists some other romance writers who have assigned unusual
jobs to their heroines (124).

31 Radway, 123.

32 Shields, interview by Eleanor Wachtel, 45.

33 Shields, interview by Anderson, 149.

34 Radway, 15.

35 *Bookclub*, BBC Radio 4, broadcast 5 March 2000, 4 P.M., presented
by James Naughtie.

The Stone Diaries, *Jane Eyre*, and the Burden of Romance

DIANNE OSLAND

I

A year after Clarentine Flett had walked out of her marriage, her husband, Magnus, we are told, discovers four little books in the bottom of Clarentine's sewing basket: 'Romantic books, he supposed they were called, ladies' books with soft paper covers. Nine cents each, the price was stamped on the back. The Nine-Penny Library.'[1] Where they had come from he can only guess – she must have bought them from 'the old Jew peddler ... and read them in secret' (99–100) – though he cannot understand the need for secrecy: 'as if he would ever have denied her so trifling a pleasure' (100). The imputation of meanness clearly rankles. His only explanation for Clarentine's desertion is that she thought him 'mean with money' and 'wanting in soft words and ways' (99), though the meanness with money he denies: he had, after all, once bought her, unsolicited, a ribbon-trimmed hairpin glass (which she had subsequently given away) and had on another occasion surprised her with an ice-box (which had, unaccountably he thinks, thrown her into a rage). And the soft words and ways – 'womanish blathering and carrying on' (99) – she ought never to have expected from a rough Orkney stonecutter. But when he discovers those soft words and ways, a year later, in the cheap romantic novels she had been secretly reading, he commits them to memory so that, if 'this talky foolishness was her greatest need' and she should ever return home, he would be ready. Clarentine never returns, but by the end of the novel Magnus's time, it would seem, has not been wasted: at 115 years of age, he has earned the double distinction of being the oldest man in Great Britain, and of being able to recite the whole of his favourite of Clarentine's novels by heart. By the time his daughter-in-law tracks him down to a nursing home in the Orkneys, however, his grip on the novel has weakened to the extent that he can now recite only the opening lines of the opening paragraph: 'There was no possibility of taking a walk that day. We had been wandering, indeed, in the leafless shrubbery ...'

What *Jane Eyre*, 'that jewel of English literature' (299), is doing at the bottom of Clarentine's sewing basket, together with the other 'ladies' books' from the Nine-Penny Library, is a question of interest, not simply to Magnus, but also to the reader, who might in other circumstances shrink from putting *Jane Eyre* in the same basket with Clarentine's other purchases: '*Struggle for a Heart* by Laura Jean Libby, *What Gold Cannot Buy* by one Mrs. Alexander, *At the World's Mercy* by Florence Warden' (100). But, whatever our qualms about lumping together classics and 'trash,'[2] every genealogy of popular romance lists *Jane Eyre* in its lineage, and most critics are prepared to admit that the enduring popularity of this novel, if not its lasting merit, has something to do with the symbolic satisfactions provided by romance. In her essay on Shields's rehabilitation of the love story in *The Republic of Love*, Faye Hammill has explored these satisfactions, together with the intellectual, social, and emotional pressures that, in the last decade of the twentieth century, have emptied romance of meaning. For Magnus, however, in the first decade of the twentieth century, the language of love has not yet become 'shallow rhetoric' exhaling 'the vapour of stale breath,'[3] and Magnus warms to the task he has set himself, until he is 'a pump primed with words full of softness and acknowledgement' (101), with words that speak of love's deepest needs.

But, as a romance primer, *Jane Eyre* has bestowed on Magnus, and on generations of its readers, a legacy of mixed blessings – and of mixed messages – which it is the intention of this essay, in part, to explore.

For Magnus's daughter-in-law, Daisy Goodwill Flett, the initial puzzle is not so much what Magnus gets out of *Jane Eyre* but what possessed him to read such a book in the first place, let alone commit it to memory: 'He was literate; he could read the Bible or the mail order catalogue if needs be, but he was not a man who would ever have sat himself down to read a book. Mrs. Flett knows this without being told: No, it would not enter his head to read a book. Particularly not a novel. Not a novel by an Englishwoman named Charlotte Brontë. And never that jewel of English literature, *Jane Eyre*' (299). The explanation given for Magnus's initial fascination with *Jane Eyre* suggests satisfactions rather more pragmatic than symbolic: alone in his parlour on wintry evenings, Magnus began reading Clarentine's books because it was a change from listening to the clock tick. And he kept reading to commit to memory soft words and ways, in earnest of his wife's return. And he kept reading *Jane Eyre*, in particular, until he knew it by heart, 'chapter by chapter, every sentence, every word' (296), because it brought Clarentine back: 'there were turnings in the story that filled the back of his throat with smarting, sweet pains, and in those moments he felt his wife only a dozen heartbeats away, so close he could almost reach out and stroke the silkiness of her inner thighs' (100).

Magnus's longings have a name – 'Clarentine' – and with that name a certain legitimacy and propriety beyond the silkiness of inner thighs, though Daisy also attributes to him another longing, the desire for home, which at the age of sixty-five had carried him from Tyndall, Manitoba, where he had emigrated at the age of eighteen, back to the Orkneys, a country he could barely remember and where he had no living relatives. Had Daisy thought about it, she might have found in this supposed longing for home an explanation of sorts for his obsession with *Jane Eyre*. For Daisy thinks of Magnus, and identifies with him (albeit without ever knowing him), as 'the wanderer,' and like Jane Eyre (who feels 'a wanderer on the face of the earth'),[4] Daisy believes 'herself to be a wanderer too, with an orphan's heart and a wistful longing for refuge, for a door marked with her own name' (305). But more revealingly, perhaps, Magnus's return to the Orkneys does not seem to be prompted by any particular, conscious need for family and roots. He simply goes 'home' in the hope that this will fix whatever is wrong with him – but in much the same way as Jane Eyre often feels that the answer to her restless discontent must lie in simply being somewhere else: 'What do I want? A new place, in a new house, amongst new faces, under new circumstances' (*JE* 100). The fact that she also happened to find her nearest living relatives on one of these excursions was not part of the plan.

The question of whether *Jane Eyre* has had a hand in shaping Magnus's longings – putting ideas into his head, for example, that drag him half way round the world – is not one that *The Stone Diaries* explicitly addresses, though it is hard to imagine this kind of obsessive rereading not having some effect, beyond enabling him to repeat the novel by heart. Certainly, other echoes of *Jane Eyre* emerge in Magnus's life – most notably in his 'broken cry,' his call to his lost Clarentine: 'Clarentine, come home, come home, my darling one, my only, only love' (101).[5] Magnus now has a strong line in 'soft words' that is a considerable improvement on the satisfied grunts that were his former tokens of intimacy with Clarentine, but if, as it appears, 'this talky foolishness' is now also expressing *his* greatest need – 'my darling one, my only, only love' – is *Jane Eyre* responsible, not simply for providing a vocabulary that can give the 'smarting, sweet pains' in the back of Magnus's throat a name, but also for *creating* the ache that he identifies first with Clarentine, and then with the desire to go home?

II

I ask this question because of related, and largely untested, assumptions concerning what addiction to popular romances must do to the women who read them, sometimes two or three or more each week. They may not, like Magnus, be reading the one book over and over again, but it is essentially the one story to which they return insatiably, and from which, it is often argued, they cannot possibly emerge unscathed. The question of what Magnus's reading has done to him – at least in the way that question has been framed – may seem to demean this simple man's search for meaning in his empty life, but I would be surprised if it had not occurred to some readers that those romances secreted in the bottom of Clarentine's sewing basket are not simply a symptom of Clarentine's discontent but have somehow contributed to it. For a start, they are hidden – but is it only because, as Magnus assumes, she thinks that he would deny her 'so trifling a pleasure' (100)? According to the readers surveyed in Janice Radway's *Reading the Romance*, romance readers today still hide their books, though not only because of criticism of the money spent on them, but also because of guilt at satisfying a pleasure recognized to be in some way shamefully, or at least embarrassingly, self-indulgent. At the same time, they also claim to be convinced that romance reading changes women, though in ways they seem reluctant to make explicit.[6] So perhaps it is shame that prompts Clarentine to hide her books, shame at wasting her time and money on trifles; perhaps it is even guilt at harbouring the unfulfilled desires that romance satisfies but that marriage does not. Or more troubling still is the possibility that romance actually *plants* the desires that marriage cannot satisfy, and that Clarentine is incited to rebellion by fictional example: 'I am no bird; and no net ensnares me,' Jane tells Rochester, 'I am a free human being with an independent will; which I now exert to leave you' (*JE* 284). Clarentine is grateful 'that "God who so loved the world" had chosen to let her go her own way' (75), but has Clarentine also been taking lessons from Jane?

Certainly, Brontë was accused in her own day of fomenting 'ungodly discontent.' For example, Elizabeth Rigby related Jane's unrest to the same 'tone of the mind and thought'

evident in the political agitation that had 'overthrown authority and violated every code human and divine' at home and
abroad.[7] Jane herself claims to speak for the 'millions' who are
already 'in silent revolt against their lot' (*JE* 125), though
romance has more commonly been attacked for creating rather
than simply voicing discontent. There is, in fact, a long tradition of blaming romance for all manner of female shortcom-
ings, and over the centuries the catalogue of dangers to which
women were considered vulnerable has become so extensive
that no facet of a woman's life – physical, social, moral, intellectual, or spiritual – has been deemed safe from corruption.[8]
But the most common complaints have been that romance
reading encourages indolence and a dereliction of household
duties, and that it breeds discontent, inflaming the imagination and softening the heart. And these are the symptoms that
Clarentine exhibits before she walks out of her marriage: for
hours she sits 'locked into paralysis over her mending basket,
watching a fly creep across the table' (11), until, late with the
laundry, she hangs out her washing in the mid-afternoon,
'faint with longing' (16) but without knowing for what, 'a
woman whose desires stand at the bottom of a cracked pitcher,
waiting' (15).

As Clarentine lets the housework drift, unable to resist the
'teasing seduction of ease and secrecy' (11), her daydreams
also exhibit signs of the sexual transgressiveness that Jacqueline
Pearson suggests is implicated in the more virulent attacks on
romance reading.[9] The reproachful God whom Clarentine en-
visages condemning her sloth would no doubt object to the
way her daydreams progressively encroach on time that should
be devoted to caring for others, but presumably he would
also be less than impressed by their explicitly erotic content.
Intriguingly similar to the sensations – the 'smarting, sweet
pains' that fill the back of the throat, the silkiness of 'inner
thighs' – that *Jane Eyre* evokes for Magnus, Clarentine's daydreams enclose her in 'tenderness': 'It rises around her like a
cloud of scent. There's no face or voice to it, only a soft, steady,
pervasive fragrance, a kind of rapturous wave that enters her

throat, then moves downward through her body, bringing tightness to her female parts and the muscles of her softened thighs' (12).

Behind the professed concern for the romance reader's moral and mental well-being may well have been, as William B. Warner argues, a more acute anxiety regarding her sexual awakening, an anxiety fed by a commodity that could be purchased and consumed in secret.[10] But no more than Magnus is she roused to realize her sensual dream in more tangible form. If Clarentine envied Mercy Goodwill's 'secret hoard of tenderness and the soft words her young husband pours into her ear' (18) – if these are 'the endearments a woman needs to hear' (35), if 'this talky foolishness was her greatest need' (100) – then it might seem surprising that when she leaves Magnus (whose romantic overtures are confined to 'If you're willing, Mother'), she does not go looking for a man who will supply his deficiencies. Instead she opts for 'a new servitude' (*JE* 99) – the care of someone else's daughter – and hard labour, observed by Magnus, 'working in that garden of hers with her back bent over double like the Galician women did' (99). If Clarentine has been taking lessons from Jane, they would seem to have little to do with the search for either the perfect soulmate or passionate love.

Clarentine's amorphous longing takes the form of a desire for a new life elsewhere, but without a clear understanding of what exactly she hopes to find, beyond simply the possibility of another kind of life. Like Magnus, who waits 'for the bare Orkney landscape to rise up and inform him, to advise him, of what he must do next' (95), and like Daisy, who returns to Canada hoping that 'something might happen,' praying, 'Please, please let something happen' (132), Clarentine eventually walks out of one life and into another: 'Ahead waited chance and opportunity of her own making ... she would wait, watchful and alert, to see what came her way' (49). In this she might also be said to be following in the footsteps of Jane Eyre, who longs 'to go where there was life and movement' (*JE* 103), to 'reach the busy world, towns, regions full of life [she] had heard of but never seen' (*JE* 125), but also without hoping for anything more specific than 'a complete change at least' (*JE* 103). But Jane, for all her unconventionality, is a conventionally fictional heroine whose steps are guided by the narrative imperative of 'tellability,' which demands that something *must* happen,[11] whereas life holds no such guarantees. 'Unluckily, a good part of the world falls through the narrative sieve,' Shields observes in her essay 'Narrative Hunger and the Overflowing Cupboard,'[12] and for women, in particular, the expectation of a tellable life, or at least of a life that meets the criteria of tellability established by traditional narrative structures, might well be one of the heaviest burdens of romance.

III

The legacy of *Jane Eyre* in Clarentine's life, however, is as difficult to pin down as it is in Magnus's – a legacy as difficult to pin down, in fact, as the effects of reading are in anyone's life. Carol Shields herself has admitted that 'a lot of my experience of what a woman's life could be ... came from reading fiction, not from reality. Just seeing other patterns of being.'[13] This is one source of our 'narrative hunger,' 'a natural ... longing to expand [our] own lives and their narrative possibilities' ('Narrative Hunger' 20). But how, or even if, this consciousness of another kind of life translates into actual behaviour is another question. As Radway comments in her new Introduction to *Reading the Romance,* 'it matters enormously what the cumulative effects of the act of romance reading are on actual readers. Unfortunately, those effects are extraordinarily difficult to trace.'[14] In the case of Clarentine, certainly, we cannot tell what those effects might be. We cannot tell, for example, whether romance simply awakened in Clarentine a consciousness of 'other patterns of being,' or whether, more specifically, Jane Eyre's declaration of independence provoked resentment of limited horizons intense enough to incite Clarentine to seek liberty and opportunity outside her marriage of twenty-five years.[15] We cannot know, in fact, whether the novel had any effect at all. But, more to the point, we cannot know whether she or Magnus even read the novel because Daisy cannot know what happened when Magnus was alone in his parlour on wintry evenings, and she cannot know what has been going on inside the privacy of Clarentine's home, where only God, and not the biographer, can enter as 'The Unseen Guest' (12).

All we do know is that, given that this is Daisy's autobiography, that Daisy has read the novel, and that she, if not Magnus and Clarentine, has apparently been taking lessons from it. It certainly appears amongst the books she has (presumably) read (355), and it emerges periodically in irreverent echoes throughout the story, and, suspiciously, not simply in the lives of those characters who are represented as having a narrative stake in it. Some correspondences are perhaps tenuous enough to resist attribution. Both novels, for example, dabble in symbolic naming, the earth, air, fire, and water of *Jane Eyre* paralleled by the flowers and stones of *The Stone Diaries*.[16] Both also engage in epistemological reflections on autobiography, and both narrators appear, whether independently or in collusion, to be uncomfortable with the presumptuousness of biographical compressions. 'Even the sentence parts seize on the tongue,' Daisy observes, 'so that to say "Twelve years passed" is to deny the fact of biographical logic' (27). In a similar vein, Jane comments that 'this is not to be a regular autobiography: I am only bound to invoke memory where I know her responses will possess some degree of interest; therefore I now pass a space of eight years almost in silence' (*JE* 97). More interestingly, there is the shared distrust of men who do not know how to treat a flower properly. In *Jane Eyre* one of the most telling contrasts between Rochester and St John Rivers is the antithesis between a Rochester who stoops 'towards a knot of flowers, either to inhale their fragrance or to admire the dew-beads on their petals' (*JE* 279), and a St John who demonstrates a cavalier disregard for daisies, distractedly crushing 'the snowy heads of the closed flowers with his foot' (*JE* 406). In *The Stone Diaries,* Clarentine characterizes God as 'the petulant father blundering about in the garden, trampling on all her favourite flowers' (113), and Harold Hoad's crass obduracy is demonstrated when, ignoring Daisy's reproach, he continues to swing his stick through the air, 'lopping off the heads of delphiniums, sweet william, bachelor buttons, irises' (116).[17]

Harold's death also recalls, in a bizarrely twisted fashion, the death of Rochester's first wife, Bertha, who, having set fire to Thornfield, stands on the roof, 'waving her arms, above the battlements, and shouting out till they could hear her a mile off,' before leaping to her death as Rochester approached and called her name: 'she yelled, and gave a spring, and the next minute she lay smashed on the pavement' (*JE* 476).[18] In *The Stone Diaries* it is not the mad wife who falls to her death but the husband, perhaps the victim, like Bertha, of hereditary madness, but certainly, on his honeymoon in France, comprehensively drunk. Perched on a third-storey window sill, a bottle in one hand and tossing coins to children in the square below, he is 'laughing, a crazy cackling one-note sound' (119), when Daisy suddenly sneezes.[19] Jane's role in Bertha's death may have been quite as innocent, the unwitting instigator of the jealous rage that prompted Bertha to set fire to the bed in which Jane had slept, but for Jane as well as Daisy 'the obligation of tragedy and its insistence on moving in a forward direction' (*SD* 119) brings a blessed relief.

IV

In one of Daisy's reflections on her imaginative reconstructions, she acknowledges that 'she enlarges on the available material, extends, shrinks, reshapes what's offered; this mixed potion is her life. She swirls it one way or the other, depending on – who knows what it depends on? – the fulcrum of desire, or of necessity. She might drop in a ripe plum from a library book she's reading' (282). But which are the ripe plums? There is corroborating evidence for some of the circumstances of Harold's death that she relates – a death certificate, an inquest, and newspaper reports – though culpable details, such as Daisy's sneeze and her physical and emotional paralysis for a good minute before getting up to investigate the squelch, she admits to suppressing, and maudlin embellishments attach themselves (presumably without Daisy's help) to the story that circulates afterwards. In Daisy's account of her own life, she freely admits to extending, shrinking, reshaping 'the available materials,' as any good postmodernist should, but it is in her account of the characters who impinge on her life that the potion is most suspiciously concocted.

Much of Magnus's story would seem to originate, for example, from Daisy's identification in the Orkneys of the 115-year-old Magnus Flett as her father-in-law. The evidence is slim. Flett was a common Orkney name, and the man had no relatives, no friends, no letters, no personal papers, no birth certificate (314); he could scarcely see or hear, and, apart from reciting the first few lines of *Jane Eyre*, could barely string two words together. But she believes this to be her Magnus, believing 'the evidence of her eyes, her ears, her intuition, that mythical female organ' (307), though before she can reconcile her belief with the few stray facts she already knows about Magnus, there is work to be done: 'Naturally it will take some time for her to absorb all she's discovered. A conscious revisioning will be required of her: accommodation, adjustment. Certain stray elements which are anomalous in nature, even irrational, will have to be tapped in with a jeweller's hammer. Reworked. Propped up with guesswork. Balanced. Defended' (307). And chief among these stray elements is this man's obsession with *Jane Eyre* – because Daisy *knows* that her Magnus would never have read such a book: 'Impossible' (299).

In critical discussion of *The Stone Diaries* there has been a tendency to accommodate the anomalous and irrational elements by taking (albeit fictional) authorship out of Daisy's hands, effectively denying her a voice at the same time as insisting that her erasure from her own writing reflects the way women have always been silenced.[20] Simone Vauthier, for example, in an analysis of 'ruptures' in *The Stone Diaries,* argues that some discrepancies in the narrative 'can be accounted for only by positing a narrator who knows more than Daisy knows or invents. To give but one example, if Daisy recounts (or invents) the story of Magnus Flett's memorizing *Jane Eyre,* how does she not identify the old man in Orkney on being told about his prodigious achievement?'[21] The discrepancy can also be accounted for, however, by positing a Daisy who constructs the story of Magnus's obsession with *Jane Eyre* only *after* identifying the old man as her father-in-law. Daisy admits to imposing 'the voice of the future on the events of the past, causing all manner of wavy distortion' (148), and it is telling that the story she comes up with neatly accounts for *all* the material facts of the gentleman's life: not simply his extraordinary achievement in memorizing *Jane Eyre,* but also the fact that he has no letters or personal papers tying him to his life in Canada (in Daisy's story, he decides to shed the excess baggage of his past life at the railway station in Thurso before crossing to the Orkneys) but possesses a photograph of 'The Ladies Rhythm and Movement Club' (in Daisy's story, the words written on the back are in a hand that Magnus cannot identify, conveniently dispensing with the problem of Daisy not recognizing Clarentine's 'large, loopy, uneducated hand' [49]).[22] Other elements of Magnus's story are also tenuously grounded in the 'historical' record. The meanness with money, for example, is corroborated by, or manufactured to fit, his consistent refusal to help out with his wife's upkeep; his self-education in 'soft words and ways' might have been prompted, or germinated in Daisy's mind, by Barker's letter suggesting that if he wants his wife back, an appeal on his part, 'if sincerely expressed and softly worded, might encourage her to reflect on her situation and eventually return home' (50). We are still left, however, with the problem of why Magnus would turn to *Jane Eyre* for help – unless he comes across it by accident, left, perhaps, in the bottom of her sewing basket by Clarentine.

Assuming that it has been Daisy who has been doing the tinkering with the jeweller's hammer, there is not a lot of evidence to support her conjectures about Clarentine, and she cannot have known much from Clarentine herself since she is only eleven years old when Clarentine dies. Her discontent might be inferred from the fact that after twenty-five years she walks out of the house with a bare 'Good-bye' and refuses to return. But her reading of romantic novels, her unsettling discovery of the 'secret hoard of tenderness' (18) in the house next door, and 'her lost hours, her vivid dreams and shreds of language' (12) seem to have little more to substantiate them than an unusually fervent and possibly derivative phrase from next door in a letter to Cuyler in which she declares, 'I loved your dear wife Mercy with all my heart' (50), and the peculiar fact recorded (presumably) by Skoot Skutari in *The Skutari Tales* (another in Daisy's list of reading) that on the day his grandfather discovered Daisy's mother giving birth, he had arrived in town mid-afternoon, and when he went next door to get help, the neighbour was hanging out her clothes – an odd time for a diligent housewife to be doing the washing. What had Clarentine been doing with the rest of the day? Reading romances and daydreaming?

The tenuousness of Daisy's grip on the substance of her characters' lives might be seen as part of the postmodernist assault on the deceptions and betrayals of conventional autobiography. It might be seen, for example, as a strategy that 'destabilises the authority of the narrating voice(s)'[23] or in which 'a transparent, essentialized, centred self or text is surrendered to an indeterminate, non-linear one of opacity, dispersion, gaps, and boundaries.'[24] And it is true that a dawning recognition of the inconsistencies and impossibilities of Daisy's narrative can slowly undermine confidence in the narrative verities that sustain the formative accretions of the coherent self, until the entire narrative fabric begins to unravel and *everything* becomes provisional, *anything* invented (including letters, reading lists, recipes, and even limestone towers). But it is surprising, and perhaps worrying, how many discontinuities we are prepared to overlook, how many simply do not register, how willingly we re-establish the terms of the contract between an external verifiable reality and life reconstituted in, or as, language.[25] And it is not simply that getting lost in a story is more fun than deconstructing it. At least in *The Stone Diaries*, recognition of the potential scope of Daisy's invention is inevitably retrospective, since we cannot know just how little Daisy has to go on until the possibility of witnesses is exhausted. We are warned very early, for example, that there are no witnesses in Mercy's kitchen, but we do not know that we need any until after the mother has died, eliminating Mercy herself as the source of the tale. We do not know how to distinguish – or even that there is reason to distinguish – unlicensed conjecture from factual testimony until there are no more potential witnesses left. As Cuyler lies dying, for example, struggling to remember what it was he had buried at the base of his pyramid, we do not understand, until we learn that Maria does not return in time and he dies alone, that even the ring at the base of the pyramid is, in all likelihood, just another piece of Daisy's creative accounting, an explanation for why she does not possess anything of her mother's, not even her wedding ring, just as Cuyler's dying, and unspoken, decision to bulldoze the pyramid rather too conveniently sanctions the action taken to sell the property after his death.

If Daisy's imaginative recuperation of the past is seen as action taken *within* the narrative to reconcile what she knows with what she needs or desires, her stories can also be seen as reassertions of the self that Daisy fears she has allowed to be written out of her life. 'I'm still in here' (322), she insists at the end, and she is, not simply in the sense that she resists being prematurely 'written off,' but also in the sense that her 'startling ability to draft alternate versions' (190) of the life around her enables her to write herself into the lives she reinvents, even to the point of feeling momentarily that she 'has given birth to her mother, and not the other way around' (191). And in one sense, of course, she has: the story of her own birth and her mother's death has been deduced from the flimsiest evidence, 'adding up ... what has been off-handedly revealed, those tiny allotted increments of knowledge' (340). A tiny scrap of knowledge such as Cuyler's description of her mother to the eleven-year-old Daisy as 'a young woman uniquely skilled with pies and preserves and household management' (89) can be fashioned into her preoccupation on the day of Daisy's birth with the elaborate preparation of a Malvern pudding; another scrap of knowledge, the fact that no one knew Mercy was pregnant, can burgeon, in Daisy's mind, into the image of an 'immense, bloated wife' whose pregnancy might pass unnoticed (16), rather than (if we are to believe the evidence of the photo) a moderately plump young woman several inches shorter (rather than, as Daisy would have it, touching up the contrast, taller) than her 'boy-bodied' husband (33). But 'her inability to feel love,' despite Cuyler's 'immense, unfathomable ardour,' her loneliness, 'separated from the ordinary consolation of blood ties,' the way she 'seems always to be waiting for something fresh to happen' (7), but without knowing what that 'something' could be – all these seem to be a projection of Daisy's own anxieties onto her mother, 'the bringing together of what she fears' (340). And Mercy's 'secret hoard of tenderness' might also be seen as Daisy's gift to her mother, supported, plausibly enough, by Cuyler's subsequent oratorical exuberance, but driven, perhaps, by Daisy's own deprivation: amongst the list of things she has not done or experienced in her life that is recorded near the end we learn: 'Nor, though she knew she had been loved in her life, did she ever hear the words "I love you, Daisy" uttered aloud (such a simple phrase), and only during the long, thin, uneventful sleep that preceded her death did she have the wit (and the leisure) to ponder the injustice of this' (345).

V

All of Daisy's storytelling seems to be speaking to her own needs. She tells us, for example, that she 'is cursed with the lonely woman's romantic imagination and thus can support only happy endings' (149), and the story she constructs of Magnus's life certainly succeeds in transforming him from a sad case into a national celebrity, from the man she still imagined, when she set out on her trip to the Orkneys, to be 'unhappy,' 'aggrieved,' and 'bitter' into a man who had not only discovered a depth of passion welling within him but who also managed to turn his grief for the loss of his 'only, only love' into a monumental performance. At the same time, Magnus's story, like Cuyler's, also attests to one of Daisy's grievances: 'Men ... were uniquely honoured by the stories that erupted in their lives, whereas women were more likely to be smothered by theirs. Why? Why should this be? Why should men be allowed to strut under the privilege of their life adventures, wearing them like a breastful of medals, while women went all gray and silent beneath the weight of theirs?' (121). Buried at the bottom of both Magnus's and Cuyler's stories is a lost love of such passionate intensity – if we are to believe the words that embody it – that each is driven by grief to perform a prodigious feat: Cuyler's limestone tower, thirty-foot high yet held together only by gravity and balance, 'a dream structure made up of sorrow mingled with bewilderment' (58), but capable of winning him fame and fortune; and Magnus's memorization of *Jane Eyre*, 'his thing' (296), earning him a profile in the *Sunday Times* and an appearance on BBC television. Magnus and Cuyler make names for themselves from their grief, but in each case the woman at the bottom of it all is lost: Cuyler has 'forgotten the impulse that launched the tower' (73), and Magnus ends up simply reciting a book. The memorial honours the man, but not the memory.

The stories that erupt in Daisy's own life leave her, she claims, 'blinded,' 'throttled,' 'smothered,' 'swamped,' 'crowded out of her own life' (190), 'erased from the record of her own existence' (76). These are essentially the stories that people tell about her: the stories we learn to live by, fashioned from 'the available materials,' but shaped by gender, social, and cultural assumptions – and flavoured also by the odd 'ripe plum' from narrative configurations that belong in the library but that often embellish our expectations of life. These configurations make Mercy and Cuyler, for example, the 'beautiful young wife' and the 'handsome young husband' in the eyes of the tower picnickers, even though they have never seen Mercy, and Cuyler in the flesh is 'no longer handsome by the day's standard' (71); they assign a 'tragic broken engagement' to the past of young Barker Flett simply because he is handsome and inexplicably unattached; they turn the 'gorgeous' Harold Hoad into a philanthropist 'distributing money ... to these poor little street children' (124), and the abrupt curtailment of the fairy-tale marriage into tragedy, the stuff of which nightmares are made.

These stories also assign roles to Daisy, telling her what it is a young woman is allowed to want: to mend a man, to make other people happy, to be a good wife and mother. She marries Harold, for example, because 'she honestly believes she can change him, take hold of him and make something noble of his wild nature ... This, in fact, is her whole reason for marrying him, this and the fact that it is "time" to marry – she is, after all, twenty-two years old. She feels her life taking on a shape, gathering itself around an urge to be summoned. She wants to want something but doesn't know what she is allowed. She would like to be prepared, to be strong' (117). But Daisy does not get a Rochester, charmed and gratified by her capacity to do him good; she gets instead a man who is so looking forward to a spot of correction – 'love like a scalpel, a whip' (117) – that it seems part of a perverse erotic fantasy: speeding drunkenly through the French countryside with his new wife pleading, whimpering, shouting for him to stop, 'he almost groans with the pleasure of what he is hearing, his darling scolding bride who is bent so sweetly on reform' (118). Nor does Daisy receive Jane's summons, supernatural or otherwise. She sneezes, and Harold is gone, with Daisy rescued from a disastrous marriage but cast in the role of the shattered bride, though in fact grieving, not for Harold but 'for her own bungling. For what she allowed. For the great story she let rise up and swamp her' (125). In retrospect, she may think, 'rather grandly,' of her role in this great story in terms of 'the obligation of tragedy' (119), but it is a role into which she has simply drifted and which culminates in an untellably bathetic climax: 'Daisy told her dear old trusted school friends everything – everything except the fact that she had sneezed just before Harold fell out the window, also that she had remained frozen on the bed for a minute or more afterward, her eyes staring at the ceiling, feeling herself already drifting towards the far end of this calamity' (125).

After a mother dead in childbirth and a husband killed on their honeymoon, Daisy's marriage to Barker Flett would seem to have saved her from her 'ragbag history' (122) and given her everything a woman could want: 'a distinguished husband and a large well-managed house and three beautiful children' (184). Like her friend Beans, who, once 'she is settled into married life with two babies, is always going on about making other people happy' (131), and like her own mother, 'dear, dear, willing Mercy,' Daisy buries herself in domestic life. 'Deeply, fervently, sincerely desiring to be a good wife and mother' (185), she reads every issue of the twentieth-century's conduct books, *Good Housekeeping*, *McCalls*, and the *Canadian Home Companion* (which offer such useful advice on how to please your husband in bed as 'Try to make your husband believe that you are always ready for his entreaties,' and 'The wearing of pyjamas has driven many a man to seek affection elsewhere' [186]). But if this is everything a woman could want, Daisy also realizes that it might hardly be called living at all, and no more than in the story of the mother dead in childbirth or the husband killed on his honeymoon does Daisy exert narrative control. As Daisy can imagine her unmarried friend, Fraidy, thinking: 'I see you're still breathing, Daisy ... I notice you continue to wake up in the morning and go to bed at night. Now isn't that interesting. I believe your life is still going along, it's still happening to you, isn't it?' (184–5).

When Daisy falls into a profound depression following the loss of the newspaper column that she had made her own after Barker's death, her existence is in fact reduced to these bare vital signs: she breathes, she wakes up in the morning, she goes to bed at night. In her own mind, she theorizes about what is wrong with her, and about what other people think is wrong with her: what it is she wants so much but doesn't have, whether 'the shaping satisfaction' of 'a job of work' (240), sex, a functioning intellect, a good cry, another husband, a mother, or relief from loneliness and the fear of abandonment. It is a formidable catalogue of deprivations, all of which seem plausible enough, even Fraidy's scornful contribution, which undercuts the lot of them: 'What do women want, Freud asked. The old fool, the charlatan. He knew what women wanted. They wanted nothing. Nothing was good enough' (246).

Wanting nothing because nothing is good enough, whether in the sense that women's needs are inconsequential or in the sense that they are insatiable, exemplifies the deep-seated ambivalence that undermines female desire in *The Stone Diaries*. It can be seen in the irresistible hunger that overwhelms the female characters, literally in the case of Mercy's compulsive eating, but also in Clarentine's addictive daydreams, in Fraidy's fifty-odd lovers. It can also be seen in the guilt at indulging what is perceived as illicit longing – regardless of its object, or, as is often the case, regardless of its lack of a specific object. Daisy, for example, even in the act of voicing her desires, pulls back, conscious of the shameful self-indulgence that a preoccupation with her own needs reflects. Trained in the business of making other people happy, she shrinks from offending, shrinks from saying what she wants (thinking, 'Go away, please just go away,' saying, 'It's so good of you to come' [314]). Even in her dying reminiscences, she is ashamed of abusing the patience of her captive audience, 'always going on and on about her own concerns. Instead of thinking of others. Putting others first' (340).

VI

In her analysis of the satisfactions provided by romance reading, Janice Radway highlights precisely this expectation of a woman's self-abnegating solicitude for the well-being of others as the primary motivating force in romance readers' desire to lose themselves in a book: 'it creates a time or space within which a woman can be entirely on her own, preoccupied with her personal needs, desires, and pleasure.' But it also creates guilt: guilt at the 'wasted' time and money that could have been devoted to others, and guilt at the shameful fascination with what is presumed to be a wish-fulfilling fantasy.[26] This is one of the burdens of romance: it feeds and intensifies the sense of unrest it addresses even as it temporarily assuages that unrest. Another lies in the urge to reproduce its repetitive paradigms, as if the fictional solutions indeed provided 'patterns for living.'

But there is also another burden of romance: its tenor or underlying meaning, its 'undersong' or muted refrain,[27] carried by its latent, as distinct from its manifest, content.[28] The plot of *Jane Eyre* would seem to imply, for example, that what Jane wants is a man who needs her, but this is not what Daisy's Clarentine takes away with her from the novel. What Clarentine seems to want – and what Jane *says* she wants – is the same as what a man wants: an adequate field for her endeavours.[29] Jane happens to find such a field in a dank corner of the English countryside caring for a maimed and blinded Rochester; Clarentine happens to find it in some waste land adjacent to her son's lodgings in Winnipeg while she is caring for her neighbour's child. But the obstacle for Daisy is that endeavour implies purpose, and her problem, as a woman of her age, is to know what she wants.[30] She feels that she lacks a 'kernel of authenticity,' a lack which she associates with the solitariness of orphanhood, and with the absence of witnesses to testify to her 'moments of courage or shame' (339).[31] But authenticity also comes from knowing what you want and acting upon it, and Daisy's – and, she suggests, a woman's – characteristic response is just 'to let her life happen to her' (356). As a thirty-one-year-old woman riding the train to Canada, for example, she compares her own life to that of the men journeying with her. When the train arrives in

Ottawa, these men will 'hurry off into the contained nexus of their real lives, while she is about to hurl herself into whatever accident of fortune awaits her. She will accept "it" without protest, without question, for what choice has she? ... She is powerless, anchorless, soft-tissued – a woman. Perhaps that is the whole of it, that she is a woman. Yes, of course' (150).

But 'Yes, of course' sounds a warning note: it is too glib, too lazy, too complacently 'soft-tissued,' despite the younger Daisy's satisfaction with a 'flash of insight' she thinks worthy of recording in her journal. The Daisy who lies dying at the end of the novel, however, does not accept '"it" without protest, without question.' She may resent being termed 'feisty,' but she has learned how to fight back;[32] she may deny being tough but is certainly not 'an old softie' (327); and while her last words, 'I am not at peace,' may be unspoken, she has hardly been silenced if we grant her 'a real gift for making a story out of things' (222). As she lies, in her last dreams, seeing nothing 'but the deep, shared common distress of men and women, and how little they are allowed, finally, to say' (359), she imagines herself turning to stone like the effigies of bishops and saints in the cathedral of Kirkwall. It is an image that she enjoys, but, however 'hugely imposing' (358), this final resting place 'wasn't good enough for them, and it isn't for her either' (359). A monument need not be built of stone; it can also be a 'written record,' 'a piece of information given in writing,'[33] and the monument that Daisy constructs – *The Stone Diaries* – is, like Cuyler's stone tower, held in place by nothing more than 'gravity and balance,' its cohesion based simply on the snugness of fit of the pieces it puts together. '[S]haped in a slant / of available light,' it is partial and prejudiced, and 'set to the movement / of possible music,' it is certainly speculative,[34] but, if Daisy is still in there, the burden of its song has not been silenced.

In 'Warren's Theory' about his mother's depression, Warren laments the squandered intellect of the woman who 'could write earnestly, even passionately' about 'Camillo Cavour: Statesman and Visionary' in 'an obscure period of nineteenth-century Italian history'(251). 'When I think about my mother's essay,' he thinks (or Daisy imagines him thinking), 'I can't help feeling cheated, as if there's some wily subversion going on, a glittering joke locked in a box and buried underground' (251–2). If, as I have been arguing, Daisy herself – like the ring buried beneath Cuyler's stone pyramid, like Mercy's lovelife and the circumstances of her daughter's birth, like Clarentine's sensual daydreams and Magnus's infatuation with *Jane Eyre* – is the product of Daisy's imaginative making, then the 'glittering joke' that is buried with Daisy is Shields's own 'wily subversion' of a narrative tradition that makes it seem as if people like Daisy have had their heads cut off or their tongues 'yanked out' (252). It is a tradition that has privileged the lives of national figures (even when, like Warren, we have never heard of them), that has consigned domestic life to the margins of its literary canon, and that has 'trafficked too freely in moments of crisis, searched too diligently for large themes and too preciously for graceful epiphanies' ('Narrative Hunger' 34). At the end of her life, Daisy may not be at peace, but neither has her tongue been stilled, and to the extent that Daisy makes this story her own, she becomes a woman who makes things happen, in the process restocking the narrative cupboard by redefining the parameters of a tellable life.

Notes

1 Carol Shields, *The Stone Diaries* (London: Fourth Estate, 1993), 99. All subsequent references to this edition (*SD*) will be made parenthetically.
2 'Trash' may be a bit harsh, especially since the distinction between 'serious' and popular novels can be difficult to maintain. Angela Carter, for example, suggests that 'of all the great novels in the world, *Jane Eyre* veers the closest towards trash' (*Expletives Deleted: Selected Writings* [London: Chatto and Windus, 1992], 162). But Clarentine's other purchases do not have a great deal to recommend them in terms of literary style.

3 Carol Shields, *The Republic of Love* (London: Flamingo, 1993), 319.

4 Charlotte Brontë, *Jane Eyre*, ed. Michael Mason (Harmondsworth: Penguin, 1996), 256. All subsequent references to this edition (*JE*) will be made parenthetically.

5 When Rochester is struggling to convince Jane to stay with him after the aborted marriage, he pleads: 'Oh! come, Jane, come! ... Oh, Jane! my hope – my love – my life!' (*JE* 357).

6 Janice Radway, *Reading the Romance: Women, Patriarchy, and Popular Literature* (1984; rpt. Chapel Hill and London: U of North Carolina P, 1991), 87–102.

7 Elizabeth Rigby, *Quarterly Review*, December 1848, in *The Brontës: The Critical Heritage*, ed. Miriam Allott (London and Boston: Routledge and Kegan Paul, 1974), 109–10. Margaret Oliphant claimed Jane's 'startling and original' doctrines were copied by a 'host of followers and imitators' (*Blackwood's Magazine*, May 1855, in *The Brontës: The Critical Heritage*, 313), though Anne Mozley cast *Jane Eyre* as a 'dangerous book' for reasons closer to home and hearth, in its failure to 'appreciate the hold which a daily round of simple duties and pure pleasures has on those who are content to practise and enjoy them' (*Christian Remembrancer*, April 1853, in *The Brontës: The Critical Heritage*, 208).

8 Avid romance reading has been held responsible for an extraordinary variety of unwholesome effects, ranging from physical debilities caused by lack of exercise and sleep, to mental laziness, an unbridled imagination, loose morals, and disastrously illusory expectations. 'M. d. L, Chirugien,' for example, quoted in a review of *De l'Homme, et de la Femme* in the *Monthly Review* (July 1773), claimed that 'of all the causes which have injured the health of women, the principal has been the prodigious multiplication of romances within the last century ... A young girl, instead of running about and playing, *reads*, perpetually reads; and at twenty, becomes full of vapours, instead of being qualified for the duties of a good wife, or nurse' (547). But morality, more than health, was the chief concern. Typical of the sweeping attacks on the moral dangers of romances was 'A

Letter to a Lady, concerning Books of Piety and Romances' in the *Universal Spectator,* no. 91 (1 August 1730), in which the writer claimed that romances 'ruin more Virgins than *Masquerades* or *Brothels*' because 'they strike at the very Root of all Virtue, by corrupting the Mind: and by raising People's Passions, and encouraging their vicious Inclinations'(quoted in Robert D. Mayo, *The English Novel in the Magazines 1740–1815* [Evanston: Northwestern UP, 1962], 57).

9 Jacqueline Pearson, *Women's Reading in Britain, 1750–1835* (Cambridge: Cambridge UP, 1999), 8.

10 William B. Warner, *Licensing Entertainment: The Elevation of Novel Reading in Britain, 1684–1750* (Berkeley: U of California P, 1998), in particular chapters 3 and 4. The fact that these stories are predominantly (though not exclusively) about love no doubt troubled society's moral guardians, but while from the Middle Ages onwards romance reading has been thought unsafe, it was not until these books became objects of mass consumption – cheap (within the purchasing power of pin-money or house-keeping savings), plentiful (initially thanks to circulating libraries), and portable (no longer massive, multi-volumed tomes, but small, light, and even, eventually, soft-covered books that could be read in private, and even slipped out of sight) – that fears about what women might be getting out of romance began to focus on their sexuality.

11 Peter J. Rabinowitz proposes that the expectation 'that something happens, that things change in a way that is not *entirely* the result of inertia,' is a basic 'rule' of reading, and is, 'for some theorists, the fundamental characteristic of narrative' *(Before Reading: Narrative Conventions and the Politics of Interpretation* [Ithaca and London: Cornell UP, 1987], 117). Furthermore, he suggests, the 'something' that happens in narrative also needs to satisfy Mary Louise Pratt's criterion of 'tellability': what happens needs to be 'unusual, contrary to expectations, or otherwise problematic' since 'in making an assertion whose relevance is tellability, a speaker is not only reporting but also verbally displaying a state of affairs, inviting his addressee(s) to join him in contemplating it, evaluating it, and responding to it'

(Mary Louise Pratt, *Towards a Speech Act Theory of Literary Discourse* [Bloomington: Indiana UP, 1977], 136). Needless to say, in ordinary life the something that happens next is not always, in these terms, 'tellable.'

12 Carol Shields, 'Narrative Hunger and the Overflowing Cupboard,' p. 20 (in this volume). All subsequent references will be made parenthetically.

13 Eleanor Wachtel, 'Interview with Carol Shields,' *Room of One's Own* 13.1/2 (1989): 26.

14 Radway, 17.

15 The current critical consensus, such as it is, is inclined to view addictive romance reading as compensatory or preventative rather than subversive (perhaps in the absence of a mass outbreak from confining marriages on the part of millions of romance readers). See, for example, Fredric Jameson, 'Reification and Utopia in Mass Culture,' *Social Text* 1 (1979): 141; Tania Modleski, *Loving with a Vengeance: Mass-Produced Fantasies for Women* (1982; rpt. New York and London: Routledge, 1990), 43; Radway, 112–13; and Jan Cohn, *Romance and the Erotics of Property: Mass-Market Fiction for Women* (Durham and London: Duke UP, 1988), 5–6.

16 If anything, the symbolic naming is more obtrusive, even if less inclusive, in *The Stone Diaries*, partly because metaphors of stones and flowers are incorporated into the discursive fabric of the narrative, and partly because the elemental alignment of the characters of *Jane Eyre* requires a bit of etymological homework to unearth the meaning of names such as Brocklehurst and Rochester.

17 Presumably, Barker is a more sensitive soul, given his fondness for flowers (and given that he 'cannot imagine any finer or more fitting gift for a young woman about to begin her life' than his wedding gift to Daisy on her marriage to Harold, Catharine Parr Traill's *Wild Flowers of Canada* [113]). But his fondness for the lady's slipper, and his particular fondness for its 'regenerative mechanics,' Daisy finds a touch perverse.

18 The links between Harold's death and Bertha's may be a little tenuous, but the bizarre twists are in keeping with 'the note of

mild mockery' that Faye Hammill suggests is typical both of Shields's attitude toward romance and of her fondness for what Shields herself describes as 'usurping traditional structures' (quoted in Hammill; see p. 79 above).

19 Harold's 'crazy cackling one-note sound' is perhaps reminiscent of Bertha's clamorous 'syllabic' peal, which the notes to the 1996 Penguin edition of *Jane Eyre* suggest 'should be imagined as a distinct "Ha! Ha!" ... a linguistic utterance rather than a mere noise' (513). But perhaps not.

20 See, for example, Winifred M. Mellor, '"The Simple Container of Our Existence": Narrative Ambiguity in Carol Shields's *The Stone Diaries,' Studies in Canadian Literature* 20.2 (1995): 96–109; Simone Vauthier, 'Ruptures in Carol Shields's *The Stone Diaries,' Anglophonia* 1 (1997): 177–92; Gordon E. Slethaug, '"The Coded Dots of Life": Carol Shields's Diaries and Stones,' *Canadian Literature* 156 (Spring 1998): 59–81. I am not arguing that the silencing of women is a peripheral issue in *The Stone Diaries,* only that it is a problem Daisy eventually grapples with rather than simply illustrates. As Wendy Roy suggests in her article 'Autobiography As Critical Practice in *The Stone Diaries,'* in this volume, 'whether Daisy's is the controlling consciousness of the narrative remains ambiguous,' particularly in the light of ironic references to Daisy in the third person, but 'the repeated references to her autobiographical project strongly suggest that she is imagining others' responses, as well as events in her life and others' lives, as she writes her autobiography with invisible ink' (121).

21 Vauthier, 184.

22 On the basis of the other photographs of Clarentine included in *The Stone Diaries,* it is difficult to identify Clarentine in the photograph of the Ladies Rhythm and Movement Club, despite Magnus picking her out as the one 'in the front row, a wee bit shorter than the others, slim, pretty, mischievous, cheeky ... biting down on her lower lip as if life was one wonderful lark' (97). The dissonance between the text and the photographs may be contributing to the metafictional exploration of the status of the real and the imaginary in this 'documentary age,' which

honours the real, 'never mind how suspect it sounds' (330), but as a device within the narrative it can also be seen as Daisy's doing, in that, in her reinvention of the past, she 'has a little trouble with getting things straight; with the truth, that is' (148).

23 Vauthier, 177.

24 Slethaug, 62.

25 A confession: on first reading *The Stone Diaries*, I did not recognize that there was a problem with the narrative that needed 'fixing.' I registered the novelty of Daisy describing her own birth, for example, but it was not the first time that I had encountered, and accommodated, third-person hearsay rendered as personal recollection.

26 Radway, 61. Radway locates this guilt in contemporary romance's reputation for soft porn, but the guilt precedes the recent trend toward sexual explicitness.

27 The *OED* lists several meanings for 'burden' in its musical context, including 'the bass, "undersong," or accompaniment' (possibly a variant spelling of 'bourdon,' literally 'drone') and 'the refrain or chorus of a song,' as well as the figurative sense of 'the leading idea.'

28 The distinction between manifest and latent content is Freud's, employed in the context of the interpretation of dreams, where the 'façade' created from the everyday materials of waking life is distinguished from the hidden, and often unacceptable, 'dream-thoughts' (see, for example, *An Outline of Psycho-Analysis*, trans. and ed. James Strachey [London: The Hogarth Press and the Institute of Psycho-Analysis, 1969], 22). In using the terms, however, I mean only to distinguish between the particular material expression of wish-fulfilling fantasy and its underlying or disguised meanings. This question of what popular romance is 'really' about, given the prevalence of repetitive formulas suggesting a highly specific matching of product to need, is a common preoccupation of critics. On the basis of the focus of intense interest on the heroine, and of the particular qualities valued in the hero, Radway, for example, argues that 'the romantic fantasy is ... not a fantasy about discovering a uniquely interesting life partner but a ritual wish to be cared for,

loved, and validated in a particular way' (83). Moreover, when the qualities of this ideal man are analysed, Radway suggests, what popular romance seems to exemplify is 'the ongoing search for a mother and her characteristic care' (13). Modleski, in contrast, focuses on elements of revenge fantasy and the consolations of bringing a hero to his knees.

29 See *Jane Eyre*: 'women feel just as men feel; they need exercise for their faculties, and a field for their efforts as much as their brothers do; they suffer from too rigid a restraint, too absolute a stagnation, precisely as men would suffer' (125).

30 In Shields's short story 'A Scarf,' from the collection *Dressing Up for the Carnival* (London: Fourth Estate, 2000), Reta Winters, a middle-aged novelist on a book tour promoting her modestly successful first novel, finds herself surrendering without protest to a friend's mistaken appropriation of the gift she had bought, after some exhaustingly serious shopping, for her daughter. It is a small sacrifice – 'A scarf, half an ounce of silk, maybe less' (27) – but emblematic of what Daisy's friend Beans in *The Stone Diaries* insists is a woman's fate: 'It's not so much a question of one big disappointment ... It's more like a thousand disappointments raining down on top of each other' (254). Or, as Reta concludes in 'A Scarf': 'Not one of us was going to get what we wanted ... We're too soft in our tissues ... We are too kind, too willing, too unwilling too, reaching out blindly with a grasping hand but not knowing how to ask for what we don't even know we want' (27).

31 In her short story 'Edith-Esther' in *Dressing Up for the Carnival,* Shields attributes the search for this 'kernel of authenticity' to the critic-biographer who is determined to uncover life-enhancing qualities in Edith-Esther's fiction, despite her resolution to refuse 'her readers the least crumb of comfort' (143). The phrase sounds spurious and pretentious, particularly when glossed as 'you're exactly who you are' (143), and suggests a certain uneasiness, on Shields's part, with the rhetoric of the search for self.

32 When a nurse describes Daisy, in her hearing, as 'feisty,' Daisy is not sure she likes it and asks her daughter what it means. Alice

tells her it means 'tough,' but Daisy thinks it sounds superior or condescending, and complains: 'It's got a bad smell ... Overripe. Like strawberries past their prime' (329). She is probably confusing 'feisty' with 'fusty' (meaning musty or mouldy), but she is right, it does have a bad smell – its derivation can be traced back to the obsolete 'fist,' meaning to break wind (which gives an added resonance to the advertisement of a large fast-food company that once described its seasoned french fries as 'feisty').

33 From the *OED* entry for 'monument.'

34 From the epigraph to *The Stone Diaries*.

Autobiography As Critical Practice in *The Stone Diaries*

WENDY ROY

'Biography is my consuming passion,' Carol Shields told an interviewer in 1999.[1] Her writing career bears out that self-assessment. While Shields was a graduate student at the University of Ottawa during the 1970s, she completed a study of nineteenth-century Canadian autobiographical writer Susanna Moodie; during that same decade, she made a fictional biographer of Moodie the narrator of her first published novel, *Small Ceremonies*, and wrote an essay on intersections between autobiography and fiction ('Three Canadian Women'). Shields has since written a novel that focuses on the posthumous reconstruction of a murdered poet by biographers and academics (*Swann*) and a short popular biography of Jane Austen for James Atlas's biography series. As critics and reviewers have pointed out, however, her most detailed commentary on biography and autobiography appears in her 1993 novel, *The Stone Diaries*.[2] Winifred Mellor argues that *The Stone Diaries* 'foregrounds the problems of writing autobiography'; Margery Fee points out that the novel is 'about the limitations of biography and autobiography'; Gordon Slethaug notes that its main character 'redeems and transforms her experiences into an exuberant auto/biography, which imitates and ironizes autobiography'; and Chiara Briganti suggests that Shields is concerned with 'the epistemological implications of life writing.'[3]

Although Shields's novel does comment on biography (for example, through the narrator's assertion that 'biography, even autobiography, is full of systemic error, of holes that connect like a tangle of underground streams' [196]), it is structured at least initially as a fictional autobiography, as is evident from the use of first-person narration in the first chapter. The narrative also addresses theoretical perspectives related specifically to autobiography, and to women's autobiography in particular. While many writers have noted the connection of *The Stone Diaries* to autobiography, few (with the exception of Briganti) have commented on this more complex engagement with theories of autobiographical writing. I argue that instead of simply modelling itself upon autobiography and thus following in the footsteps of predecessor fictional autobiographies such as Charlotte Brontë's *Jane Eyre* (an explicit intertext, as Dianne Osland points out in the previous essay), *The Stone Diaries* instead turns autobiography into critical practice by engaging with feminist theories of life writing. By redefining what Osland calls 'the parameters of a tellable life' (105), Shields's novel undermines autobiography's traditional privileging of linear and cohesive narratives. At the same time, it questions the efficacy of the discontinuous and relational nature of autobiography as proposed by feminist theorists, and provides a critique of social structures that define both women's writing and their lives.

The Stone Diaries evokes the genre of autobiography repeatedly, through the title, the family tree, the table of contents, the opening *my* and *I*, the middle section of photographs labelled with the names of the novel's characters, and the more or less chronological birth-to-death narrative. Shields's novel does not just mimic autobiography, however; it acts as a critical comment on it, in part by subverting conventions of autobiography. In contrast to what the title implies, the book is clearly not a diary, the table of contents refers only ironically to the actual contents of each chapter,[4] the first-person narrative is periodically replaced by other narrators and other narrative strategies, the photographs provide a jarring counterpoint to, rather than correspondence with, the descriptions of characters in the text, and the narrators muse repeatedly about the genre of autobiography. Because *The Stone Diaries* both imitates and undermines autobiography, it can be classified as meta-autobiography, or a work of literature that comments on the genre.

In particular, Shields's novel comments on the traditional notion that autobiographers write to set themselves apart from their communities. Georges Gusdorf argued in 1956 that autobiography was a relatively recent genre because earlier generations of men did not have the 'conscious awareness of the singularity of each individual life' required to write personal history: 'Throughout most of human history, the individual does not oppose himself to all others; he does not feel himself to exist outside of others, and still less against others, but very much *with* others in an interdependent existence that asserts its rhythms everywhere in the community.'[5] Not only is Gusdorf's language gender exclusive, but also his description of the 'interdependent existence' that is anathema to autobiography appears much like the life many women lead, and his description of self within the rhythms of community much like the writing about the self in which many women engage. Gusdorf's and other similarly limited characterizations of autobiography are one reason works by many women writers typically have been omitted from discussions of the genre. Another reason is the narrow definition of accepted forms of autobiography; as William Spengemann points out, only 'self-written biograph[ies]' and not 'letters, journals, memoirs, and verse-narratives' traditionally have been admissible to the genre.[6] Because women's writings about the self have often taken the form of diaries and letters, they have often been ignored by conventional autobiographical critics.

Since 1980, feminist theorists of autobiography have challenged gender-exclusive categorizations, arguing that autobiography by women is often different from autobiography by men, and in particular that narrow definitions need to be broadened to include writings by women that stress their lives in relation to others. Mary Mason writes, for example, that 'the disclosure of female self is linked to the identification of some "other,"' while Françoise Lionnet argues that because 'the human individual is a fundamentally relational subject,' it is not through one *other*, but in relation to a broader community that women are able to write about themselves. Tackling Gusdorf's theories directly, Susan Stanford Friedman posits that the female autobiographical self 'often does not oppose herself to all others, does not feel herself to exist outside of others, and still less against others, but very much *with* others in an interdependent existence that asserts its rhythms everywhere in the community.'[7] One relationship of interdependence upon which feminist researchers have focused is the autobiographer's connection with her mother. Adrienne Rich writes that she begins her autobiographical book *Of Woman Born* 'as a woman who, born between her mother's legs, has time after time and in different ways tried to return to her mother, to repossess her and be repossessed by her, to find the mutual confirmation from and with another woman that daughters and mothers alike hunger for, pull away from, make possible or impossible for each other.' That desire for maternal connection is especially evident, Bella Brodzki argues, when the autobiographer's mother is absent or dead: 'now inaccessible (literally or figuratively), she is the pre-text for the daughter's autobiographical project.'[8]

As well as noting the relational nature of women's writings about the self, some contemporary feminist theorists argue that women's autobiographies tend to be more fragmented and inconclusive than men's. Estelle Jelinek writes, for example, that while men as autobiographers often shape their lives into coherent wholes by using 'chronological, linear' narratives, literary self-portraits by women are often 'disconnected, fragmentary, or organized into self-sustained units rather than connecting chapters.' Her arguments have been echoed, restated, and expanded upon by subsequent theorists who write about gaps, voids, fissures, and 'black holes' in women's writing.[9] Feminist autobiographical critics have examined in detail one particular gap in women's autobiography: the lack of sexualized portrayals of the body.[10]

The Stone Diaries explores and critiques the relational and fragmented nature of women's writings about the self, including the writer's relationship with her mother and the difficulty of the autobiographer in representing her bodily experience. It also reflects on recent postmodernist and feminist arguments about the permeability of borders that separate fiction from autobiography. Linda Hutcheon argues, for example, that 'to write of anyone's history is to order, to give form to disparate facts; in short, to fictionalize,' while Liz Stanley writes that feminist autobiography is 'characterised by its self-conscious and increasingly self-confident traversing of conventional boundaries between different genres of writing.'[11] The putative fictional nature of autobiography puts into question another humanist and modernist tenet of autobiography: that it can be directly related to a specific life. Janice Morgan argues that as a result of the 'post-structuralist rejection of the author as a unified, originating subject,' the belief that autobiography 'is easy, factual, and transparent' has been cast into doubt.[12]

Shields's book crosses boundaries between autobiography and fiction in that it is what Nathalie Cooke calls 'fictive autobiography,' or 'autobiography composed by a fictional protagonist, which draws attention to its own problematical status as a fictive construct.'[13] But can *The Stone Diaries* be called autobiography? Marlene Kadar argues that autobiography (or, in her terminology, 'life writing') should include not only more fragmented forms such as letters, journals, and diaries, but also 'the fictional frame in which we might find an autobiographical voice.' That 'fictional frame' perfectly describes a work such as *The Stone Diaries*, which has a distinct, although fictive, autobiographical voice. Kadar argues, further, that life writing, especially life writing that is metafictional, is not only a genre but also a 'critical practice.' She comes to this conclusion because, in her view, 'reading a kind of metafictional life writing, one that overtly resists a proof-positive reading, leads us to ask questions about our critical practice.' This type of life writing thus becomes 'both the "original genre" and a critical comment on it.'[14]

The Stone Diaries is metafiction that makes a critical comment on the genre of life writing. It draws attention to its generic status in order to question the relationship of fiction to autobiography, and autobiography to some version of reality.[15] Shields's book questions the shape of women's life histories as discussed not just by traditional autobiographical theorists and their feminist counterparts, but also by feminist social theorists such as Betty Friedan. In blurring the boundaries between autobiography and fiction, it helps to enlarge the reader's understanding of women's lives and how they are written.

Autobiography As 'An Assemblage of Dark Voids and Unbridgeable Gaps'

Shields responds most directly to feminist theories of autobiography by making voids and gaps the main characteristic of her fictive autobiography of Daisy Goodwill Flett. Early in *The Stone Diaries*, Daisy comes to believe that 'her autobiography, if such a thing were imaginable, would be, if such a thing were ever to be written, an assemblage of dark voids and unbridgeable gaps' (75–6).[16] The novel's increasingly discontinuous and assembled narrative indeed represents women's autobiography as fissured and as portrayable only within and through a network of relationships. Daisy's voice is replaced by numerous other voices and other modes of narration, and her story is displaced by the stories of others around her. Her authorial 'I' fades in and out of the narrative, replaced through much of the novel by an omniscient or judgmental narrator who refers to Daisy in the third person, who undercuts her version of events, but who may represent the ironic or questioning voice of Daisy herself. As that voice is supplanted by a proliferation of outside accounts – newspaper clippings, letters, theories of family and friends presented in their voices, photographs, grocery lists, recipes, lists of books Daisy has read and lingerie she has purchased – the novel provides a graphic illustration of the way that a woman can be 'crowded out of her own life' (190). Although 'hers is the only account there is' (149), Daisy's story is almost taken over by a multiplicity of other voices. Shields's construction of fictive autobiography through a community of voices and stories suggests that women's autobiography is, indeed, often based upon relationship, while also revealing the limitations of that communal representation of the self; for if a woman can only represent herself in relation, she may, like Daisy, become lost in the interconnections that constitute her sense of self.

The Stone Diaries is an autobiography made up of voids: it is sparked by 'the vacuum [Daisy] sensed, suddenly, in the middle of her life' (75), and it is 'written on air, written with imagination's invisible ink' (149).[17] The process of writing autobiography is explored at several points throughout the book, as its first- and third-person narrators talk about 'biographical logic' (27), tell the reader that 'the recounting of a life is a cheat' (28) and that 'there are chapters in every life which are seldom read, and certainly not aloud' (111), and point out that biography and autobiography are 'full of systemic error, of holes that connect like a tangle of underground streams' (196). Daisy is the purported author of this particular unwritten autobiography, and, as the reader is told,

> all she's trying to do is keep things straight in her head. To keep the weight of her memories evenly distributed. To hold the chapters of her life in order ... And the question arises: what is the story of a life? A chronicle of fact or a skillfully wrought impression? The bringing together of what she fears? Or the adding up of what has been off-handedly revealed, those tiny allotted increments of knowledge? (340)

By referring to life as divided into chapters, the novel constructs Daisy's life as a narrative and Daisy as an autobiographer. By asking whether the story of a life is fact or impression, its narrator consciously theorizes autobiography in a post-modern way, approaching Hutcheon's argument that 'to write of anyone's history is ... to fictionalize.'[18]

Only the first chapter of *The Stone Diaries* reads consistently like autobiography, but not traditional autobiography, or even traditional fictional autobiography such as *Jane Eyre*. Daisy as autobiographer describes, not events she can remember experiencing or straightforward accounts of what she has been told, as Jane does, but imaginary accounts of her parents' motivations, their sex lives, and her own birth. As first-person narrator, Daisy emphasizes the fictionality of her story and thus undermines her self-representation. She corrects herself as she describes the doctor 'pulling a sheet – no, not a sheet but a tablecloth' – up over her dead mother's face (38), and she notes that as a wailing infant, she is 'swaddled in – what? – a kitchen towel. Or something, perhaps, yanked from Clarentine Flett's clothesline' (39). Daisy's revisionary mode of narration undermines the reader's sense of both the accuracy and importance of the events related: 'Everyone in the tiny, crowded, hot, and evil-smelling kitchen ... has been invited to participate in a moment of history,' she says of her own birth, then adds, 'History indeed! As though this paltry slice of time deserves such a name' (39). Her account of her history in *The Stone Diaries* is self-consciously presented as neither objective nor transparent. Instead, the reader is reminded of the subjective and constructed nature of autobiography (and, indeed, history in general) by being given different versions of events, initially by Daisy herself.[19]

After chapter 1, the first-person voice appears only sporadically, especially in straightforward narration such as when Daisy describes 'the summer I turned thirty-one' (121). The story of her life is even more radically undermined by the third-person narrator who appears in the second chapter. As that narrator says, Daisy's autobiography is 'a primary act of imagination,' and in articulating it, she will be 'getting the details wrong occasionally, exaggerating or lying outright' (76–7). In case we as readers miss the point, the narrator later addresses us directly:

Maybe now is the time to tell you that Daisy Goodwill has a little trouble with getting things straight; with the truth, that is ... Which is why you want to take Daisy's representation of events with a grain of salt, a bushel of salt.

She is not always reliable when it comes to the details of her life; much of what she has to say is speculative, exaggerated, wildly unlikely ... Daisy Goodwill's perspective is off. (148)

The assessment of Daisy as unreliable autobiographer appears to come from the ironic voice of an intrusive, judgmental, outside narrator, but that voice may be Daisy's, displaced into the third person to allow her to comment on herself. As the narration shifts from first- to third-person, Daisy appears to be taking literally the autobiographical convention of a hidden third-person narrator who turns the self into an object to be investigated.[20] Even when narration is in the third person, it is sometimes still clearly Daisy who is doing the recording, as when the narrator describes 'a very private moment, she will not discuss it with anyone, though she records it here – in which [Daisy's husband] had extolled her smooth-jointed fingers, comparing them to wonderful flexible silken fish' (230). Whether Daisy's is the controlling consciousness of the narrative remains ambiguous, although the repeated references to her autobiographical project strongly suggest that she is imagining others' responses, as well as events in her life and others' lives, as she writes her autobiography with invisible ink.

The undermining of Daisy's narrative authority and the related vacillation between first- and third-person narration work together to distance Daisy from her own story. This distancing is especially evident in sections of the narration that waver from naming Daisy as *I* or *me* to naming Daisy as *her* or *she* in the space of a single sentence. An example appears in the account of Daisy's recovery from measles and pneumonia, when her autobiographical project begins: 'The long days of isolation, of silence, the torment of boredom – all these pressed down on *me*, on young Daisy Goodwill and emptied *her* out' (75, italics added).[21] Another example occurs near the end of the novel, as Daisy's death approaches: 'She's lost track of what's real and what isn't, and so, at this age, have I' (329). A third example clearly distinguishes between the *I* of the judgmental narrator and the *her* of Daisy, the person being judged: 'In a sense *I* see *her* as one of life's fortunates, a woman born with a voice that lacks a tragic register' (263, italics added). In *The Stone Diaries*, Daisy's displacement from the centre of her story is evident each time *I* or *me* is replaced by *she* or *her*, each time Daisy is constructed – or constructs herself – as an other.

Daisy is transformed almost completely into a relational other as her life is increasingly mediated by the stories of the people around her. As the *I* fades after the first chapter, the narrative names her more and more frequently in terms of her relationships: as Barker Flett's 'niece,' Cuyler Goodwill's daughter, Mrs Flett, Alice's mother, Victoria's great-aunt, Grandma Flett. The narrative of each chapter also diverges from the chronology indicated by its title to provide details about the lives of others with whom Daisy is in relation. 'Birth, 1905' devotes scant space to Daisy's birth and her mother's subsequent death; most of the chapter is taken up by an account of Daisy's parents' early life and marital relationship, and by an exploration of the unfulfilled desires of neighbour Clarentine Flett, who becomes Daisy's foster mother. 'Childhood, 1916' only briefly describes the experiences of eleven-year-old Daisy; the chapter focuses mostly on how Cuyler Goodwill fills his life after Mercy's death, on the reason Clarentine leaves her husband, Magnus, to live with her son, Barker, and on Barker's suppressed sexual feelings for Daisy. 'Marriage, 1927' describes Daisy's marriage and her young husband's death on their honeymoon, but focuses in even more detail on her three 'fathers': Cuyler, Magnus, and Barker. In each chapter of the book, other people's stories repeatedly eclipse Daisy's, and her life is repeatedly constructed as the sum of others' with whom she is in relation.

The dislocation of the narrative centre away from Daisy is especially evident in the chapters that present her life from

1955 to 1965. 'Work, 1955–1964' is told entirely in letters of the sort that Daisy might have kept in an old shoebox in the back of a closet. Not one is written by Daisy; they are from her lawyer, her dead husband, her friends, her children, the newspaper editor who is her boss (and perhaps her lover), and the readers of her gardening column. Daisy's voice is absent, and each letter tells more about the person writing than it does about Daisy. 'Sorrow, 1965' consists almost entirely of theories of Daisy's friends, family members, and acquaintances about the reasons she has fallen into a depression. Each theory is presented in the voice of another person, and again each reveals much more about that *other* than it does about Daisy. As Daisy imagines the responses of her relatives, friends, and acquaintances, not one of them, not even those supposedly closest to her, knows much about her. Instead, all are preoccupied with their own lives and filter their insights about Daisy's life through their own experiences. The theory of Daisy's daughter Alice is that her mother is depressed because she has lost her job as a gardening columnist; Alice believes that, as Betty Friedan argues, 'we are our work! ... Work and self cannot be separated' (242).[22] Daisy's friend Fraidy, on the other hand, argues that Daisy's depression is related to her suppressed yearning for sex; Fraidy herself carries a pocket diary containing cryptic details about her sexual encounters with fifty-four men, including 'duration, position, repetition, degree of response, and the like' (246). Daisy as autobiographer never expresses her own theory about her depression, at least not in a first-person voice. Instead, her experience is self-consciously presented through letters and gossip, and thus she is located in the gaps that are created by other people's contiguous and sometimes overlapping accounts of her.

In the final chapter of *The Stone Diaries*, 'Death,' Daisy's autobiography is reduced to fragments. The chapter begins with two versions of her obituary notice (her 'real' one and one she imagines) followed by two versions of the inscription on her headstone, and includes lists of organizations she belonged to, illnesses she suffered, books she read, things she never did, addresses where she lived, and overheard or imagined conversations about her illness, her work, her marriages, and the flowers on her coffin. Among this diverse collection of voices, her voice is almost entirely silenced, although Daisy as autobiographer paradoxically appears to be imagining the experience of death in 'a series of mutable transparencies gesturing not backward in time but forward – forward toward her own death' (358). Although her last unspoken words, 'I am not at peace,' are recorded (361), her voice in this chapter is for the most part subsumed in the myriad relationships that constitute her.

Shields said of her earlier novel *Swann*, 'I wanted to try writing from a void, completely masking the narrator.' With *The Stone Diaries*, she at times comes close, as Daisy is 'erased from the record of her own existence' (76) and 'crowded out of her own life' (190). Mellor writes that Daisy 'occupies a cavern of vacancy at the centre of the text,' while Fee suggests that 'the narrative figures Daisy as a hole in a complex social network,' and Briganti argues that in Shields's novel, 'the centre, or that which is assumed to be the centre, is made purposefully and relentlessly void.'[23] Readers indeed must construct Daisy's story through the gaps and silences in others' stories, others' voices, other types of narration. But, in contrast to what Lisa Johnson argues elsewhere in this volume, I argue that the novel's focus on Daisy's 'empty centre' may in itself be redemptive. Indeed, it puts into concrete terms Seyla Benhabib and Drucilla Cornell's argument that a woman's individuality traditionally 'has been sacrificed to the "constitutive definitions" of her identity as a member of a family, as someone's daughter, someone's wife and someone's mother.'[24] As a way of illustrating this sacrifice of individuality, *The Stone Diaries* constructs Daisy Goodwill Flett almost entirely in relation to others. Because this construction both reveals and obscures her, Shields's book exemplifies ideas that a woman's self-representation is necessarily fragmented and her life relational, and at the same time critiques the notion that portraying a woman through her place within relationship can be an effective way to represent her life. It also emphasizes the inadequacy, and yet the necessity, of portraying a woman through gaps in her life story.

'Telling the Truth about [Her] Own Experiences As a Body'

One of the most obvious unbridgeable autobiographical gaps in *The Stone Diaries* is its spotty description of experiences of the body. The gap between body and text in women's autobiographical writings was recognized by Virginia Woolf when she wrote that 'telling the truth about [her] own experiences as a body' was one of her unfulfilled goals.[25] Like Woolf, the fictional autobiographer of *The Stone Diaries* tacitly admits that she cannot represent the truth of her own body, but must remain silent about important details such as her first sexual encounter and the births of her three children. She breaks the silence about sexuality and childbirth only through imaginative renderings of others' intersecting life stories.

Gaps and misdirections in representation of bodily experience reflect an autobiographical tradition that discourages sexualized portrayals of the body. As Shirley Neuman argues, representations of bodies traditionally have been repressed in autobiography because the genre is 'synonymous with spiritual quest.' For women autobiographers, the spiritual rather than corporeal focus of autobiography results in what Neuman calls 'a double handicap': in the mind-body dichotomy, woman is most commonly associated with body, while at the same time, she is discouraged from writing about that body in autobiography. As a result, the female autobiographer is 'in the position of either not writing at all, or of having to invent a self that is female and non-corporeal.' These difficulties of representation, Sidonie Smith argues, mean that the female body may be either 'a source of subversive practice, a potentially emancipatory vehicle for autobiographical practice, or a source of repression and suppressed narrative.'[26] In *The Stone Diaries*, both subversion and suppression are explored. The corporeal omissions and the images of the body that rupture the surface of the narrative are evidence of repression and of an awareness that representing the body in autobiography has the potential to be emancipatory. When the body *is* described, it becomes a 'naming of an unspeakable' that figures as a political act.[27]

The absence of the female autobiographical body in *The Stone Diaries* is made concrete through the exclusion of Daisy from the photographs, borrowed from museums, photographic services, and Shields's family albums, that appear designed to illustrate the novel's characters and that form the central section of the book. Daisy's parents are pictured, as are her husbands, friends, children, and grandchildren, but Daisy herself is absent. Disparities are evident between what readers have imagined and what they see in the photographs, reinforcing perceptions of the fictional and constructed nature of autobiography. (The photograph labelled with the name of Daisy's mother, for example, pictures her as not nearly as obese as the written text suggests.)[28] As far as images of Daisy are concerned, however, the centre of Shields's fictional autobiography is not just disjunctive; it is a void.

Shields has shown in other books such as *Small Ceremonies*, *The Republic of Love*, and *Larry's Party*, and in the short story 'Eros,' that she can write with comfort about sexuality and pregnancy.[29] In *The Stone Diaries*, however, details of sex and childbearing are repressed, at least as they relate to the novel's fictional autobiographer. Shields has explained that in presenting Daisy's life at ten-year intervals, 'I knew ... I would be losing moments like childbirth, which I think is probably the most dramatic moment of any woman's life, and her education, and her sexual initiation – but I decided to miss those moments and to go for other moments.' This explanation may strike the reader as inadequate, since Shields could have used the retrospective techniques she employs in other parts of the narrative to include details of Daisy's experiences of sex, pregnancy, and childbirth (just as in *A Fairly Conventional Woman* she presents Brenda Bowman's wedding night through a flashback).[30]

A better explanation for the omissions in *The Stone Diaries* is that discussions of sex and childbirth have traditionally been taboo in our culture, especially in autobiography. Whether such discussions are avoided altogether or are only partially represented, they provide examples of women's 'double handicap' in the genre of autobiography. Thus we might expect a woman's autobiography (even a fictional one) to display a continual conflict between resistance to revelation of details about sexuality and childbirth, and revelation of those details. In *The Stone Diaries*, the suppression of Daisy's first sexual experience and the birth of her children alternates with explicit revelations about Daisy's own birth and about the sexuality of her husband, her parents and parents-in-law, her friend, and even her great-niece. As these narratives rupture the surface of the text, they provide a critique of social strictures governing women's bodies, especially the tenets that women's sexuality must be focused on others' pleasure and must have reproduction as its goal.

Daisy's adult ambivalence toward sexuality is represented in a conversation with her older daughter. Although Daisy responds to Alice's disgust with the comment 'It's a beautiful thing between a man and a woman,' she is not convincing (166). The distancing of the narrative voice, which refers to her, not as 'I' or even 'Daisy,' but as 'Alice's mother,' emphasizes her ambivalence. The subsequent tragicomic section titled 'Mrs. Flett's Intimate Relations with her Husband' reveals that Daisy has learned to define what she can and cannot desire from articles in popular magazines for women. The articles she has read dictate her use of contraceptives and her choice of nightdress, and mar her experience of sex and orgasm. Just as Brenda Bowman's experience of sexuality is damaged by books and magazine articles that require her, during sex, to be 'constantly thinking, evaluating, planning, counting, asking herself what was the next move? And the next?' (*FCW* 155), Daisy tries 'through a helix of mixed print and distraction, to remember exactly what was advised in the latest issue of *McCalls*, something about a wife's responsibility for demonstrating a rise in ardour; that was it – ardour and surrender expressed simultaneously through a single subtle gesturing of the body; but how was that possible?' (191). Throughout this section, Daisy is named 'Mrs. Flett,' a woman who exists only in relation to her husband, a narrative strategy that serves to further distance the ostensible autobiographer from her own desire.

In those parts of the novel that Daisy narrates as 'I,' the sexual experiences she describes in detail are those of her parents, which must be primarily conjecture. Although her father finds sexual joy night after night and reflects on his days 'rounded by rapture' (36), her mother views his ardour as 'immense, unfathomable' (7). Cuyler's sexuality is in fact performed as a solitary act because Mercy is acted upon but is never a participant. She is always the object rather than the subject of desire. Mercy's sexual energy is instead subsumed in her desire for food, and results in her continuing obesity. *The Stone Diaries* repeatedly contrasts Mercy's fat body with the 'spare, neat' bodies of Daisy (59), Clarentine (9), and Cuyler (17). At the same time, the book eroticizes fat by turning the obese Mercy into a sexual object. In an era when toxic thinness of the female body is considered ideal, and when fat is viewed as evidence of excess, the representation of fat as erotic is startling. Shields's act of taking the cultural construction of woman as body, and giving the reader BODY in the form of an overwhelming corporeal and sexual presence, is a compelling critique of media representations of women as primarily bodies, but as bodies that are sexually desirable only when they conform to the ideal.

The sometime result of sexuality – pregnancy – is explored in a similarly graphic but second-hand way. Daisy's pregnancies and labours are absent from the narrative, but the experience of the childbearing body is present in her detailed depictions of her own birth, a subject about which her dead mother has been unable to speak. Her birth is told instead in the first-person of the child, now an adult commentator imagining that she is present: 'It is a temptation to rush to the bloodied bundle pushing out between my mother's legs, and to place my hand on my own beating heart, my flattened head and infant arms amid the mess of glistening pulp' (23). Daisy's description of her birth is a vivid rendering of the experience of childbirth and of a woman's genitalia during childbirth. Yet, although she imagines this scene in all its bloodied detail, her impulse is to distance herself from it by labelling it with Latin or biblical terminology: 'I feel compelled to transform [it] into something clean and whole with a line of scripture running beneath it or possibly a Latin motto,' she says (23). The expressed need for distancing through traditional forms of narration recognizes that childbirth, like sexuality, is culturally constructed as unclean and unwhole(some). At the same time, Daisy's compulsion to transform the birth into something whole reflects her desire to take the 'dark voids and unbridgeable gaps' (76) of her woman's life history and to fill them in.

If sex and childbirth are present in her fictional autobiography, albeit distanced as part of others' experiences, the body during illness and death is represented more immediately through Daisy's own experience. The narrative speaks graphically of Daisy's bodily deterioration, evidence of the progress toward death in someone still living – a progress seldom seen in autobiographies, which must of necessity end before their subjects' deaths. Daisy as a seventy-two-year-old woman is defined physically by decay: 'the fissured broken flesh of her once presentable calves,' the eyes that have 'sunk into slits of marbled satin,' 'the appalling jowls or the slack upper arms that jiggle as she walks' (280). During her illness and decline eight years later, 'her body is all that matters' (309). Daisy is recast in this passage as entirely body – no longer a sexual entity invaded by the individual male body of a husband, but a set of organs invaded by the masculinized body of medicine: a catheter to take away urine, a drainage tube in her nose, an intravenous needle in her arm.

Shields's earlier fiction has acknowledged the unspeakableness of women's illnesses: in *Swann*, Rose Hindmarch is unable for months to speak about the fibroid tumours from which she suffers, while Judith Gill of *Small Ceremonies* goes into hospital for 'a minor operation, a delicate, feminine, unspeakable, minimal nothing' (22). In *The Stone Diaries*, in contrast, illness and bodily decline actually produce speech by fostering Daisy's autobiographical impulse. Provoked to thought by bodily weakness, Daisy uses autobiography as a recuperative.[31] The book engages most directly with her autobiographical undertaking at five times in her life when she lies quietly in bed and has the opportunity to consider her life: when she is ill as a child; when she waits as a married woman for her husband to return from a trip; when she wakes in the morning in her Florida retirement home; when as an elderly woman she recovers in hospital from a heart attack; and when she dies. During her initial writing of her autobiography on air, sparked during that childhood illness, 'she understood that if she was going to hold on to her life at all, she would have to rescue it by a primary act of imagination' (76). Following the heart attack, 'pictures fly into her head, brighter by far than those she sees on the big TV screen in the patients' lounge' (327), and 'she knows that what lies ahead of her must be concluded by the efforts of her imagination' (340).

In the fictional autobiography of *The Stone Diaries*, as in women's autobiography in general, the body becomes both a site of politicized exploration and an avenue for expression. Smith argues that 'writing her experiential history of the body, the autobiographical subject engages in a process of critical self-consciousness through which she comes to an awareness of the relationship of her specific body to the cultural "body" and to the body politic,' and argues that 'that change in consciousness prompts cultural critique.'[32] By showing the difficulties of representing the body, and by forging beyond those difficulties to discuss cultural constructions of sexuality, *The Stone Diaries* makes a critique of both autobiography and society. Briganti writes that 'what is genuinely postmodern in this autobiography is the reclaiming of the maternal body and the elaboration of its relation to language in a genre that has traditionally banished the body from representation' (185). I would argue that such a reclaiming is also, and perhaps more strikingly, genuinely feminist. Smith concludes that in autobiography, 'if the body is the source of an identity that leads to oppression, the sexed body, the racialized body, then the body must be taken back and honoured on the way to speech and writing.'[33] By showing the struggle to adequately represent sexuality and birth, illness and death, and by exploring the ambiguous presence of the body in photographs, Daisy Goodwill's fictional autobiography helps to take back and honour the repressed female body.

Mother As 'Pre-text' for the Autobiographical Project

The body that is most honoured in *The Stone Diaries*, as Briganti also argues in her essay later in this volume, is that of Daisy's mother. Hers is the novel's most overwhelming corporeal presence, and at the same time its most startling absence. Mercy's body dominates the book's first chapter, while Daisy's search for the lost body of her mother is a thread that runs throughout her life story and that is resolved only in the imagined physical reconnection with her mother at her own death. In *The Stone Diaries*, Daisy has missed out on the primary source of language from her birth mother, and thus, as Bella Brodzki argues of many woman autobiographers, she seeks to reconstruct and reclaim her mother's message through her own autobiographical narrative.[34] That her mother is the 'pre-text' and compelling motivation for Daisy's fictional autobiography is evident from its first chapter, its first line, and even its title. The *Stone* of the title is not the traditional patronymic of husband or father, but rather the name of the author's mother, an orphan whose surname is taken from a substance mined in the town where she is born. As a fictional autobiographer, Daisy opens the novel with the words 'My mother's name was Mercy Stone Goodwill,' introducing herself in relation to that one essential other whose absence is conspicuous in the past tense of the verb. In the first chapter, the body of the mother is extraordinarily visible in Daisy's imagined rendering of 'the vault of her [mother's] flesh, her wide face, her thick doughy neck, her great loose breasts and solid boulder of a stomach' (7). As already discussed, that body is also visible in a sexual context, as Mercy is eroticized in Daisy's imagination of her father's sexual response, and in a childbearing incarnation, as Daisy recounts her mother's labour and her own birth. For the majority of the book, however, the body of the mother is a glaring absence, although never quite invisible to the daughter who longs to connect with her.

For Daisy, the lack of her mother is first and most physically evident in the lack of the breast just after birth. As the adult autobiographical narrator who retroactively imagines, views, and records her own birth, Daisy describes her infant mouth searching for the 'filament of matter we struggle to catch hold of at birth' (39). The only physical connection Daisy will have with her mother is a more tenuous one – the 'last of her breath,' which Mercy has given to her child as a way of calling her to life (40). By representing the life-giving properties of the mother's breath, Daisy as autobiographical narrator reappropriates the female creative ability that has long been patriarchally appropriated in the biblical rendering of a male God breathing life into dust as a means of generating human life (Genesis 2.7). Images of the tenuous connection to the maternal through the breath that calls Daisy to life, and the missed connection with the filament of matter that is the mother's nipple, recur as Daisy thinks about her mother late at night while she awaits the arrival of her husband. A 'filament of sensation' and a 'lightly drawn' breath connect Daisy again with the body of her mother, and in 'a flash of distortion,' Daisy imagines herself to have 'given birth to her mother, and not the other way around' (190–1). Like Adrienne Rich, Daisy is 'a woman who, born between her mother's legs' tries 'to return to her mother, to repossess her and be repossessed by her.'[35] Of course, Daisy as autobiographer *has* created her mother. She has imaginatively filled in the gaps of

Mercy's life and death, and in the process has included a graphic portrayal of an experience of childbirth that reveals more about Daisy's experience than it does about her mother's. In death, Daisy is at last joined to her mother, as she feels herself 'merge with, and become, finally, the still body of her dead mother' (359). As she once imagined that she gave birth to her mother, she now imagines that she *is* her mother, lying 'silent and still as a boat' after her death during Daisy's birth (40).[36]

Daisy has several fathers (Cuyler, Barker, and Magnus) and several adoptive mothers, both good and bad (her beloved 'Aunt' Clarentine; her father's housekeeper, Cora-Mae Milltown; her first mother-in-law, Mrs Hoad; and her father's second wife, Maria). Nevertheless, because her mother's sudden death incapacitates her father as a parent, throughout much of the narrative Daisy functions as an orphan. *Jane Eyre*, a novel with which *The Stone Diaries* purposefully engages, features a more traditional orphaned heroine whose motherless status 'gives her the freedom necessary to circumscribe her own developmental course.'[37] In her essay in this volume, Dianne Osland points out many fascinating interconnections between the two novels. *The Stone Diaries* certainly echoes *Jane Eyre* by taking the form of a woman's fictional autobiography (the original title of the earlier novel is *Jane Eyre: An Autobiography*) and by representing the central character as an orphan who is initially cast adrift but eventually integrated into social and family networks. It diverges from the earlier book in striking ways, however, including in its vivid rendering of the mother whose death makes way for the heroine's story. Jane as fictive autobiographer repeats a version of what she has been told about her parents, but she does not try to reconstruct her mother through body memory in the way that Daisy does. And although Daisy's story begins in the romance-plot manner, with the heroine's mother dying in childbirth, it subsequently becomes a 'writing beyond the ending' of the plot that views heterosexual romance and marriage as the only acceptable conclusion to a woman's life story.[38] The novel refuses Daisy's 'romantic imagination' that 'can support only happy endings' (149). Rather than concluding with *Jane Eyre*'s 'Reader, I married him,' *The Stone Diaries* reveals the groom as an alcoholic who is sexually uninterested in his bride, then shows the bride in a second marriage, as a mother and grandmother, and finally in death. Because Daisy's mother is the 'pre-text' for her daughter's autobiography, her absence does not limit Daisy to the traditional path of the orphaned heroine. By continuing the narrative past Daisy's wedding, Shields offers readers a glimpse into the imagined life not only of a young, questing, motherless woman, but also of a middle-class housewife and mother, the sort of person who, according to Patricia Meyer Spacks, seldom features in traditional autobiography.[39]

Diaries and the Domestic

I want to close with a discussion of the role of housewife and mother as represented in *The Stone Diaries* and with a return to the book's beginning – its title. As that title might suggest, a myriad of images and representations of stone are both inscribed and destabilized in the novel.[40] One significant image, in terms of autobiography, is that 'the stone in [one's] throat' must become 'dislodged' in order for speech to occur (84). The form that speech will take, the title further implies, is that of a collection of diaries, a version of autobiography that has traditionally been excluded from theoretical discussions. But *The Stone Diaries* does not consist of the diaries of Daisy Goodwill Flett, even though its readers are continually reminded of diary-writing through references to diaries in the hands of the book's characters: Daisy (132), her husband, Barker (112, 198), her mother (189, in a diary wishfully imagined by Daisy), her older daughter (234), and her friend (248). Diaries are even part of the ironically unsound advice Daisy receives when she is depressed; she is told to 'keep a diary like Virginia Woolf' (262), although Woolf committed suicide at close to Daisy's age after having written in her diary, 'This trough of despair shall not, I swear, engulf me.'[41] Shields's book evokes the process of diary-writing primarily by paying the kind of attention to daily activity that is often characteristic of diaries.

The domestic nature of women's diary entries is made explicit in *Swann*, when literary critic Sarah Maloney expresses profound disappointment about poet Mary Swann's unassuming 'pocket scribbler' that contains only 'jottings' (49) such as 'Creek down today,' 'Green beans up,' or 'Door latch broken' (55). Swann's diary and the details *Swann* provides about her life and Sarah Maloney's indeed reflect the ordinariness, the dailiness, and the domesticity of many women's lives. Shields has said that she purposefully set out to write books that included domesticity: 'I have never for one minute regarded the lives of women as trivial, and I've always known that men and women alike possess a domestic life that very seldom finds its way into our fiction.'[42] While all of the protagonists of Shields's novels have careers at some point in their lives, all of them (even male protagonists such as Jack Bowman of *Happenstance*, Tom Avery of *The Republic of Love*, and Larry Weller of *Larry's Party*) also have domestic lives. *The Stone Diaries*, like Shields's other books, is in part an exploration and affirmation of the domestic aspects of life often left out of literature, but it also provides a critique of enforced domesticity.

The novel opens with the fundamentally domestic: a recipe and a menu. On a hot July day, Mercy Stone Goodwill is 'making a Malvern pudding for her husband's supper' (1), which will consist of 'cold corned beef with a spoonful of homemade relish, some dressed potatoes at the side, cups of sweet tea, and then this fine pudding' (3). The richness of detail about the making of the meal culminates in the suggestion that for women like Mercy, the domestic is a concrete kind of creativity. Daisy as narrator says of her mother that 'like an artist – years later this form of artistry is perfectly clear to me – she stirs and arranges and draws in her brooding lower lip' (2). Later in the novel, Daisy's own recovery from her depression is linked to the domestic details of life: 'She'd like to tie a crisp clean apron around her waist once again, peel a pound of potatoes in three minutes flat and put them soaking in cold water. Polish a jelly jar and set it on the top shelf with its mates' (263). The domestic is further validated as much of the narrative is presented in the form of household details such as recipes and grocery lists.

Yet despite its references to what is characterized in *Swann* as the 'redemptive' nature of dailiness (19), *The Stone Diaries* is far from an uncritical celebration of household duties. Chapter 1 is only Daisy's imaginary rendering of the joys of domestic life, and while chapter 5 echoes this rendering as it opens with Daisy preparing a cold supper for her family in the heat of a July day, the differences between the two parallel scenes are striking. In 'Motherhood, 1947,' Daisy is not the first-person narrator, and the chapter presents the reality of her experience of wifedom and motherhood rather than the imagined ideal. While for her mother, preparing and eating food is 'heavenly' and her 'notion of paradise' (2), Daisy's culinary enterprises are described using the language of hell and damnation: her kitchen is 'hot as Hades' (157), and she says 'Damn it' five times under her breath as she prises the veal loaf out of the pan (158–9). Daisy's recipe is not from a cookery book passed down from woman to woman, as is her mother's recipe, but from the pages of *Ladies Home Journal* (158). Her young son thinks she looks 'straight from the Oxydol ads' (160), and inside her shabby house, the only thing she is proud of is her glass-topped coffee table, which she uses to display photographs of her children and a copy of her marriage announcement. The idea is not original; she got it from a *Canadian Homes and Gardens* article ironically titled 'Putting the Essential You into Your Decor' (193–4).

The details of Daisy's life (including, as noted previously, her sex life) and her ideas about domestic duties reflect analyses by Betty Friedan about the mystique that developed around middle-class women in the middle of the twentieth century. Friedan argues that 'domestic aspects of feminine existence – as it was lived by women whose lives were confined, by necessity, to cooking, cleaning, washing, [and] bearing children' – were turned 'into a religion, a pattern by which all women must now live or deny their femininity.'[43] That religion, she suggests, was promulgated through women's magazines of the type referred to repeatedly in *The Stone Diaries* (158, 164, 185, 191, 194). As Daisy's kitchen language shows, she finds domesticity a kind of hell, but she nevertheless slavishly takes as her Bible the magazines that Friedan decries as essentializing and restrictive. Like the women in an issue of *McCalls* that Friedan analyses, Daisy is 'almost childlike.'[44] Barker recognizes her 'girlishness' (160), and even Alice speculates that the age difference between her parents 'kept [Daisy] girlish, made her a kind of tenant in the tower of girlhood. There she remained, safe, looked after' (235–6). Daisy's life may have the illusion of safety, but hers is a trapped, Rapunzel-like state, and she is not safe from disillusion about the limited nature of her life's rewards: 'A little sigh escapes the lips of Mrs. Flett (Daisy), who is suddenly exhausted and who can't help noticing that no one has asked for a second helping of jellied veal loaf' (161–2). Daisy may not be able to define her own situation, but evidently she suffers from what Friedan called 'the problem that has no name, a vague undefined wish for "something more" than washing dishes, ironing, punishing and praising the children.'[45]

The Stone Diaries refers directly to Friedan's book when it comments on the 'good jabber about *The Feminine Mystique*' (242) between Alice and Fraidy. Alice endorses Friedan's solution to 'the problem that has no name' – work outside the home – while Fraidy, having worked at less-than-satisfying jobs all her life, 'tak[es] issue with Betty Friedan's exaltation of work as salvation' (242). Unlike her daughter and her friend, Daisy as autobiographer does not admit to having read Friedan's book. Carol Shields read it, however, and it influenced her life as much as it influenced her fiction. Shields has said that after having dreamed of fulfilling her society's domestic ideal, she was never able to 'doze off quite the same again' after she read *The Feminine Mystique* in 1963, the year it was published.[46] She linked Friedan's book to her own representation of women's roles in *The Stone Diaries* when she wrote that Daisy

> believed what the women's magazines said about women's work. She absorbed, unquestioningly, the notion of what a woman's life might consist of, its rewards, its bargains. If only one person had said to her: Your life is your own and there is work you can do. (A lot of women never heard this articulated before *The Feminine Mystique* was published.)[47]

By writing in *The Stone Diaries* about Daisy Goodwill's perceived lack of choice, about her unquestioning adoption of models of women's lives presented in popular media, and about the fact that she is 'blinded, throttled, erased from the record of her own existence' (76), Shields explores, makes concrete, and criticizes theories learned from Friedan about women's lives and women's work. Shields has described her fictive autobiography as a comment on women's silencing and on their erasure from the centre of their own lives.[48] In *The Stone Diaries*, Daisy's son muses on the silencing and marginalization of his middle-class, middle-aged North American mother. He says, 'Something, someone, cut off her head, yanked out her tongue ... [Y]ou would expect her to land somewhere near the middle of the world. Instead she's over there at the edge. The least vibration could knock her off' (252). Daisy is indeed teetering on the margins, and her tongue has indeed been yanked out, as is attested by her autobiographical project, which is thought but not articulated and is often presented through others' stories and others' voices.

Liz Stanley argues that 'our understanding of "lives" and how they become "written lives"' is gained not only from autobiographies based on 'real' lives, but also from fictional autobiographies such as *Jane Eyre*.[49] Shields herself has said:

> It is through fiction that I've learned about the lives of women. And about how people think; biography and history have a narrative structure, but they don't tell us much about the inte-

rior lives of people. This seems to me to be fiction's magic, that it attempts to be an account of all that cannot be documented but is, nevertheless, true.[50]

The Stone Diaries merges fictional content with autobiographical form and theory to provide the story of a woman's life that cannot otherwise be written, 'but is, nevertheless, true.' The book is indeed a 'life,' the traditional descriptive title for biography and autobiography, but it is also a sophisticated critique of both autobiography and theories of autobiography. It critiques notions of women's life stories as necessarily fragmentary and relational; it reflects and resists the repression of a female physical existence in much autobiographical writing; it examines the figure of mother in life writing; and it alternately validates and critiques the domestic as an integral part of women's life histories. By exploring theoretical and practical constraints on the representations of women's stories, Shields's novel examines and critiques social constraints on women's lives.

Notes

I would like to thank Susan Gingell for her helpful comments on an earlier version of this essay.

1 Carol Shields, 'A Likely Story: A Conversation with Carol Shields,' interview by Katie Bolick, *Atlantic Unbound* 283.1 (14 Jan. 1999), http://www.theatlantic.com/unbound/factfict/ff9901.htm (consulted 14 March 2000).

2 *Susanna Moodie: Voice and Vision* (Ottawa: Borealis, 1977); *Small Ceremonies* [*SC*] (1976; rpt. Toronto: Random House, 1995); 'Three Canadian Women: Fiction or Autobiography,' *Atlantis* 4.1 (1978): 49–54; *Swann: A Mystery* (1987; rpt. as *Swann*, Toronto: Random House, 1995); *The Stone Diaries* (Toronto: Random House, 1993). In subsequent references, Shields's works will be cited parenthetically.

   Swann engages with autobiography as well as biography.

After one of *Swann*'s main characters says that most people could write their autobiographies in 'one *long* sentence' (227), the narrative subsequently provides two pages titled 'Frederic Cruzzi: His (Unwritten) One-Sentence Autobiography' (228–9). The book's title evokes Marcel Proust's autobiographical fiction *Swann's Way*, while the life history of Mary Swann evokes the unwritten biography of Vancouver-born poet Pat Lowther, who was bludgeoned to death by her husband in 1975 and whose fourth, posthumous book of poetry is called *A Stone Diary*.

3   Winifred M. Mellor, '"The Simple Container of Our Existence": Narrative Ambiguity in Carol Shields's *The Stone Diaries*,' *Studies in Canadian Literature* 20.2 (1995): 96; Margery Fee, 'Auto/Biographical Fictions,' review of *The Stone Diaries*, by Carol Shields, *Canadian Literature* 144 (1995): 173; Gordon E. Slethaug, '"The Coded Dots of Life": Carol Shields's Diaries and Stones,' *Canadian Literature* 156 (1998): 59; Chiara Briganti, 'Fat, Nail Clippings, Body Parts, or the Story of Where I Have Been: Carol Shields and Auto/biography,' p. 176 (in this volume).

4   As Shields points out, 'the chapter headings speak ironically to what [is] in the chapter, so that in fact the chapter on Love isn't really about love, and the chapter on Childhood only touches on childhood' ('The Golden Book: An Interview with Carol Shields,' interview by Joan Thomas, *Prairie Fire* 14.4 [1993–4]: 58).

5   Georges Gusdorf, 'Conditions and Limits of Autobiography,' in *Autobiography: Essays Theoretical and Critical*, ed. and trans. James Olney (Princeton: Princeton UP, 1980), 29.

6   William Spengemann, *The Forms of Autobiography: Episodes in the History of a Literary Genre* (New Haven: Yale UP, 1980), xi. Regenia Gagnier has demonstrated that working-class Victorian narratives also were disqualified from the genre because their subjects 'did not express themselves in individuated voices with subjective desires' (*Subjectivities: A History of Self-Representation in Britain, 1832–1920* [New York: Oxford UP, 1991], 28).

7   Mary G. Mason, 'The Other Voice: Autobiographies of Women Writers,' in Olney, ed., *Autobiography*, 210; Françoise Lionnet, *Autobiographical Voices: Race, Gender, Self-Portraiture* (Ithaca: Cornell UP, 1989), 27; Susan Stanford Friedman, 'Women's Autobiographical Selves: Theory and Practice,' in *The Private*

Self: Theory and Practice of Women's Autobiographical Writings, ed. Shari Benstock (Chapel Hill: U of North Carolina P, 1988), 56.

The view of women's autobiography as grounded in relationship is not shared by all feminist theorists; Leigh Gilmore, for example, argues that the theory that women autobiographers 'represent the self in relation to "others"' proposes a 'unitary, transhistorical female experience' that does not exist (*Autobiographics: A Feminist Theory of Women's Self-Representation* [Ithaca: Cornell UP, 1994], xiii, xii). Patricia Waugh, meanwhile, argues that women's writing in general 'foregrounds the construction of identity *in relationship*' (*Feminine Fictions: Revisiting the Postmodern* [London: Routledge, 1989], 10).

8 Adrienne Rich, *Of Woman Born: Motherhood As Experience and Institution* (1976; rpt. New York: Norton, 1986), 218; Bella Brodzki, 'Mothers, Displacement, and Language in the Autobiographies of Nathalie Sarraute and Christa Wolf,' in *Life/Lines: Theorizing Women's Autobiography*, ed. Bella Brodzki and Celeste Schenck (Ithaca: Cornell UP, 1988), 245.

9 Estelle C. Jelinek, ed., *Women's Autobiography: Essays in Criticism* (Bloomington: Indiana UP, 1980), 17; see also Jeanne Perreault, *Writing Selves: Contemporary Feminist Autography* (Minneapolis: U of Minnesota P, 1995), 4; Benstock, ed., *The Private Self*, 29; and Helen Buss, *Mapping Our Selves: Canadian Women's Autobiography in English* (Montreal: McGill-Queen's UP, 1993), 15. A dissenting voice comes from Domna Stanton, who argues that some women's narratives are linear, and notes that some male critics, especially those who approach autobiography from a post-modernist perspective, posit that all autobiography is fragmentary (*The Female Autograph: Theory and Practice of Autobiography from the Tenth to the Twentieth Century* [Chicago: U of Chicago P, 1987]).

10 Shirley Neuman, '"An Appearance Walking in a Forest the Sexes Burn': Autobiography and the Construction of the Feminine Body,' *Signature* 2 (1989): 1–2; Sidonie Smith, *Subjectivity, Identity, and the Body: Women's Autobiographical Practices in the Twentieth Century* (Bloomington: Indiana UP, 1993), 6.

11 Linda Hutcheon, *The Canadian Postmodern: A Study of Contemporary English-Canadian Fiction* (Toronto: Oxford UP, 1988), 82; Liz

Stanley, *The Auto/Biographical I: The Theory and Practice of Feminist Auto/Biography* (Manchester: U of Manchester P, 1992), 255. Northrop Frye wrote as early as 1957 that autobiography is 'prose fiction' because it is 'inspired by a creative, and therefore fictional, impulse to select only those events and experiences in the writer's life that go to build up an integrated pattern' (*Anatomy of Criticism: Four Essays* [Princeton: Princeton UP, 1957], 307). For variations on this argument, see Philippe Lejeune, *Le Pacte autobiographique* (Paris: Éditions du Seuil, 1975), 26; William L. Howarth, 'Some Principles of Autobiography,' in Olney, ed., *Autobiography*, 86; and Paul Jay, *Being in the Text: Self-Representation from Wordsworth to Roland Barthes* (Ithaca: Cornell UP, 1984), 16. For discussions of feminist traversing of boundaries between fiction and autobiography, see also Marlene Kadar, ed., *Essays on Life Writing: From Genre to Critical Practice* (Toronto: U of Toronto P, 1992), 5, and Stanley, 255.

12 Janice Morgan, 'Introduction: Subject to Subject / Voice to Voice: Twentieth-Century Autobiographical Fiction by Women Writers,' in *Redefining Autobiography in Twentieth-Century Women's Fiction: An Essay Collection*, ed. Janice Morgan and Colette T. Hall (New York: Garland, 1991), 3, 6. The theoretical rejection of the notion that autobiography necessarily refers to a real human life worries some feminist critics of autobiography, who argue that women must continue to insist upon some form of referentiality in their life writing in order 'to claim a self, to speak [their] oppression, to name oppressors' (Stanley, 16).

13 Nathalie Cooke, 'Reading Reflections: The Autobiographical Illusion in *Cat's Eye*,' in Kadar, ed., *Essays on Life Writing*, 164.

14 Kadar, 7, 3, 10, 12.

15 I draw here on Patricia Waugh's definition of metafiction as 'fictional writing which self-consciously and systematically draws attention to its status as an artefact in order to pose questions about the relationship between fiction and reality' (*Metafiction: The Theory and Practice of Self-Conscious Fiction* [London: Methuen, 1984], 2).

16 Lisa Johnson, in her essay in this volume, '"She Enlarges on the Available Materials": A Postmodernism of Resistance in *The Stone Diaries*,' takes exception to the repeated critical quotation

of what she calls 'bruised phrases' (202). I argue that these undeniably striking parts of the novel form part of Shields's critique of the notion that a woman's autobiography can be adequately expressed through its voids and gaps. Simone Vauthier's interesting article, 'Ruptures in Carol Shields's *The Stone Diaries*' (*Anglophonia* 1 [1997]: 177–92), which I discovered after this essay was prepared, analyses these gaps in terms of the paradigm of chaotics. (Note that in many editions of *The Stone Diaries* 'unbridgeable' is misspelled as 'unbridgable.' We have corrected this throughout this volume [editors].)

17 Shields has pointed out that Daisy is not *writing* her autobiography: 'She's thinking it, in exactly the same way that we all think our own life. We carry around this construct that is our own life. But no, she doesn't actually put pen to paper ... She's building it, and she's building it out of the scraps of what she knows and what she imagines' ('Golden Book' 58). Daisy's task in *The Stone Diaries*, as is the task of the biographer-narrator of *Small Ceremonies*, is to fill 'gaps' (*SC* 33), to engage in a 'careful daily accumulation of details,' to 'enlarge on available data' (35).

18 Hutcheon, 82. Shields has explored the shifting boundaries between biography and fiction in earlier works of fiction and nonfiction. Her 1978 essay 'Three Canadian Women,' for example, concludes that 'there is no such thing as pure autobiography or pure fiction, but only varying degrees of assimilated and transformed experience' (54). Her 1987 novel, *Swann*, is structured as the fictional recreation of a woman's biography; its last chapter, a film script that begins with a director's note that 'the main characters ... are fictional creations, as is the tragic Mary Swann, *poète naïve* of rural Ontario' (293), emphasizes the book's fictionality.

19 Winifred Mellor discusses the postmodern narrative ambiguity of *The Stone Diaries*, arguing that the subversion of autobiographical egotism evident in Daisy's undercutting of her own narrative 'recognizes the self-aggrandizing impulse in the writer of autobiography and destabilizes it by mocking it, and at the same time it enforces the accepted premise that events become history once they are written down' (102).

20 For a discussion of this convention, see Shari Benstock, 'The

Female Self Engendered: Autobiographical Writing and Theories of Selfhood,' in *Women and Autobiography*, ed. Martine Watson Brownley and Allison B. Kimmich (Wilmington: Scholarly Resources, 1999), 9. Autobiographers have frequently written about themselves in the third person, but Gertrude Stein self-consciously plays with this convention in *The Autobiography of Alice B. Toklas*, which purports to be written by Stein's companion, but is actually Stein's own autobiography, written in the third person 'as simply as Defoe did the autobiography of Robinson Crusoe' ([New York: Harcourt, 1933], 310). In contrast to my analysis, Vauthier argues that 'some discrepancies can be accounted for only by positing a narrator who knows more than Daisy knows or invents'; thus she suggests that the narrator oscillates between autobiographer and biographer. She does acknowledge, however, that Daisy as autobiographer may also be writing about herself in the third person (184–5, n183).

21 Along a similar vein, Briganti argues that the passage cited 'enacts the precariousness of the subject even down to the shifting pronoun assignations' (186).

22 I explore Shields's response to Friedan's 1963 criticism of media constructions of women's roles later in this paper.

23 Carol Shields, 'A Little like Flying: An Interview with Carol Shields,' interview by Harvey De Roo, *West Coast Review* 23.3 (1988): 48; Mellor, 106; Fee, 173; Briganti, 190–1.

24 Seyla Benhabib and Drucilla Cornell, eds., *Feminism As Critique: On the Politics of Gender* (Minneapolis: U of Minnesota P, 1987), 12.

25 Virginia Woolf, 'Professions for Women,' in *The Death of the Moth and Other Essays* (London: Hogarth, 1942), 153.

26 Neuman, 2; Smith, 23. According to Smith, although the writing subject attempts to 'contain, control, and co-opt' the marginalized body, it remains on the 'horizon of experience' and thus 'can never be "jettisoned entirely," nor can it be wholly contained' (6). In twentieth-century life writing, women's bodies have in fact become less and less contained; see, for example, Maxine Hong Kingston's *The Woman Warrior*.

27 Julia Watson, 'Unspeakable Differences: The Politics of Gender

in Lesbian and Heterosexual Women's Autobiographies,' in *De/Colonizing the Subject: The Politics of Gender in Women's Autobiography*, ed. Sidonie Smith and Julia Watson (Minneapolis: U of Minnesota P, 1992), 140.

28 See Deborah Schnitzer, 'Tricks: Artful Photographs and Letters in Carol Shields's *The Stone Diaries* and Anita Brookner's *Hotel du Lac*,' *Prairie Fire* 16.1 (1995): 28–39, as well as previously cited articles by Vauthier and Briganti, for analyses of photographs in *The Stone Diaries*.

29 'Eros' (in *Dressing Up for the Carnival* [Toronto: Random House, 2000]) traces a woman's increasing awareness of herself as a sexual being; *Larry's Party* (Toronto: Random House, 1997) has a chapter called 'Larry's Penis, 1986'; chapter 1 of *The Republic of Love* (Toronto: Random House, 1992) opens with female protagonist Fay McLeod in bed with her long-time lover, whose thumb is 'twiddling away' on her clitoris (5); and *Small Ceremonies* includes several references to the sexual relations of a married couple, features a birth in chapter 8, and uses gestation as a structural element: the book consists of nine chapters, titled with nine consecutive months from September to May.

30 Shields, 'Golden Book,' 58; *A Fairly Conventional Woman* [*FCW*] (1982; rpt. as *Happenstance: The Wife's Story*, Toronto: Vintage, 1994).

31 Fee suggests that Daisy's account of her life is 'a kind of fantasy she has during her long decline into death after a heart attack at 80' (173). By contrast, I argue that Daisy thinks out her autobiography throughout her life, although she clearly revises as she grows older and her sense of generic conventions with which to compare her narrative becomes more developed.

32 Smith, 131.

33 Smith, 177.

34 Brodzki, 246.

35 Rich, 218.

36 *The Stone Diaries* is not the first time in Shields's fiction that the body, absent through death, is an overwhelming presence. In *Swann*, the murdered and dismembered body of poet Mary Swann haunts the text. Biographer Morton Jimroy even recalls

her body in order to think and speak about her poetry in relation to literary theory: 'It was just a matter of time before the theoreticians got to Mary Swann and tore her limb from limb in a grotesque parody of her bodily death' (95).

37 Marianne Hirsch, *The Mother/Daughter Plot: Narrative, Psychoanalysis, Feminism* (Bloomington: Indiana UP, 1989), 44.
38 Rachel Blau DuPlessis, *Writing beyond the Ending: Narrative Strategies of Twentieth-Century Women Writers* (Bloomington: Indiana UP, 1985), 197.
39 Patricia Meyer Spacks, 'Selves in Hiding,' in Jelinek, ed., *Women's Autobiography*, 112.
40 See articles by Leona Gom ('Stone and Flowers,' *Prairie Fire* 16.1 [1995]: 22–7), Slethaug, and Vauthier for detailed discussions of stone imagery in *The Stone Diaries*.
41 Virginia Woolf, *A Moment's Liberty: The Shorter Diary*, ed. Anne Olivier Bell (Toronto: Lester & Orpen Dennys, 1990), 501–2.
42 Shields, 'A Little like Flying,' 47.
43 Betty Friedan, *The Feminine Mystique* (1963; rpt. New York: Dell, 1964), 38.
44 Friedan, 30.
45 Friedan, 54.
46 Carol Shields, 'Interview with Carol Shields,' by Eleanor Wachtel, *Room of One's Own* 13.1/2 (1989): 20.
47 Carol Shields, '"Writing Must Come Out of What Passionately Interests Us. Nothing Else Will Do": An Epistolary Interview with Carol Shields,' by Joan Thomas, *Prairie Fire* 16.1 (1995): 127.
48 Shields, 'Golden Book,' 60.
49 Stanley, 14.
50 Carol Shields, 'Interview with Carol Shields,' by Marjorie Anderson, *Prairie Fire* 16.1 (1995): 150.

The problem for feminist biographers, as O'Brien explains it, is two-sided. On the one hand, 'deconstruction's questioning of the unitary, representable self and the fixed correspondence between signifier and signified leads to a questioning not only of the concept "identity" but also of the concept of "woman." From the perspective of deconstruction, to posit a female voice or a woman writer's creation of identity is to confuse the social construction "woman" with an experiential reality.'[4] On the other hand, many feminists have 'opposed ... deconstruction's dismantling of the unified subject and the category "woman"' because, in their attempts to refute the notion that masculine experience is the universal experience, they have looked specifically to narratives of 'self-creation or self-discovery' for a 'means to rescue the self from male definitions and to construct a female self.'[5] As Kineke suggests, the problem with this predominant feminist theory of biography is that it 'repeat[s] the patriarchal construction of the single coherent subject' by '[plotting] life-stories that are concerned with their subjects' heroic progress from the status of woman-as-victim to the status of woman-as-writer and ... [eliding] the possibility for multiple and contradictory selves to inhabit the biography.' Kineke argues for a form of feminist literary biography that uses a 'methodology of contrast, of contradiction, of different and inconsistent versions of a life positioned side-by-side without trying to tie up all the loose ends; a method, in other words, that writes the possibility for irreconcilable differences both within and among portrayals of the subject.' Such a strategy would '[challenge] masculine authority and authenticity and [create] an alternative methodological space from which to tell a different life story.'[6]

In *Jane Austen* Shields has written the very type of literary biography that Kineke proposes while finding a means of reconciling the conflict between postmodern and feminist theories of biography that O'Brien identifies. First, she undermines the notion of a stable self, an essential biographical subject. While she records many of the few known facts of Austen's life in an attempt to point toward the presence behind the novels, her interest clearly lies in the fictions of

Austen's life: both the numerous fictitious Austens other critics, readers, and biographers have created, and the fictitious selves Austen herself created or experienced in her life and her novels. Thus, just as Wendy Roy has argued in this volume that *The Stone Diaries* 'can be classified as meta-autobiography, or a work of literature that comments on the genre' (115), I argue that Shields's *Jane Austen* functions as postmodern meta-biography, a meta-biography whose end is to present Austen not as a stable identity, an essential self, but as what Shields has called elsewhere 'a multitude of selves.'[7]

But *Jane Austen* is a work about a woman writer written by a woman writer. If, as Sarah Gamble suggests earlier in this volume, 'the innate self-reflexiveness of Shields's [writing] ... opens her work up to postmodern interpretation' (40), Shields's deep interest in Austen as a *woman* writer and a literary foremother means she does not abandon Austen completely to the potentially nihilistic postmodern notion that there is no self to identify. Rather, Shields manipulates postmodernist theory from a feminist standpoint. Her method is one Patricia Waugh has identified when she asserts that 'many women writers are using postmodern aesthetic strategies of disruption to re-imagine the world in which we live.'[8] In this case, Shields uses postmodern aesthetic strategies of disruption to suggest that Austen was a woman writer who used her novels to reinvent herself imaginatively, creating those multiple selves as a response to varied life situations. More importantly, however, Shields uses these same strategies to imagine and re-imagine the Austen we all feel we know and love, and in so doing to join with Austen in acts of creation. Thus, although Shields identifies Austen's multiple fictive selves, she also sees the very creation of those selves as an example of the fertile and affirmative power of creative thought.

Biography As Fiction

In her interview in the *Atlantic Monthly* Shields defends the value of literary biography, explaining that although her teachers advocated the methods of the New Criticism, she has since become alert to the failures of that methodology:

> We were taught to look only at the text, and not to get involved in who the writer was, and how that corresponded to the writing. There was even a period where author photos weren't published on the backs of books. I think the New Criticism failed because there's always a presence behind a novel, and you can never forget that presence. We need to know the connection between the words and the person who makes them up.[9]

As a writer, Shields is keenly aware of what she calls our narrative hunger, our deep need 'for the glimpse of the human dilemma, the inaccessible stories of others,'[10] or, in the case of famous authors like Austen, 'the connection between the words and the person who makes them up.' Such assertions might seem to pit Shields against the postmodern concept of the death of the author, a concept that, like the New Critical method, causes critics to dismiss questions of authorial intention or agency when considering a literary work. They might seem instead to ally her with those feminist biographers who seek to identify an essential self.

Yet Shields is not so naïve as to think that the connection between author and text is straightforward or that the biographer can unearth all of the facts of a subject's life and neatly establish that connection. A writer whose works repeatedly dip into questions of biography, Shields is certainly familiar with what Marjorie Garber has called the 'old truth' that all biography 'is a species of fiction-making.'[11] As Sarah Gamble points out earlier in this volume, Shields explores the fictive nature of the biographical craft in her 1976 novel, *Small Ceremonies*. Early in the novel, the work's narrator and protagonist, Judith Gill, who is writing a biography of Canadian writer Susanna Moodie, both hints at and resists the recognition that the literary biographer constructs a subject who is largely fictitious. Noting that she looks for 'the cracks in the surface' of Moodie's novels, which present a picture of a neatly 'glazed' life, Judith explains that Moodie's 'reticence'

> makes her a difficult subject to possess. But who, after all, could sustain such a portrait over so many pages without leaving a few chinks in the varnish? Already I've found, with even the most casual sleuthing, small passages in her novels and backwoods recollections of unconscious self-betrayal, isolated words and phrases, almost lost in the lyrical brushwork. I am gluing them together, here at my card table, into a delicate design which may just possibly be the real Susanna.[12]

Of course, Judith's language reveals an instance of her own 'unconscious self-betrayal.' Her metaphor of gluing together the key pieces of Moodie's identity suggests that the picture obtained will in the end always remain a collage of assembled fragments, even though Gill thinks she might 'possess' the 'real' author. By the novel's conclusion, Judith acknowledges that the 'real' Susanna has escaped her. Judith has found one of Moodie's novels in particular, what she calls Moodie's fictionalized autobiography, invaluable to her own work. While to her it seems that the novel is 'Susanna's own story,' she also comes to see that the novel is nevertheless 'an idealized picture,' 'an autobiography in fictional form.' The autobiography thus reveals something that 'isn't really Susanna; it's only a projection, a view of herself' (155). Finally, the Judith who once optimistically sought to possess Moodie admits that even Moodie 'seemed to have had little real understanding of herself.' As she sends off the final manuscript of her biography, she reflects, '[I]s it any wonder that I don't understand her?' (153). Having functioned under the assumption that she could unearth the truths about this female literary figure, Judith ends up serving as an object lesson in the failures of the feminist essentialist biographical method.

As Sarah Gamble explains elsewhere in this volume, Judith's search for the real Susanna 'is bound to fail' because Susanna Moodie is 'not a person but a linguistic cipher [that] points to nothing but more words, more manuscripts' (43). Gamble enlarges on this point by arguing that *Small Ceremonies* 'presents biography as a kind of boderline genre, not quite history, not quite fiction' (43). Shields the biographer also stands on this border between history and fiction, albeit more self-consciously than her somewhat naïve heroine Judith Gill. I want to suggest that Shields leans toward the fiction side of that borderline; she downplays the historical orientation of the traditional biographical form in order to emphasize biography's fictional qualities, and thus challenges both the assumptions that undergird that form and the methods that typify it.

If it is indeed a truth universally acknowledged that all biographies are works of fiction, it is also true that most biographers do not bring this notion to the fore in their writing. Rather, the typical biographical stance is to assert, as Judith Gill does, that in this particular biography the reader will finally meet the 'real' subject. Ironically, while literary biographies are about inventors of fictions of various kinds, these biographies seldom explicitly acknowledge their own fictive qualities. Their stance is rather, as Sharon O'Brien argues, based on that of the nineteenth-century omniscient narrator:

> [T]he assumptions made about biography accord with those made by readers and writers of realistic fiction: language is a transparent medium capable of representing the world; character and the self are knowable; the cause and effect linearity implied by the chronological plot is a reliable way of ordering reality; and the author is a trustworthy narrator who understands the relationship between the private self and the public world. Given these assumptions, it is easy to see why a traditional biographer or critic would distrust the presence of *any* acknowledged theory in biography.[13]

Shields herself did no original research for her biography of Austen. Rather she relied, as do most authors of the Penguin

Lives series, on reading existing biographies, compilations of letters, and works of criticism.[14] A look at the biographies Shields consulted reveals that *all* of them participate in the tradition O'Brien identifies, arguing either overtly or covertly that they have discovered the 'real' or knowable Austen where others have failed. Park Honan (1996), for example, claims to have written 'the most complete, realistic life of Jane Austen.'[15] John Halperin (1984), David Nokes (1997), and Claire Tomalin (1997) have all written biographies that contest the long-accepted notion that Austen was a virtuous woman who led a largely uneventful life. Each replaces this earlier version of Austen with his or her own construct of a knowable character: Halperin asserts that Austen was essentially characterized by 'detachment ... moral distance ... coldness' and used irony as a way of maintaining her distance from both her own feelings and from others.[16] Nokes, who also claims to have written a biography that has 'the virtue of greater authenticity,' suggests that Austen was actually 'rebellious, satirical and wild.'[17] Tomalin argues that Austen's life 'was, in fact, full of events, of distress and even trauma, which left [permanent] marks upon her,' but that she 'overcame' these traumas 'and made them serve her purposes.'[18] And, true to traditional biographical form, each of these biographies presents Austen's life through the other patterns O'Brien identifies, assuming cause-and-effect linearity, assuming that language accurately represents the world, and assuming that they, as authors, are the reader's trustworthy guides to the 'real' Austen.

Yet the cumulative effect of reading all these biographies in a relatively short time, as Shields must have done, is to sense that there are numerous possibilities for how to interpret Austen's life and that no one interpretation can be privileged over any other. Having read through these biographies en route to writing her own, and being herself a writer of postmodern fiction, Shields must have come to this conclusion. Her biography differs significantly from those she consulted; in O'Brien's terms, it '[exposes] the framework the biographer is using to interpret the subject' and 'moves biog-

raphy into the realm of ... postmodernist novel, a fictional
world in which characters do not "come to life" according to
the conventions of nineteenth-century realism.'[19] In so doing,
I would add, Shields's biography effectively deconstructs the
traditional biographies of Austen by pointing out the numerous fictive versions of Austen that have been invented by
critics, biographers, and readers.

Even the opening of Shields's biography resists the traditional biographer's stance. Most Austen biographies begin
the process of identifying the stable self in the manner of the
prototypical nineteenth-century *Bildungsroman*, either by telling the story of Austen's birth or by examining Austen's
lineage, focusing gradually on her parents, and then turning
to the moment of her birth. Thus the subject becomes the
identifiable product of an identifiable series of historical events:
parentage, birth, childrearing, schooling, and so on. Shields,
by contrast, starts with intractability, with the questions and
problems an Austen biographer faces. The first sentence of
chapter 1 declares that 'today Jane Austen belongs to the
nearly unreachable past,' and in the sentences and paragraphs
that follow, Shields writes of the lack of tangible remnants of
Austen's existence (no diary, no voice recording, no photograph, few surviving letters, no portrait), the 'intractable silences' that 'throw long shadows on [Austen's] apparent
chattiness' (5). Most of all, Shields undermines the authority
of her own biography by emphasizing the 'opacity of
[Austen's] life' (5). The cumulative effect of these paragraphs
is to suggest that any Austen biography is largely a work of
conjecture, constituted predominantly by the absence rather
than presence of facts and artefacts. Unlike Honan, Tomalin,
Halperin, and Nokes, then, Shields reflexively highlights the
fictionality and unreliability of what will follow.

Structurally, Shields's biography also contests the notion of
Bildung. While Shields does present the events of Austen's life
in chronological order, she does not write anything like a
linear narrative. The biography shifts from moments of linear
narrative, to moments of analysis or observation about her

novels, to moments of speculation and rumination, to moments of discussion of the novel, novel writing, and novel reading, among other things. A certain slippage results; Shields's book refuses to stay grounded in its own purported biographical mode, or at least in what readers have come to expect of that genre. Chapter 3, for example, begins with a discussion of Austen's heroines, then moves to readers' responses to Austen's novels, to Austen's overall role in the development of the novel, to the novel reading Jane and her family did at home, to the influences of that reading and of her family on her early writing style, to questions of what kind of a child Austen was, and then back to the development of her earliest writing style. The chapter contains no dates, very few concrete events, very few of the titles of Austen's juvenilia, and no references to the order in which the juvenilia were written, even though the period of Austen's youth when she wrote the juvenilia and the nature of Austen's development as a writer via this juvenilia turn out to be the overall topic of the chapter. This method suggests that whatever *Bildung*, whatever development, occurs is neither linear, historical, nor factual but is rather the result of a jumble of simultaneous interests and influences glimpsed only through the smudged lens of biographical interpretation.

In addition to deconstructing the concept of *Bildung* through this postmodern narrative strategy, Shields directly interrogates critical and biographical assumptions about Austen, playfully taking to task those vague but commonly accepted assertions about Austen's character that rest on shaky underpinnings. One such perception Shields identifies, a perception that she suggests has 'become enamelled and precious and ready for museum sanctity,' is the notion that Austen was 'possessed of a small soul marked by a profound psychic wound' (9). Even as Shields suggests the likely source of inspiration for this notion ('The defensive tone of her letters and the cheerful mockery that characterizes her unsentimental novels support this belief to a point' [9]), she also makes clear the ultimately speculative nature of such accepted assertions by pointing out that 'we can only guess at the degree of her alienation and its cause. It might amount to little more than simple contagion. She lived, after all, in an age of satire, and as near as we know, she was the child of unsentimental parents' (9). By pointing out the guesswork involved in much of Austen scholarship, Shields emphasizes the contingency of the enshrined understandings of Austen's character. Shields's choice of language here and elsewhere in her biography highlights this idea of the contingent nature of biographical speculation. In response to the assertion that Austen had a 'small soul marked by a profound psychic wound,' Shields offers, not a counter assertion, but rather a counter possibility couched in terms of what might have been. Shields is careful, then, not to claim to have the answer that will set the Austen record straight (as tends to be the case with most biography). She instead offers an account of what might have been; she poses her response as a tenuous position, and in so doing also underscores the tenuous nature of the long-accepted picture of Austen with which she takes issue.

But Shields's suggestion here also points to the idea that not only might our conception of Austen's character be contingent, but that Austen's voice itself might be contingent upon cultural trends. Biographers have failed to recognize that the defensive tone in Austen's letters and the cheerful mockery in her prose might be merely the products of an era rather than the signs of a distinguishing identity. Even Austen's letter-writing voice, Shields points out, offers the calculated effect of candour: 'She writes quickly so that the text will mimic the sound of her own voice, a letter-writing technique that was encouraged in her time, and so the scattered and somewhat breathless nature of her correspondence is not the result of carelessness but of deliberation' (6). Austen's authorial tone might be merely a construct, a persona, rather than a key to her essential identity. Austen's 'sense of irony,' Shields notes, 'often throws biographers off course when assessing the Austen personality' (86). The product of an era when authors used irony as a form of sleight of hand, Austen fools us into believing we know who she is.

Shields uses numerous other strategies that undermine the stability of the omniscient biographical voice. While generally biographies are written in the declarative, particularly when it comes to issues about which there is scant evidence, Shields's biography frequently slips into or gestures toward the interrogative. It is worth listing several examples here:

> Who was she really? And who exactly is her work designed to please? One person? Two or three? Or an immense, wide, and unknown audience that buzzes with an altered frequency through changing generations, its impact subtly augmented in the light of newly evolved tastes and values? (5)

> We don't know what Cassandra made of such comments, and perhaps she made nothing ... Nor do we know how she received Jane Austen's remarks about her sister-in-law Mary following childbirth. (78)

> The next nine years of Jane Austen's life were unsettled and ... almost entirely silent. This long silence, in the middle of a relatively short life is bewildering ... The silence asks questions about the flow of Jane Austen's creative energies and about her reconciliation to the life she had been handed. (85)

By asking or pointing out questions, by acknowledging all that 'we don't know,' by affirming that *perhaps* something happened (implying also that perhaps it did not), by admitting bewilderment, Shields points out the mystery, the inconclusiveness, fundamental to all biography and therefore by extension to all notions of a stable subject. By implication, then, those biographies that pose answers to these questions in a manner that is not self-reflexive are being disingenuous, masking uncertainty behind the voice of authority.

Particularly telling in this light are the moments when Shields uses the interrogative not only to point out how little we know about Austen's life, but also to point out how frequently asserted interpretations often crystallize into presumption. For instance, Shields has this to say about Austen's famed disclosure that she would frequently lie on three chairs during her final illness:

> Jane Austen, in her final illness, reports she was too weak to walk upstairs and so she sometimes rested on three sitting-room chairs lined up together, leaving the sofa for her mother. What can we make of this improbable scene? Did her mother not notice the unusual furniture deployment? Or was Jane Austen in the full throes of a bizarre martyrdom? Were the mother and daughter playing out an old and rivalrous claim? Or was Mrs. Austen – and this is the interpretation that has hardened in the record – a demanding and self-absorbed woman, careless of her daughter's comfort and too insensitive to see the signs of serious illness? (16–17)

Shields folds the myth that Austen's mother was a selfish woman into a series of other questions; in so doing she lifts it from the realm of accepted fact and sets it firmly back into the realm of speculation. The notion becomes just one in a number of possibilities, an amusing fiction.

Life As Fiction

Not only does Shields's life of Austen point to the many ways in which biography functions as a work of fiction, but it also highlights the ways in which both Austen's reported experiences and her lived experiences, the very foundations upon which biography is based, are also works of fiction. For example, Shields makes it abundantly clear that Austen's family members played an enormous role in inventing the Jane Austen we think of today:

> The story of the marriage proposal, its hasty acceptance and its reversal twelve hours later, entered the leaves of the Austen legend. Each family member had a theory, an explanation, about why Jane, normally so determined in her resolutions, so *sensible*, should have entered into a hasty agreement and then, with great clumsiness, extricated herself. (108–9)

Here Shields freezes a moment when a story, in this case a story that is not fictive (it is a fact that Austen accepted a marriage proposal from Harris Bigg-Wither, only to break off the engagement the following morning), enters the realm of interpretation and becomes romanticized myth. As Shields notes elsewhere in the biography, such stories become 'too much the traditional material of opaque family legends, which represent, perhaps, the wish to sprinkle a little fairy dust on a life that was sadly lacking in romance' (105). Moreover, by emphasizing the idea that those who knew Austen most intimately could only offer different theories about what motivated her actions, Shields suggests the elusive nature of both the original event and the personality centrally involved in that event. As Sarah Gamble argues earlier in this volume about the works of Mary Swann, Austen's self is 'systematically cut loose from the defining signifier of the author and [passes] into common ownership.' Her identity becomes the work of 'communal endeavor' (59). By pointing out the common ownership of the Austen identity, Shields also suggests that any biography not only invents a fiction, but also bases that very fiction on a substructure of the numerous fictions that precede it. The core event of the story is stratified, overlaid with a palimpsest of its later versions, and an understanding of the true nature of the event or the individuals who took part in it is at times deferred indefinitely.

Not only does the core event itself become stratified, but the nature of the self also becomes subject to conjacency, to its juxtaposition with other selves. Shields makes this point when she discusses the relationship between Jane and her sister Cassandra, a relationship that has been of particular interest to Austen scholars both because of its closeness and because Cassandra, by destroying many of Jane's letters to her, acted as a *de facto* editor and biographer. Shields notes that Cassandra 'censored [Austen's] correspondence so that the world would understand the angel of goodness her sister had been' (175). Shields writes of a 'small chip of an incident,' 'a sort of half story' Cassandra told that when staying in Devon her sister Jane once met a young man. According to Cassandra, the two fell in love, the young man declared his intention to continue seeing Jane, and then died while on a trip out of town. Shields explains that the story 'was related by Cassandra to her niece Caroline years later and is, sadly, unreliable in its turnings, being too much a mirror image of Cassandra's tragic engagement' (105). This formulation suggests not only that Cassandra might have confused the events of Jane's life with her own, but that Cassandra could not always distinguish between herself and her sister. Shields emphasizes this point at the opening of her biography by suggesting that 'in part, the opacity of [Jane's] life may rest on the degree to which it was fused with that of her sister Cassandra, providing a mask or at the very least a subsuming presence. Each sister's life invaded the other, cancelling out parts of the knowable self' (5). Thus the close identification between the sisters might have resulted in either a sort of covert identity or an identity overshadowed by the presence and identity of another. Austen's character is not insular; it does not stop at the borders of the mind or body. Rather it is fluid, often located precisely in the moments of exchange, sharing, and overlap between the two sisters. Moreover, by suggesting that parts of Austen's identity might have been fused with and indistinguishable from that of her sister, Shields hints at pockets of non-identity, rifts in Austen's experience of herself as a self.

All such notions lead, of course, to the postmodern idea of the self as a construction, and Shields, as a postmodern writer, has made it clear that she not only accepts this notion, but works it into her fiction. When discussing *The Stone Diaries*, for example, Shields has asserted that Daisy Goodwill is 'thinking [her autobiography], in exactly the same way that we all think our own life. We carry around this construction that is our own life.'[20] Similarly, in the Austen biography, Shields notes that when Jane and her parents moved to Bath 'there would be new people to meet, new social patterns offered, new circumstances in which to recreate herself' (91). But Shields makes it clear that that recreation depends upon context, that it cannot be completely autonomous. Elsewhere she has said,

'We're just a bundle of impressions of other people, after all.'[21] And in *Jane Austen* what Shields shows is the degree to which Austen had to sort out the possibilities for her identity, to accept or reject others' impressions of her and repeatedly invent herself anew. For instance, Shields argues that 'the erasure of the private self from Jane Austen's early work suggests a confusion concerning that self or else a want of permission from those around her. Her maturing sensibility must be read today through the scrim of an increasingly subtle voice as she attempted to close the gap between longing and belonging, between wanting to please herself and placate her audience' (35–6). Austen's identity shades off into or is contingent upon her family's identification of her, her interpretation of that identification, and the strength of her desire to realize that identification. Her novels show us the voice that results from this process. Thus, although we read only one side of a story when we read an Austen novel, Shields nevertheless makes us aware that even these novels participate in the dialogic process; they are part of a conversation between writer and reader, 'written and revised,' Shields notes, 'in concert with a remarkable communal consultation' (141). This recognition forces us to ask the question: if Austen's novels were indeed written in part to please and entertain her family members, if they were written in fact through a sort of dialogue with family and friends, how can the voice we find in them be exclusively that of Jane Austen?

By locating questions of Austen's identity in the matrix of the relationship between her writing and her family as audience, Shields suggests the degree to which even Austen's narrative voice is contingent. She refuses to fall into the trap of conflating Austen's ironic narrative voice and her personality as other biographers have done. She argues that 'to write is to be self-conscious, as Jane Austen certainly knew. What flows onto paper is more daring or more covert than a writer's own voice, or more exaggerated or effaced' (120–1). The narrative voice is thus an overlay for the writer's own unknown and unknowable voice, a sort of willed distortion of the already distorted self.

If we cannot look to Austen's narrative voice for clues to her identity, then, we also cannot look to her novels for straight-forward autobiographical self-revelation. As Shields points out, the elusive identity of Austen becomes entangled in that of the fictive selves she imagines in her novels. In this sense Austen's fiction might be construed as 'good novels' Austen 'imagine[s] herself into' (50). Or, we might further construe them as imaginative autobiographies, autobiographies in which she creates other possibilities for her experience rather than trying to represent her own identity. When pondering *Persuasion*, for example, Shields suggests that in the novel Austen 'might be desperately rewriting the trajectory of her own life and giving it the gift of a happy ending' (170). Or she might not be. The most Shields will say for sure is that at best Austen's 'real life [is] engraved roughly, enigmatically, be-neath [the] surface' (69) of any particular novel she has writ-ten. Our ability to delineate in which ways Austen's fiction represents aspects of her true self (if such a self exists) and in which ways it represents her imagined self is tenuous at best. Reading Austen's novels for clues to a singular identity, as so many biographers do, has severe limitations. 'The two ac-counts,' Shields writes, 'will always lack congruency and will sometimes appear to be in complete contradiction' (175).

And, as Shields points out in an interview, all art tran-scends and in some senses supersedes its creator:

[T]he real mystery, the one that interests me, is the mystery of human personality and the creation of art, a question that pops up in all of my books ... the fact that art is bigger than those who make it, that it comes from unexpectedly common clay, and that its actual creation resists the analytical tools we apply to it. I've known writers to blink when reading their own books and ask themselves: 'Did I really write this?' It's as though a writer enters a sort of trance while working, or, by working on a book over a long period of time, is able to draw into that work a multitude of selves.[22]

That Austen's selves are multitudinous, that they are fictions of her own, of her time, of her family members, of her biographers, of her critics, and of her audiences, becomes a central message of Shields's biography. In Shields's hands, then, biography becomes a self-reflexive genre, a postmodern form that comments on itself.

Biography As Feminist Fiction

Shields's biography of Austen also makes clear the extent to which all biography becomes intermingled with the interests and imagined selves of the biographer. The quotation above serves as a case in point. It is no coincidence that the writer whose interests lie in the multiplicity, contingency, and constructedness of identity should write a biography that presents its subject as one whose selves are multiple, contingent, and highly constructed. Nor is it a coincidence that the author of *The Stone Diaries*, a novel that presents its main character as 'a woman thinking her autobiography in which she is virtually absent,'[23] should write a biography that focuses largely on the gaps and 'silences,' the questions, slippage, and absences of an author's 'opaque' life.[24]

Such an assertion seems at first to place me in the camp of those who think Shields's work lands on the postmodern side of what Lisa Johnson later in this volume calls 'the largely unresolved conflict between feminism and postmodernism' (202). If the self is unstable, fictive, elusive, then we might indeed be tempted to agree with Roland Barthes that the author 'enters into his [*sic*] own death' when writing begins, that 'writing is that neutral, composite, oblique space where our subject slips away, the negative where all identity is lost, starting with the very identity of the body writing.'[25] But if Shields thoroughly espoused Barthes's view, she wouldn't have written a literary biography in which she tries to connect the author and her works, however tenuous and qualified that connection might be.[26] And while for Barthes there is finally no 'voice of a single person, the *author* confiding in us,'[27] for Shields the author the fact that there *is* a 'person who makes [the words] up'[28] is crucial; the author cannot finally be amputated from her texts.

Certainly, the methods I've described in the preceding sections also distance Shields from the feminist essentialist theory of biography; an author whose identity is multiple and fictive cannot be seen as a unified subject whose experiences represent women's struggles to construct a female identity. But if for Shields making the connection between author and works is essential, and if Austen's identity is multiple, veiled, fragmented, incomplete, and absent, then how does Shields resolve that tension and connect the author to her words?

It should come as no surprise that Shields the fiction writer looks to Austen's novels as a starting point, despite her acknowledgment of the difficulties inherent in doing so. *Jane Austen* is, after all, a literary biography, and although Shields toys with the genre, she does not toss it completely away. When confronting the myriad problems that faced her as an Austen biographer, Shields admits that in the end she always found herself turning, not to the facts of Austen's life, but to her novels: 'This is, in the end, what matters: the novels themselves, and not the day-to-day life of the author, the cups of tea sipped with her neighbours, the cream cakes she bought at the bakery. Even her extraordinarily revealing letters must be separated – somehow – from the works of fiction that have survived' (10).

Later in this collection of essays, Lisa Johnson argues convincingly that *The Stone Diaries* exemplifies the concept of *'embodied postmodernism'* advocated by feminist aesthetic and cultural theorists, that Shields uses a *'tactile aesthetics'* in order to '[turn] postmodernism toward the material conditions of women's lives' (205) Johnson suggests that Shields manipulates postmodern techniques in order to ground her novels in the lived, bodily, sensory experiences of her female characters. What interests me about Shields's biography of Austen is that is does not try to re-enact this strategy with Austen herself. Shields largely abandons the steaming teas and tasty cream cakes in favour of the mental Austen, the most disembodied Austen. Her explanation of why is worth quoting at length:

> The novelist George Gissing wrote that 'the only good biographies are to be found in novels.' He was speaking about the genuine arc of a human life, that it can be presented more authentically in fiction than in the genre of biography. Biography is subject to warps and gaps and gasps of admiration or condemnation, but fiction respects the human trajectory.
>
> Traditionally Jane Austen's biographers have nailed together the established facts of her life – her birth, her travels, her enthusiasms, her death – and clothed this rickety skeleton with speculation gleaned from the novels, an exercise akin to ransacking an author's drawers and drawing conclusions from piles of neatly folded handkerchiefs or worn gloves. In so doing, the assumption is made that fiction flows directly from a novelist's experience rather than from her imagination. (10–11)

Shields does not claim here that by looking at Austen's novels she can piece together the 'real' Austen for us where others have failed – no Judith Gill she. In fact, Shields makes it clear that Austen 'is not a writer who touches close to the autobiographical core' (70). What she does suggest is first, that the novels allow us to catch glimpses of Austen's imagination, and second, that the purpose of biography is to enable the writer and reader to participate in analogous imaginative acts. Thus, by employing deconstructive notions of identity even as she emphasizes the power of one woman's imagination, Shields engages in an *imaginative aesthetics* of postmodernism in order to connect with the female creative imagination, and in so doing suggests one way to carry out the feminist project of 'using postmodern strategies of disruption to re-imagine the world in which we live.'[29]

For clarification of this idea we can look to the curious thing that happens at the end of Shields's biography. Rather than concluding with Austen's death, which she treats in the penultimate chapter, Shields takes an opportunity in the final chapter of her biography to revisit and condense an article she wrote for the journal *Persuasions* in 1991 titled 'Jane Austen Images of the Body: No Fingers, No Toes.'[30] In it Shields notes the 'infrequency of bodily images or bodily reaction' (180) in Austen's novels. Shields points out that the infrequency of bodily images makes their occasional use all the more powerful: 'When Mr. Knightley draws Emma's arm within his and presses it against his heart, we are fully persuaded of his yearning, since he has never done anything like this in the hundreds of preceding pages. When he presses the arm yet again in the following paragraph, we understand we are in the presence of a grand passion' (181). Yet such moments notwithstanding, Shields argues in this section of the biography that 'Jane Austen's writing is indifferent to the human body' (181). Shields even counts up the number of times Austen mentions body parts in her novels, and finds that 'except for the brain, the human body is infrequently mentioned in Jane Austen's work' (177).

It is here, in this emphasis on the brain, that Shields finds a connection between Austen and her works:

> Austen's narrative intricacies and turns were propelled for the most part by incident or by reason, and not by the needs or responses of the body. The brain – for Jane Austen does frequently refer to that particular fleshy organ – presides over the rest of the corporeal body that is treated with what? Indifference? Incuriosity? Disregard? Or perhaps a metaphorical shrug that all but erases itself. Or else her strategy, conscious or unconscious, points to the values that she believed supported a decent community of individuals. (177)

For Shields, then, Austen's works provide not so much traces of the embodied Austen as traces of one segment of the embodied Austen, of 'that particular fleshy organ' that is most capable of extending the body beyond itself. What interests Shields, then, is not the body that made the texts but the mind that made them.

In the example I've noted, Shields overtly connects the brain to reason, placing Austen on the rational side of the mind/body divide, the side that has traditionally been allied with male writers. Elsewhere in the biography, however, Shields formulates the distinction in a significantly different way, linking the brain not so much to reason as to imagination. When discussing Austen's ability to distance herself from her own works, for example, Shields suggests that 'the detachment of Jane Austen's imaginative flight from her personal concerns is extraordinary, even given the fiction writer's license' (71). What Shields uncovers here is not an aspect of the rational impulse but rather a glimpse of a type of creative impulse in which the person and the product, the mental flight and the bodily or conscious experience, one might even say the creature and the creator, are markedly distinct. Thus, for Shields it is the imaginative flight itself that is revealing. While, as I've pointed out earlier, we can't trust Austen's novels to help us isolate her true voice, we *can* learn something of Austen's mind, and we can learn it precisely in those moments when that mind invents alternative possibilities.

Shields also suggests that if by experiencing Austen's imagination at work we connect with Austen in some way, by self-consciously engaging in imaginative acts similar to Austen's own we connect on a still deeper level. The biography enacts this process on a regular basis. In an earlier section of this essay, I argued that Shields points out the speculative nature of fiction, and that she flushes out what amounts to the covert fictions other biographers create by contrasting them with more candid speculations of her own. Shields uses this strategy of open speculation repeatedly in *Jane Austen*. The auxiliary verbs 'may' and 'might' appear frequently in this text,[31] shaking the foundations of the indicative mood, opening up possibilities rather than shutting them down. In addition to these uses of the subjunctive, Shields's frequent use of the interrogative voice also calls attention to the imaginative nature of biography, as do her suggestions that we invent our own versions of various moments in Austen's life: 'it can be imagined that the abrupt shift from mother's breast to alien thinks of a distinct female literary tradition and identifies particular key women writers as her literary foremothers. First, in 'Thinking Back through Our Mothers: Tradition in Canadian Women's Writing,' an article Shields wrote for a collection of essays titled *Re(dis)covering Our Foremothers*, ed. Lorraine McMullen (Ottawa: U of Ottawa P, 1990), Shields takes another look at books of her mother's that she read as a child and suggests that popular women's literature must be taken into account when formulating a female literary tradition. Shields suggests that her title can be read two ways: both as a reference to Shields's act of thinking back through her mother's influence, an influence exerted through choice of literature, and as a reference to the novelists themselves, who serve as literary mothers in that their novels exerted an influence on the formation of Shields's literary imagination. In an interview with Marjorie Anderson, Shields also notes that she feels 'a particular affinity with early 19th-century writers such as Jane Austen' ('Interview with Carol Shields,' *Prairie Fire* 16.1 [Spring 1995]: 145). It is also revealing to me that Shields begins her biography of Austen with a preface in which she tells the story of delivering a paper on Austen that she and her daughter (also a writer) co-authored at a conference of the Jane Austen Society in 1996, *Jane Austen* (New York: Penguin, 2001), 1–4. (All further references to this text will be made parenthetically). By opening her biography in this manner, Shields effectively sets her reader up to think of Austen in terms of a tradition of literary mothers and daughters.

3 Sharon O'Brien, 'Feminist Theory and Literary Biography,' in *Contesting the Subject*, ed. William H. Epstein (West Lafayette, IN: Purdue UP, 1991), 123–33; Sheila Kineke, 'Subject to Change: The Problematics of Authority in Feminist Modernist Biography,' in *Rereading Modernism*, ed. Lisa Rado (New York: Garland, 1994), 253–71.

4 O'Brien, 127.

5 O'Brien, 128.

6 Kineke, 264, 257, 265, 256.

7 Harvey De Roo, 'A Little like Flying: An Interview with Carol Shields,' *West Coast Review* 23.3 (Winter 1988): 50.

8 Patricia Waugh, 'Stalemates? Feminists, Postmodernists and Unfinished Issues in Modern Aesthetics,' in *The Politics of Pleasure: Aesthetics and Cultural Theory, Ideas and Production*, ed. Stephan Regan (Buckingham: Open U, 1992), 191.

9 Bolick, n.pag.

10 Carol Shields, 'Narrative Hunger and the Overflowing Cupboard,' p. 20 (in this volume).

11 Garber even goes so far as to claim that this 'truth' is 'so old that only a willed cultural amnesia can make it new' ('Introduction,' in *The Seductions of Biography*, ed. Mary Rheid and David Suchoff [New York: Routledge, 1996], 175).

12 Carol Shields, *Small Ceremonies* (New York: Penguin, 1976), 7. All further references to this text will be made parenthetically.

13 O'Brien, 125.

14 For a list of the works Shields consulted when writing the biography, see 'A Few Words about Sources,' in *Jane Austen*, 183–5.

15 Park Honan, *Jane Austen: Her Life* (New York: St Martin's Griffin, 1996), back cover.

16 John Halperin, *The Life of Jane Austen* (Baltimore: Johns Hopkins UP, 1984), 36–7.

17 David Nokes, *Jane Austen: A Life* (Berkeley: U of California P, 1997), 5, 7.

18 Claire Tomalin, *Jane Austen: A Life* (New York: Vintage, 1997), 6.

19 O'Brien, 125.

20 Joan Thomas, 'The Golden Book: An Interview with Carol Shields,' *Prairie Fire* 16.1 (Spring 1995): 58.

21 Bolick, n.pag.

22 De Roo, 50.

23 Thomas, 58–9.

24 These quotations come from page 5 of *Jane Austen*. Shields also discusses the silences in Austen's life at some length on pages 85, 105, and 110.

25 Roland Barthes, 'The Death of the Author,' trans. Stephen Heath, in *Image – Music – Text*, ed. Stephen Heath (New York: Hill and Wang, 1977), 142.

26 Others have echoed Shields's suggestion that, as one educated

through New Critical methods, she has already learned to be suspicious of any theory that forces us to disregard entirely the relationship between the author and her texts. These echoes suggest that biography need not be seen as inconsistent with postmodern theory. Arnold Rampersand has suggested that 'the "disappearance of the author" is not incompatible, as a theory, with further historical study of the author in question ... After all, the author had disappeared before, in the face of New Criticism, which was how most of us were trained to read literature' ('Design and Truth in Biography,' *South Central Review* 9.2 [Summer 1992]: 5).

27 Barthes, 143.
28 Bolick, n.pag.
29 Waugh, 191.
30 Carol Shields, 'Jane Austen Images of the Body: No Fingers, No Toes,' *Persuasions: Journal of the Jane Austen Society of North America* 13 (16 Dec. 1991): 132–7.
31 For example: 'Jane Austen, describing the childhood of Catherine Moreland in *Northanger Abbey*, might be touching on her own early years of lightly supervised freedom ...' (20); 'Jane Austen may have glimpsed the emptiness of the future' (44); 'Mrs. Austen, Jane Austen's mother, may or may not have had a spirit similar to Mrs. Bennet's ...' (18).
32 Carol Shields, 'Arriving Late: Starting Over,' in *How Stories Mean*, ed. John Metcalf and Tim Struthers (Erin, ON: Porcupine's Quill, 1993), 247.

SECTION THREE

To 'Shorten the Distance between What Is Privately Felt and Universally Known': Reaching beyond the Word

CHIARA BRIGANTI

LISA JOHNSON

DEE GOERTZ

KATHY BARBOUR

nies (1976) and *Swann* (1987) show Shields not only exposing this unsavoury aspect of the biographer's craft, but also anticipating the challenge launched by Malcolm Bradbury by descending into the self-made labyrinth of the biographer's writerly anxiety.[5] With *The Stone Diaries* (1993), by choosing as a subject the uneventful life of Daisy Goodwill, Shields has made her peace with Dr Johnson and has accepted *his* challenge: 'I have often thought that there rarely passed a life of which a judicious and faithful narrative would not be useful.'[6]

Shields's pursuit of some of the questions that have sparked the debate of theorists of biography and autobiography for the last two decades has been at times playful and self-mocking; Shields has been even willing to risk being identified with one of her characters – Sarah Maloney – an entrepreneurial female academic who is determined to show that she can 'post-mod along with the best of them' (*Swann* 53). But while Sarah has written more than she has thought and is finally dismissible, Shields has thought long and hard and has succeeded in making the epistemological implications of life writing a solid and serious concern of her fiction. While such concern has been well documented,[7] my purpose in this essay is to trace the way in which Shields's fiction both exposes her own ambivalence regarding her 'consuming passion'[8] for biography and continues to complicate what have by now become *topoi* of women's storytelling. If women's autobiographical discourse has been informed by the yearning for a point of origin figured in the maternal body, Shields has grounded the telling of a woman's life in the inescapable corporeality of the mother tongue. Furthermore, Shields's interrogation of women's life narratives goes beyond the well-established tradition of providing 'a critique of social structures that define both women's writing and their lives' (Roy, 114); I would argue, in fact, that what Roy calls 'Daisy's displacement from the centre of her story' (122) is not simply the staging of the silencing of a woman's voice, but rather the evidence of Daisy's deployment of a deliberate strategy. If a large component of recent female autobiographical discourse is the representation of the attempt to shape the viscous magma of the lived life, Shields has increasingly used the richness of her language to create a shimmering surface of teasing specificity, a manifestation of the tension between an impulse to make public and to keep private the content of personal experience.

Our curiosity is neither morbid nor ordinary. It is the kind known as devouring.[9]

At the beginning of *Small Ceremonies* (1976), Judith Gill, the protagonist, recounts the pleasures and pitfalls of her profession as a biographer. At the moment, she is engaged in writing the biography of Susanna Moodie, a subject that Shields herself, in her study entitled *Susanna Moodie: Voice and Vision*, had found 'maddeningly private.'[10] The choice of Susanna Moodie is not insignificant. As though intent on commenting ironically on her own problematic engagement with her subject in that study, Shields is careful to point out that far from finding such reticence maddening, Judith respects it. What draws Judith to Moodie are precisely those 'cracks in the surface' that make her 'a difficult subject to possess.'[11] She reflects on the difference between Moodie and her previous subject, Josephine Macclesfield, 'who, shameless, showed every filling in her teeth' (7); and, implicitly agreeing with the notion that 'selfhood is a matter of secrecy,'[12] Judith admires Susanna Moodie because she has done the brave thing: she has held back; she has never stooped to bore her reader 'with the idle slopover of her soul,' 'the detailing of her rancid sex life or the nasty discomfort of pregnancy in the backwoods.' She has had the decency 'not to dangle her shredded placenta before her public' (7).

The web of intertextuality in which Shields has allowed herself to be implicated shows Judith better capable than her author of careful self-assessment in her professional life, and of spotting in her *métier* the degrading and preying side of the biographer's sleuthing. However, it soon becomes Shields's turn to expose her character; thus she shows that despite Judith's distaste for such a dubious exhumation of corpses, she cannot always abide by her professed discretion. Judith lets the detective fever of the biographer drive her to pry into the life of John Spalding, her (failed) novelist landlord, assembling an identity out of the accumulation of debris ranging from figures in household accounts to the content of the medicine cabinet, and launching with gusto into a typical gritty Shields catalogue that doesn't spare 'an ancient douche bag ... a disintegrating diaphragm ... rubber safes ... half-squeezed tubes of vaginal jelly' (36). When she finally starts burrowing through John Spalding's unpublished novels, her language betrays the preying impulse that she has been unable to quell – 'I swallowed them, digested them whole' (36) – and finally she has to admit that it is not the literary quality of the manuscripts that has kept her in thrall, but that she has been driven by an 'unhealthy lust for the lives of other people' (38). These words – swallowing and digesting – are perhaps not simply a predictable corollary to Judith's vampiric violation of privacy and thus of selfhood; they are also the first, if tenuous, evidence of Shields's preoccupation with the relation between the physical body and the material body of language that she will explore more purposefully in *Swann* and *The Stone Diaries*, both of which originate in a woman's bloodied body.

While the concern with the motivation of the biographer is only a secondary thread in the fabric of *Small Ceremonies*, a certain distaste for the 'biographer's shameless silky greed' permeates *Swann* (113). Here, a group of scholars make a concerted effort to penetrate the mystery of Mary Swann, a poor farm woman who wrote poetry on the side and who was murdered, chopped up, and stuck into a silo by her husband. Their attempt is defeated by what is finally perceived as 'a life lived ... in the avoidance of biography'(110). Mary Swann, in unwitting conspiracy with the Death of the Author, has indeed, as Bradbury would put it, 'disappeared ... down the labyrinth of writing,' and it is here that she must be followed.

All of the characters in the novel are intent on reshaping Mary Swann. The mousy Rose Hindmarch finds in her claim to have known Mary Swann a way to appease the suspicion of her own vacuity. It is the urge to fill the vacuum in her life that inspires her to put together 'The Mary Swann Memorial Room,' which, allegedly displaying a number of mementoes of Mary Swann's life, is in fact the product of Rose's purposeful hunting in rummage sales and country auctions. It doesn't matter that nothing in the room has ever belonged to Mary Swann, for Rose can imagine her figure 'bent over the painted table scratching out her poems by the light of the kerosene lamp.' Whether *bricoleuse* or full-fledged creator, Rose has seen the room 'acquire shape with creative amazement' (163). And what of it? Who is to say that this forgery is not art?

In a moment of sincerity, Rose does admit to herself that the friendship she has claimed to have shared with Mrs Swann is her own shameless fabrication; for, indeed, she has never exchanged more than a few passing remarks with Mary Swann, a 'woman who kept to herself' (152). Rose too, albeit garrulous, is a woman who does not tell you anything about herself. In her quiet way, she also harbours mystery, whether it be the long Friday nights to which she looks forward all week, of spy novel reading and occasional masturbation, or the tumour she is convinced is eating her away. And this reserve she shares with the reclusive Swann may be what gives Rose, not a scholar, not even a reader of poetry, an edge over her competitors.

Sarah Maloney, author of the well-received *The Female Prism*, and 'discoverer' of Mary Swann, does not acknowledge a chilly void inside; but she expects that the role she will play in the canonization of Mary Swann to Canadian National Poet will allow her to shed her identity of militant feminist scholar, now *démodé*, for a new, more poised self well suited to the stylish square-shouldered wardrobe with which she has stocked her closet. Convinced as she is that a fellow scholar 'is capable of violating [Mary Swann] for his own gain' (31), it is not out of discretion but rather out of sheer embarrassment that she dumps Mary Swann's rhyming dictionary into a trash bin and refuses to make public the content of the poet's notebook; for its list of daily chores and eggs sold points to the conspicuous absence of kernels of truth from which Swann's poetry should have been born. And yes, its publication would spark unwelcome doubts about the value of Sarah's 'discovery' and ruin her dream of a scholarly scoop.

Morton Jimroy, Mary Swann's official biographer, while professing that Mary Swann is the love of his life, has grown distrustful of her and secretly convinced that it is not love but contempt that draws biographers to their subjects, and must acknowledge that what attracted him to his previous subjects, Ezra Pound and John Starman, was their sheer pettiness, 'the fatuous self-stroking' (84), their shameless self-regard. While other Swann scholars unceremoniously describe him as a 'body snatcher,' he himself reflects that 'it was a matter of time before the theoreticians got to Mary Swann and tore her limb from limb in a grotesque parody of her bodily death' (81). In the meantime, he turns thief and unremorsefully absconds with a photograph (one of only two extant) of Mary Swann, and her fountain pen.

Frederic Cruzzi, the publisher of Swann's slim collection of poems, does not turn thief, but, like Sarah Maloney, suppresses his doubts about professional ethics. Cruzzi's fastidiousness makes him shy away from writing his autobiography, for he loathes 'the cosy cherishing of self' (181) that the form implies, and 'the appalling melted fat of rumination' (181) that accompanies 'the current jejune notion of soul-baring' (177). Nevertheless, Cruzzi has disremembered (and here the word *is* a pun on 'dismember') that the little collection by the embarrassing title (his own choice) *Swann's Songs* is the product of his and his wife, Hildë's, invention. The poems, written in washable ink, were almost illegible by the time they were salvaged from the garbage bin where Hildë had dumped them by mistake. He and Hildë had spent a long night in which

> they puzzled and conferred over every blot, then guessed, then invented ... The last poem, and the most severely damaged, began: 'Blood pronounced my name.' Or was it 'Blood renounces my name'? The second line could be read in either of two ways: 'Brightens the day with shame,' or 'Blisters the day with shame.' They decided on *blisters* ... because – though they didn't say so – they liked it better. (222–3)

It is of some interest that precisely this poem should strengthen Sarah Maloney's conviction that Mary Swann's poetry 'is filled with concealed references to her mother and to the strength and violence of family bonds ... particularly those between mothers and daughters' (50–1). Sarah may be influenced by the taut twine by which she feels tied to her own mother, and by her belief that mothers and daughters are joined by 'a kind of blood-hyphen that is, finally, indissoluble' (47). As for Rose, it is only her feminine delicacy that prevents her from countering Morton Jimroy's rather pompous disquisition on the blood as a symbol 'for the continuum of belief, a metaphysical covenant with an inexplicable universe' (150), by insisting that Mary Swann had been simply talking about the messy affair of menstruation. Rose may be right in thinking that what is perfectly obvious to a woman is easily overlooked by a man; but Shields in no way grants her unfailing jury-of-her-peers insight. For Rose, too, has access only to a text that has been abundantly tampered with. Her insight, however, cannot be dismissed; and while Mary Swann's body may represent an uncertain origin for these lines, its trace haunts the poem as it haunts the novel.

We learn that by the time the Cruzzis are finished tinkering with the poetry, Mary Swann is dead, shot in the head, her body dismembered, the bloodied parts hidden in a silo. It may be an exaggeration to claim that Frederic and Hildë have perpetrated a similar act on her poems; but it may not be excessive to see in this night of Mary Swann's death the birth of Hildë as a poet. For poor Hildë, whose poems Frederic had not deemed fit for publication by the choosy Peregrine Press, has gone from filling small gaps to supplying whole lines and even parts of a stanza, claiming that 'she could feel what the inside of Mary Swann's head must look like' (223), even though Frederic has chosen to remember this substantial rewriting as simply Hildë's 'small emendations' (226).

When it is finally discovered that all the copies of Swann's collection of poems have been lost, these eager scholars set out to reconstruct the whole Swann corpus (certainly a deliberate pun) from memory. It is only appropriate that while the epigraph to the novel, a Swann poem, celebrates the poet's invisibility ('The rivers of this country / Shrink and crack and kill / And the waters of my body / Grow invisible'), the novel should close with the last reassembled poem, 'Lost Things,' which seals Mary Swann's irrecoverability and reveals a desire to regress to a state of pre-existence. These are the last two stanzas:

As though the lost things have withdrawn
Into themselves, books returned
To paper or wood or thought,
Coins and spoons to simple ores,
Lustreless and without history,
Waiting out of sight

And becoming part of a larger loss
Without a name
Or definition or form
Not unlike what touches us
In moments of shame. (313)

Art has produced forgery that has produced art. Creative impulses have been excited by this gory death, by the dismembering of a woman's body. Thus, it is hardly surprising that Shields's most imaginative novel also has its origin in a woman's bloodied body.

Bodies rarely figure in autobiography.[13]

If *Swann* relies on the format of the thriller cum film script to stage the elusiveness of its subject, *The Stone Diaries*,[14] a novel cast in the form of fictional autobiography, doesn't need complicated generic props to face the challenge of a modern epistemology that questions the notion of a unified subject. *The Stone Diaries* is not so much an example of what Sidonie Smith has called 'a non-story, a silent place, a gap in patriarchal culture,'[15] as a poignant rendition of the impossible task of writing the life story of a woman who is always already elsewhere, who seems not to have any qualms in appearing to us as a magma of blood, amniotic fluid, and flesh, but who is never indeed seen. Judith of *Small Ceremonies*, who had decried Josephine Macclesfield's dangling of 'her shredded placenta before her public' (7), would have abhorred Daisy Goodwill's indecent account of her own birth, the shameless flaunting of her own 'just-hatched flesh' (23). But even though, before her story is over, we will be quite literally acquainted with every filling in her teeth, we will soon learn that, unlike Josephine, Daisy is not 'candid to a fault'; her 'introspection' is not 'wide open, a field of potatoes' (*Small Ceremonies* 7–8). Shields teases us out of thought by staging the disappearing acts of an incredibly resilient character who, until the very end, continues to reaffirm her own unrepentant inconstancy, and whose last (unspoken) words, in an explicit refusal of the complacency of the autobiographical subject, will be: 'I am not at peace' (361).

In writing about her mother in *Landscape for a Good Woman: A Story of Two Lives*, Carolyn Steedman claimed to be writing about 'lives lived on the borderlands, lives for which the central interpretative devices of the culture don't quite work.'[16] And Shields, who writes about such lives, both in *Swann* and in this novel, seems determined to create a *mise en scène* of such inadequacy. Well aware that while men are 'uniquely honored by the stories that erupted in their lives ... women were more likely to be smothered by theirs' (121), Shields gives her heroine the ability to turn this smothering into art, thus rescuing from oblivion the contents of the 'narrative cupboard.'[17] She continues her harangue against the futile retrieval of the factual record ('we can never, never get enough facts' [330]), the choking surfeit of information. While decrying the aptness of women to be crowded out of their own lives, however, she goes further, both practising what Linda Hutcheon has described as the tendency of postmodern fiction to pursue 'a contradictory turning to the archive and yet a contesting of its authority'[18] and turning factual excess into a screen behind which her character can always escape. While in *Swann* it took a murder, a book thief, and a group of bungling scholars to insure that the reclusive country poet remain forever unknowable, in *The Stone Diaries*, Daisy Goodwill remains unknowable through her sheer pretence of being willing to expose to the public scrutiny the inner recesses of her life, literally to open every closet and cupboard. As the paucity of our knowledge about Daisy Goodwill is enhanced by the quasi-manic overflow of what appears to be an endless fund of facts – lingerie lists, menus, recipes, the contents of a drawer – any pretence of order and meaning is finally renounced. There is no hope here of reaching that 'total disclosure which is what a biographer prays for, the swift fall of facts which requires no more laborious jigsaws' (*Small Ceremonies* 36). The shape of auto/biography dissolves into the motley material for a scrapbook, simply presented as what it ultimately is – the trace of a life that is always elsewhere. And whereas *Swann*, for all its brilliance, belongs more to artistry than to art, the lavishly sensual *Stone Diaries* engages in a complex dynamics of exposure and concealment to evoke effortlessly the sense of a life shot through with intimations of absence and haunted by the spectre of a bloodied woman's body.

I said earlier that despite the shameless exposure of herself as 'just-hatched flesh' (23), Daisy is anything but a candid narrator. That is not to say, however, that the manner of Daisy's physical entry into her story ought to be dismissed as mere tease. To David Williams's claim that 'what is truly postmodern ... about *The Stone Diaries* may be its use of autobiography to decentre the figure of an autonomous subject, or to question the metaphysics of identity,'[19] I would add that beyond the decentring of the subject, what is genuinely postmodern in this autobiography is the reclaiming of the maternal body and the elaboration of its relation to language in a genre that has traditionally banished the body from representation.[20] In arguing that in traditional autobiography, 'woman, mother, and the feminine ... were part of "the mess and clutter" of the nonidentical that the autobiographer had to clear out as he struggled toward self-identity and the narrative of a coherent past,'[21] Sidonie Smith has implicitly acknowledged the Kristevean argument that 'modern ethical thought is based on repression of body and body processes connected to an abject maternal body.'[22] And indeed, in this text, the maternal body is experienced in Kristevean terms as '*both* the originating, nurturing source of subjectivity (hence desired) *and* rejected as abject ... at once a source of fascination and rejection.'[23] For, as Kristeva herself has maintained, 'devotees of the abject ... do not cease looking, within what flows from the other's "innermost being," for the desirable and terrifying, nourishing and murderous, fascinating and abject inside of the maternal body';[24] they never cease to be fascinated by the indissolubility of the blood-hyphen that ties together mothers and daughters.

A hot afternoon in Manitoba. The loud silence of desolation. An extraordinarily obese woman, Mercy Stone, an orphan whose last name comes from the home where she has been raised, is intent on shaping her last masterpiece. Absorbed in the making of a luscious Malvern pudding, unaware of being pregnant, she gives birth to a daughter and dies of eclampsia before help can reach her. Mercy's life, from the moment when she was found in a flour barrel, outside the Stone home for orphans, to her marriage to Cuyler Goodwill, appears to be contained in these first few pages. This section, entitled 'Birth, 1905,' is supposedly devoted to the coming into the world of the protagonist/narrator – Daisy Goodwill. But, in fact, it isn't. It insistently remains the scene of Daisy's mother's death, and the following sections continue to mock the expectations of sequence and refuse to bring to fruition the promises announced in their stark headings.

In an implicit rejection of the validating quality of the mundane cycle of a woman's life, each promise is betrayed. 'Childhood' does not have much to do with Daisy as a little girl. Daisy has been adopted by a neighbour, Clarentine Flett, 'a woman crazed by menopause and loneliness' (37), who, after walking out on her husband, has moved to Winnipeg to live with her eldest son, Barker, a professor of botany. And this chapter is devoted to Barker Flett's sexual yearnings, comically centred on 'the western lady's slipper' (45) and, alternately, on Daisy herself; to an exchange of letters between Clarentine Flett and Daisy's father; and to a description of Cuyler's work on a stone tower he is building as a memorial to his wife. We do get a very brief glimpse of Daisy, when, recovering from measles, she is suddenly hit with the sense that her mother's death has barred her from participating in a process of identification and repetition across generations, condemning her to live in a vacuum that can never be filled, but only mourned with that violence of feeling 'for an "object" that has always already been lost,'[25] which is Kristeva's definition of the abject: 'Something was missing ... the kernel of authenticity, that precious interior ore that everyone around her seemed to possess' (75). We meet Daisy, then, as lack, in a rich passage that enacts the precariousness of the subject even down to the shifting pronoun assignations: 'The long days of isolation, of silence, the torment of boredom – all these pressed down on me, on young Daisy Goodwill and emptied her out. Her autobiography, if such a thing were imaginable, would be, if such a thing were ever to be written, an assemblage of dark voids and unbridgeable gaps' (75–6).

Indeed, precise headings and orderly chronology notwithstanding, what we have here is not so much an autobiography as a drawerful of material for a scrapbook. In 'Marriage' we are graced with the menu of Daisy's wedding lunch, but the bulk of the chapter is about Cuyler's new-found eloquence and affluence as his talents as a stonecutter are finally appreciated. Of the marriage itself, we only learn that it is cut short by the accidental death (or suicide?) of the bridegroom. To 'Love,' supposedly the story of Daisy's second marriage, this time to Barker Flett, we come more prepared. We follow Daisy on her journey back to Canada titillated by the promise of a Lolita / Humbert Humbert story with strong incestuous overtones that has been long in the making. What we get, however, is a curiously detailed account of her encounter with a stranger at Niagara Falls, during which she experiences her only moment of sexual ecstasy recorded in the novel. It is evidence of Shields's subtlety that it is only after multiple readings that one will discern in this scene the echo of Cuyler's rapturous lovemaking: 'Niagara in all its force is what [Mercy]'s reminded of as he climbs on top of her each evening, a thundering let loose against the folded interior walls of her body' (7). Subtle though it is, this echo is proof of the irrepressibility of Mercy's body, which should have been safely enclosed in the first section of the novel. Daisy's encounter produces no thunder; in fact, it amounts to no more than the brushing of the man's sleeve against her bare arm, and yet it is indelibly fixed in her mind; almost as though it were uncannily charged with her mother's memory, it is much more fixed 'than the chronology of her tragic honeymoon' (134) and certainly more accessible than Barker's wooing, which is carefully kept out of sight.

Daisy's own thoughts on her marriage are not recorded, for she has given up the practice of keeping a private journal. Her travel diary she has lost, and 'she shudders to think whose hands it may have fallen into, all that self-indulgent scribbling that belongs, properly, to the province of girlhood – a place where she no longer lives' (156). Lost diaries and missing letters replicate the 'emptiness she was handed at birth' (281), the absence of the full freight of her mother's words, which, according to Sarah Maloney, all women carry (*Swann* 48). But as it is in this same void that Daisy finds a connection with her past, 'a pattern of infinite regress which ... pushes her forward' (281), so the narrative too seems to be propelled by a desire to pursue the last breath that Mercy Stone Goodwill has given to her daughter and to postpone the moment of folding back unto itself, when inevitably the narrated life will appear as waste and opacity, enveloped in those 'fumes of absence' (281) that never cease to haunt Daisy's dreams.

The Lady Vanishes

When *The Stone Diaries* was first published, the reviewers were quick to notice that Daisy Goodwill's photograph is the only one missing from the family album inserted in the middle of the novel. What went unnoticed at the time is that although the photograph of Daisy's mother is allegedly there, in fact, it isn't. By the time we reach the photographs, we have been lured into the uneasy role of freak-show spectators. We cannot help leafing through the pages expecting to be confirmed in the picture that Shields has conjured up for us. Why, we have almost been inside Mercy's enormous body when she devours loaves of bread to ease her discomfort and imagines 'the soft dough entering the bin of her stomach, lining that bitter bloated vessel with a cottony warmth that absorbs and neutralizes the poisons of her own body' (6). We have also been privy to Mercy's hesitant response to Cuyler's exalted desires:

> Lying together in their shallow bed, she is embarrassed about the attentions of his hands, though by accident her own fingers have once or twice brushed across his privates, touching the

damp hair encircling his member and informing him of the nature of heaven. He is not repelled by the trembling generosity of her arms and thighs and breasts, not at all; he wants to bury himself in her exalting abundance, as though, deprived all his life of flesh, he will now never get enough. (34)

We have been allowed a perhaps even more intimate glimpse of Mercy in the opening scene, when she, alone, undisturbed by the ardour of her youthful husband, revels in a celebration of self-sufficient sexuality:

> It is something to see, the way she concentrates, her hot, busy face, the way she thrills to see the dish take form as she pours the stewed fruit into the fancy mold, pressing the thickly cut bread down over the oozing juices, feeling it soften and absorb bit by bit a raspberry redness. Malvern pudding; she loves the words too, and feels them dissolve on her tongue like a sugary wafer, her tongue itself grown waferlike and sweet. (2)

In her essay in this volume, Lisa Johnson observes how 'this lavishing of affection on the solid presence of words enacts the French feminist theory of *écriture feminine*, writing at the intersection of body and text, joining the aesthetic with the erotic' (208).[26] And, indeed, words and tongue become one as Mercy experiences a *jouissance* that makes her one with her work of art. Such erotically charged language prepares us for the literally 'visceral event,'[27] to use Daphne Marlatt's phrase, that is Daisy's coming into language. Thus, later we are not startled when, in 'Motherhood, 1947,' Daisy, in telling us how 'the narrative maze opens and permits her to pass through' (190), tropes the telling of her autobiography as an act of birthing, unwittingly echoing Marlatt's explorations of the correspondences between the vocabulary of verbal communication and the language used to describe the physical body: 'matter (the import of what you say) and matter and by extension mother; language and tongue; to utter and to outer (give birth again); a part of speech and a part of the body;

pregnant with meaning; to mouth (speak) and the mouth with which we also eat and make love.'[28]

Thus we become ripe for the disappointment that the 'body-snatcher' must feel upon discovering that his subject has remained a bloodless myth distilled from letters. We realize, in fact, that the photograph refuses to ratify the vision that Shields's sensuous prose has conjured up for us. The sepia photograph that supposedly portrays Mercy with Cuyler is definitely not the picture of 'an extraordinarily obese woman ... with ... jellylike features' (17). We have missed her. As we will miss Daisy. Like mother, like daughter. As a character says in *Swann*, 'Women, women. Endlessly elusive and intent on victory' (110). Now you see me, now you don't.

And what we see is not the abstract, unified, ungendered self that autobiography has traditionally privileged. Paying only lip service to the traditional landmarks of female experience, and thus skipping quickly over courtship and marital bliss, Shields makes us stare rather at what has been traditionally sealed into oblivion, relentlessly and unmercifully insisting on the decrepitude of old age, with a stark refusal to sentimentalize it. Thus, as the pronoun 'I' fades away, emphasizing the process of Daisy's turning herself into a spectacle, Daisy lets herself be seen only when she is old. When she dies, we are left with images that underscore a refusal to ascribe wholeness to the subject – 'the (powdery, splintery) bones, ankles, the sockets of my eyes, shoulder, lip, teeth' (359) and fingernail clippings inexplicably hoarded in a velvet box. The daughter who had promised unlimited display, not hesitating to appear before us at the moment of birth as 'the pulsing, mindless, leaking jelly of my own just-hatched flesh' (23) – a powerful echo of what Kristeva has called 'a self-giving birth ever miscarried'[29] – has taken us through a journey that turns out to be a series of disappearing acts, as though she had been making sure that all the traces she has left behind will not cohere into a whole, that her life will not be open to the meddling of whimsical interpretations. The centre, or that which is assumed to be the centre, is made purposefully and relentlessly void, almost as though Carol Shields envisioned her task as that of protecting her character from the possibilities of analysis, from the greed of the body snatcher, and of insuring that the disorder of female *jouissance* be sheltered against any attempt to represent it.

Rich textures are provided for everybody else – for the enthusiastically lustful Cuyler, for Barker Flett's botanical sexual fantasies, for Clarentine Flett, down to those characters who make only a brief appearance. For all of them, the reader has the satisfying feeling that s/he has been provided with abundant cloth to stitch a story together. Slim as the evidence is concerning the crisis that drives Clarentine Flett to desert her husband, the vision of this woman standing beside the clothesline, with the words that she has overheard Cuyler murmur to his wife, 'Oh, how I love you and with all my heart' (16), etched in her memory, promises a rich unfolding. By the time Clarentine dies in a senseless accident, little as we have been with her, we are satisfied that we know her. We know the loneliness of her dreamlike afternoons, the impulse behind her gifts of tea towels with embroidered corners. We even recognize the 'shrewish tone skirling away inside her head ... the scolding voice ... so abrasive and quick, yet so powerless to move her' (11). For Mercy and Daisy, we have plenty more material, and yet cannot help knowing that 'we can never, never get enough facts' (330).

Finally what Shields offers is what Carolyn Steedman has described in another context as 'an altered sense of the historical meaning and importance of female *insignificance* ... A sense of that which is lost, never to be recovered completely.'[30] The journey through what in Chodorow's words is the 'more complex relational constellation'[31] of women's emotional lives, through the cultural obliteration of female identity to arrive at a 'self in hiding,'[32] maps a series of addresses where Daisy can never be found, an aspect that is emphasized in the Italian translation of the novel, entitled *In cerca di Daisy* (Seeking Daisy).[33] So every time we call on her we feel like the unwelcome visitors for whom 'the lady is not at home.' (Indeed,

Daisy would have endorsed the sentiment that Marina Tsvetaeva, that other exile, put so simply: 'I am absent from my life, I am not at home.')[34] The 'rhetoric of *uncertainty*'[35] in the autobiography of Daisy Goodwill is flaunted with a sort of carnivalesque rapture as the novel confronts the dilemma of the representation of the life experience of a subject who has been forbidden to experience.[36] Like other recent writers such as Steedman in *Landscape*, where the life of the narrator is intertwined with her reassembling/inventing of her mother's youth in an industrial town in Lancashire, and Jamaica Kincaid in her intriguingly entitled *Autobiography of My Mother*, or film-makers such as Ngozi Onwurah of *The Body Beautiful* and Giovanna Gagliardo of *Maternale*,[37] Shields seems to share the sentiment that Margaret Oliphant articulated in her auto-biography when she claimed that she was not always able to keep her memories separate from those of her mother.[38] These stories of enmeshed lives revel in the corporeal roots of sub-jectivity, opposing the traditional view of the subject of knowl-edge as universal, neutral, and genderless. In their search for a meaningful speaking position, these writerly daughters all share a preoccupation with the mother's body as point of origin, with that 'blood-hyphen' which is, in Sarah Maloney's words, 'finally indissoluble' (*Swann* 47), along with an aware-ness of the necessity to bring this body into language. Their approach to subjectivity claims the necessity of a grounding of the subject in the spatial dimension of the body, where the body is not a natural given but rather a field of intersections of material and symbolic forces. The body, to borrow Peter Brooks's phrase, becomes 'emblazoned with meaning ... an "epistemophilic" project.'[39]

But whereas Kincaid, for instance, gives in to the desire for determinacy and closure and, by inserting a gradually more complete photograph of her mother to introduce the various sections of the book, ultimately connives with the will to unmask and discover the mother, Shields is consistent to the end with a narrative which even in the sliding from the first- to the third-person pronoun emphasizes that identity doesn't belong to the self, that it is forever elusive, only to be briefly glimpsed in the play of language, never to be discovered or unmasked. This novel constitutes a sort of choral feminine history that culminates in the construction of a web of intersubjectivity, suggesting the inescapable bodily enmeshment of the narrator and her mother, a state of abjection which is finally experienced as rapture. An example of what Julia Kristeva has called 'female writing' – that which makes one see, feel, touch, with both pleasure and horror, a body made of organs – this novel insists on challenging our resistance to accepting the body's materiality and on viewing the body as caught in a process of decay, as it struggles to forget the impossibility of recovering the mother as mother. What is re-membered is precisely this irrecoverability.

There are bits of your body you carry around all your life but never really own. (*The Stone Diaries* 274)

Daisy has entertained the possibility that finding the burial place of her father-in-law, Magnus Flett, will ease the sense of a 'terrifying inauthenticity gnawing at her heart' (267). When her paleobotanist great-niece Victoria leaves for the Orkney Islands on a research project to find evidence of early plant life, Daisy follows her. Victoria is amused by what she considers Daisy's infatuation with 'the genealogical phenomenon' (265) that drives people (but mostly women, she has noticed) to heal the plague of displacement and disaffection by 'tramping through cemeteries' (265) and consulting library archives. In a landscape that is defiantly possessed by stone, Victoria will turn up nothing – not the 'microscopic tracing of buried life' (301), not even 'a small rock chip imprinted with the outline of a leaf' (301). But the trace that escapes Victoria is what Daisy unwittingly discovers. Her search for Magnus Flett has been, arguably, equally unsuccessful, and she won't be able to utter the word 'father' before the breathing cadaver that may or may not be the centenary Magnus Flett. However,

Daisy, who has mourned all her life her exile and the loss of 'an "object" that has always already been lost'[40] and who has never ceased to yearn for the 'wing-beat' (40) of her dying mother's breath, has not been the usual weekend genealogist. After a life-long journey, she has joined that landscape where all life turns to stone and is now ready to become that rock chip in which the 'coded dots of life' (301) are imprinted.

While I am fascinated by the way in which Lisa Johnson teases out the 'narrative of *possibility* embedded in limestone,' I would argue that it is not the Salem limestone that constitutes 'the central metaphor of feminist postmodernism in this novel' (211); for this malleable freestone is displaced by the harder rock formations that can be found only in a remote point of land in the Orkney Islands. If, as Johnson rightly notes, the limestone tower Cuyler builds in memory of his late wife 'is like a text in Braille, ridged etchings of images and words so vivid one takes the description in through the fin-gertips' (209), one cannot ignore that before the end of the novel the tower is reduced to rubble, while the language that describes Daisy's last imagined artistic act evokes the elusive tenacious rock that holds the promise of fossil patterns (but 'will always frustrate the attempt of specialists to systematize and regulate' [293]) and defies death and time:

> Stone is how she finally sees herself, her living cells replaced by the insentience of mineral deposition. It's easy enough to let it claim her. She lies, in her last dreams, flat on her back on a thick slab, as hugely imposing as the bishops and saints she'd seen years earlier in the great pink cathedral of Kirkwall. It wasn't good enough for them, and it isn't for her either, but the image is, at the very least, contained; she loves it, in fact, and feels herself merge with, and become, finally, the still body of her dead mother. (358–9)

Daisy's life has been 'written with imagination's invisible ink' (149), its fictionality displayed ostentatiously, courting the effect of numerous tentative and contradictory drafts never ready for the press. But this ink, invisible though it may be, is not washable. And her story won't be revised, dismembered, and amended like Mary Swann's poems, for she 'doesn't actually put pen to paper.'[41] It is Daisy's body that becomes the site of inscription of stories as Daisy, who has not hesitated to make a spectacle of her decrepitude, of the mutilation of the body by old age, sees herself undergoing a process of literal petrification. As she distances herself from 'her clavicle, her fat cells, her genital flesh, from her toenails and back gums, from her nostrils and eyebrows' (359) and revels in the obliteration of any certain boundary between the living and the dead, the end of this process of dissolution coincides with the end of her search for the mother. The lightness of being that has haunted all her life, the sense of being surrounded by things 'lacking in weight' (280), has been finally placated as she embraces her 'final form' (360) and reaches that 'trance of solitude' which attaches 'its weight to her faltering pendulum heart' (360).

To be sure, finding Magnus Flett has not liberated Daisy from the nagging recognition that 'she belongs to no one. Even her dreams release potent fumes of absence' (281). And the passage that I have quoted at length, with its echoes of an ecstatic pre-oedipal, dyadic union with the mother, supports Victoria's suspicion that her aunt is really in search of her mother, that 'her preoccupation with her two fathers is only a kind of ruse or sly equation' (269). Daisy may not have found her mother – she may have to make do with the 'emptiness she was handed at birth' (281) – but by the end of the novel she has found in stone/Stone a substance that is finally neither malleable nor amorphous; she has ceased to reinvent herself and has petrified around the edges of her mother's absence – thus both embracing and containing maternal chaos. 'Stone is how she finally sees herself' is indeed an appropriation of the mother's last name. This name, significantly the generic last name of every child in the orphans' home, is both signature and title of a text haunted by the spectre of displacement and disaffection. For if 'the self is not a thing carved on entablature'(231), its trace may very well be found in a stone diary that is unremittingly plural.

After much scrambling on the plates of outcropping rock, Victoria and her professor/boyfriend must renounce their dream of discovering in twenty-one days 'a microscopic tracing of buried life' (301). In the life-long search that culminates in the evocation of the figure of the fossil as a metaphor for her life, Daisy has given form to what the Italian psychoanalyst Anna Salvo has described as the burden of translating into a simple figure the daughter's profound and all-encompassing passion for the mother.[42] While Cuyler's painstakingly carved memorial to his wife crumbles to a pile of rubble, Daisy is finally able to build her own monument to Mercy and thus to appropriate a 'matrilinear consciousness,' the 'mother/daughter patterning of generations that only woman directly experiences.'[43] Daisy is finally able to fulfil her wish and 'to pull herself inside a bag of buried language, to be that language, to be able to utter that unutterable word' (266). Mercy, for whom, too, orphanhood has meant the knowledge of being apart from any coherent history and who has felt 'profoundly buried,' 'no more than a beating of blood inside the vault of her flesh' under Cuyler's 'unfathomable ardour'(7), is now given a decent burial, the deserved 'sweet black eclipse' that Judith had denied to Susanna Moodie (*Small Ceremonies* 34); and no body snatcher will be able to exhume her, no botanist will systematize and regulate her, no biographer will force a beginning and an end on her story: she has become the trace of life to which the daughter has given shape – that *mémoire des pierres* that the French translator of the novel has aptly chosen for its title.[44]

Notes

1   Malcolm Bradbury, 'The Telling Life: Some Thoughts on Literary Biography,' in *The Troubled Face of Biography*, ed. Eric Homberger and John Charmley (New York: St Martin's P, 1988), 140.

2 Carol Shields, *Swann* (New York: Penguin, 1990), 187. All subsequent citations are from this edition.

3 Samuel Johnson, 'Rambler n. 60,' in *The Works of Samuel Johnson*, vol. 2 (Oxford: Talboys and Wheeler, 1825), 286.

4 Cf. Hilary Spurling: 'This view of the humble, plodding, patient, persistent investigator ... is a reality most biographers will recognize. It is at the opposite extreme from the sensational popular view of biographers as literary scavengers, jackals or carrion crows, disgorging what had much better be hidden, dismembering their subjects, sucking them dry, gathering in droves round their death-beds, flaying them sometimes even while still alive' ('Neither Morbid nor Ordinary,' in *The Troubled Face of Biography*, 114).

5 Bradbury, 140.

6 Johnson, 286.

7 See, in particular, Wendy Roy's essay in this collection, 'Autobiography As Critical Practice in *The Stone Diaries*.' All subsequent citations are from the present volume.

8 Carol Shields, 'A Likely Story: A Conversation with Carol Shields,' interviewed by Katie Bolick, *Atlantic Unbound* 283.1 (14 Jan. 1999), cited in Roy, 113.

9 Ivy Compton-Burnett, *Daughters and Sons*, cited in Spurling, 114.

10 Carol Shields, *Susanna Moodie: Voice and Vision* (Ottawa: Borealis, 1973), 2.

11 Carol Shields, *Small Ceremonies* (New York: Penguin, 1996), 7. All subsequent citations are from this edition.

12 John Richetti, *Defoe's Narratives: Situations and Structures* (Oxford: Clarendon, 1975), 128, cited in David Williams, 'Reimagining a Stone Angel: The Absent Autobiographer of *The Stone Diaries*,' in *O Canada: Essays on Canadian Literature and Culture*, ed. Jørn Carlsen (Oakville, CT: Aarhus UP, 1995), 127.

13 Shirley Neuman, '"An Appearance Walking in a Forest the Sexes Burn": Autobiography and the Construction of the Feminine Body,' *Signature* 1.2 (Winter 1989): 2.

14 Carol Shields, *The Stone Diaries* (New York: Penguin, 1995). All subsequent citations are from this edition.

15 Sidonie Smith, *A Poetics of Women's Autobiography: Marginalities*

and the Fictions of Self-Representation (Bloomington: Indiana UP, 1987), 50.

16 Carolyn Steedman, *Landscape for a Good Woman: A Story of Two Lives* (London: Virago, 1985), 5.

17 Carol Shields, 'Narrative Hunger and the Overflowing Cupboard,' p. 34 (in this volume).

18 Linda Hutcheon, *The Politics of Postmodernism* (London: Routledge, 1989), 81.

19 Williams, 128.

20 For a discussion of the autobiographical imperative to repress the body in representation, see Neuman, '"An Appearance."' Neuman points out how 'a literary-philosophic tradition which identifies women as corporeal leaves the woman autobiographer in the position of identifying her self with her body, of creating herself through technologies of the body' (2).

21 Sidonie Smith, *Subjectivity, Identity, and the Body: Women's Autobiographical Practices in the Twentieth Century* (Bloomington: Indiana UP, 1987), 19.

22 For a fine discussion of the 'abject' in Kristeva, see David Fischer, 'Kristeva's *Chora* and the Subject of Postmodern Ethics,' in *Body/Text in Julia Kristeva: Religion, Women and Psychoanalysis*, ed. David R. Crownfield (Albany: State U of New York P, 1992), 100.

23 Fischer, 98.

24 Julia Kristeva, *Powers of Horror: An Essay on Abjection*, trans. Leon S. Roudiez (New York: Columbia UP, 1982), 54.

25 See Kristeva's *Powers of Horror*, in particular, 15.

26 In her fine discussion of Shields's 'embodied postmodernism,' Johnson also points to the similarities in the ways Carol Shields and Jeanette Winterson revitalize postmodern language (226n17).

27 George Bowering, 'Given This Body: An Interview with Daphne Marlatt,' *Open Letter* 4th ser., 3 (1979): 68, cited in Pamela Banting, 'The Reorganization of the Body: Daphne Marlatt's "Musing with Mothertongue," in *ReImagining Women: Representations of Women in Culture*, ed. Shirley Neuman and Glennis Stephenson (Toronto: U of Toronto P, 1993), 219.

28 Daphne Marlatt, *Touch to My Tongue* (Edmonton: Longspoon, 1984), 46, cited in Banting, 220.

29 Kristeva, *Powers of Horror*, 54.

30 Carolyn Steedman, 'Women's Biography and Autobiography: Forms of History. Histories of Form,' in *From My Guy to Sci-Fi: Genre and Women's Writing in the Postmodern World*, ed. Helen Carr (London: Pandora, 1989), 104.

31 Nancy Chodorow, *The Reproduction of Mothering: Psychoanalysis and the Sociology of Gender* (Berkeley: U of California P, 1978), 169.

32 Patricia Meyer Spacks, 'Selves in Hiding,' in *Women's Autobiography: Essays in Criticism*, ed. Estelle C. Jelinek (Bloomington: Indiana UP, 1980), 128.

33 Carol Shields, *In cerca di Daisy*, trans. Alessandro Cremonese Cambieri (Milano: Rizzoli, 1993).

34 Cited in Susan Stanford Friedman, 'Women's Autobiographical Selves,' in *The Private Self: Theory and Practice of Women's Autobiographical Writings*, ed. Shari Benstock (Chapel Hill: U of North Carolina P, 1988), 44.

35 Spacks, 128.

36 On this particular aspect of women's autobiography, see Marina Vitale, 'Una donna dalla memoria lunga: la scrittura autobiografica dal basso,' in *Il racconto delle donne*, ed. Angiolina Arru and Maria Teresa Chialant (Naples: Liguori, 1990), 94.

37 Jamaica Kincaid, *Autobiography of My Mother* (New York: Farrar Straus Giroux, 1996); Ngozi Onwurah, *The Body Beautiful*, 23 min. (New York: Women Make Movies, 1990); Giovanna Gagliardo, *Maternale* (Rome, 1978).

38 Cited in Vitale, 107.

39 Peter Brooks, *Body Work: Objects of Desire in Modern Narrative* (Cambridge: Harvard UP, 1993), 5.

40 Kristeva, *Powers of Horror*, 15.

41 Joan Thomas, 'The Golden Book: An Interview with Carol Shields,' *Prairie Fire* 14. 4 (1993–4): 58. It is tempting to argue that in constructing an autobiography that has never been written, but only built 'out of the scraps of what [Daisy] knows

and what she imagines,' Shields may be providing a radical illustration of what Xavière Gauthier has described as women's existence 'outside the Symbolic' ('Is There Such a Thing As Women's Writing?' [1974], in *New French Fem-inisms: An Anthology*, ed. Elaine Marks and Isabelle de Courtivron [New York: Schocken, 1981], 162–3). This would be consistent with the novel's Kristevean rejection of 'everything finite, definite, structured, loaded with meaning' (Julia Kristeva, 'Oscillation between Power and Denial' [1974], in *New French Feminisms*, 166).

42 Anna Salvo, 'Un luogo interdetto: la passione per la madre,' *Stazione di posta* 48/50 (July–Dec. 1992): 21.

43 See Stephanie A. Demetrakopoulos's discussion of matri-linearism in 'The Metaphysics of Matrilinearism in Women's Autobiography: Studies of Mead's *Blackberry Winter*, Hellman's *Pentimento*, Angelou's *I Know Why the Caged Bird Sings*, and Kingston's *The Woman Warrior*,' in Jelinek, ed., *Women's Autobiography*, 181.

44 Carol Shields, *La Mémoire des pierres*, trans. Oristelle Bonis (Paris: Calmann-Lévy, 1995).

where. The same bruised phrases appear again and again: Daisy 'blinded, throttled, erased from the record of her own existence' (76), her imagined autobiography 'an assemblage of dark voids and unbridgeable gaps' (75–6) centred precariously on a missing 'kernel of authenticity' (75). This pattern of interpretation overlooks the redeeming, even optimistic, moments of the novel, along with its trajectory toward hope and self-knowledge. In order to refocus the critical discussion, it is necessary to leave behind the pursuit of what *isn't* there – in the novel or character, in the reader or world – attending instead to what *is.*

The Stone Diaries can therefore be usefully resituated within a different, less nihilistic set of questions and concerns, such as the largely unresolved conflict between feminism and postmodernism. Suspended between these competing paradigms of art and contemporary selfhood, *The Stone Diaries* dramatizes the concept of *embodied postmodernism,* an epistemological stance and aesthetic vision which values the particular over the universal and the possible over the impossible. The power of the imagination to transform 'the available materials' emerges as a central theme in this novel: in the face of meaninglessness – we live, we are lost, we die – Carol Shields redirects our eyes to moments of agency and playfulness, producing in our bodies brief sensations of order and pleasure in the world around us. This recognition of agency in women's storytelling marks my point of departure from Briganti's interpretation, in which 'inevitably the narrated life will appear as waste and opacity' (188). In fact, my article shares more with Dianne Osland's essay in this volume, for I believe, with her, that 'Daisy's imaginative recuperation of the past' should be 'seen as action taken *within* the narrative to reconcile what she knows with what she needs or desires' (97). Far from being a novel about the impossibility of telling a self-authored woman's life story – or living one – *The Stone Diaries* gathers together the various 'reassertions of the self that Daisy fears she has allowed to be written out of her life' (Osland, 97). Key to reconceptualizing Shields's vision as a *postmodernism of resistance*, that is, a conjoining of postmodernity with *jouissance*, is the reader's willingness or drive to recognize it as such. Osland again: 'while her last words, "I am not at peace," may be unspoken, [Daisy] has hardly been silenced if we grant her "a real gift for making a story out of things"' (104). Let's do.

A Plurality of Postmodernisms

In *The Stone Diaries*, Shields employs common postmodern aesthetic strategies – the fragmented narrator, hybrid genre, and metafictional narrative, for example – but she joins them with a thematic insistence on the transformative female imagination, foraying into new parts of this aesthetic field, enacting an *embodied, woman-centred,* and *politicized* postmodernism. Because my interpretation depends for its meaning on recognizing the existence of 'many *different* postmodernisms,'[3] a brief review of two key articles will be useful in distinguishing among them. In 'Stalemates? Feminists, Postmodernists and Unfinished Issues in Modern Aesthetics,' Patricia Waugh criticizes 'the generally apocalyptic vision of much postmodern thought,' asserting that 'many women writers are using postmodern aesthetic strategies of disruption to re-imagine the world in which we live, while resisting the nihilistic implications of the theory.'[4] In the same vein, Marilyn Edelstein's 'Resisting Postmodernism; or, "A Postmodernism of Resistance"' outlines the tension between postmodernism and feminism – forces often seen as irreconcilable – and highlights their potentially common ground:

[S]ome critics of postmodernism claim that, by problematizing identity and rejecting essence, postmodernism eliminates the possibility of agency (both individual and cultural) and thus cannot be useful for feminist or antiracist struggles ... Since most versions of postmodern theory assume the social, ideological, psychoanalytic, and/or linguistic construction or determination of the subject, the argument runs, how can such a theory include the possibility of not-always-already-determined acts and choices? Linda Hutcheon argues that postmodernism *has* no theory of agency, where feminism must.[5]

The glimmer of a 'not-always-already-determined' zone in women's lives and artistic *oeuvres* holds out hope to the reader for choice, agency, desire. Theorizing this space of possibility, Edelstein draws on bell hooks's cultural theory to propose 'a postmodernism of resistance':

> We often talk about postmodernism with metaphors of loss, rejection, abandonment – of meta-narratives, foundations, absolutes, faith. Yet it is also possible to see postmodernism as a moment of regeneration, as a time of proliferating possibilities: new discourses, media, voices, identities, and social and political relationships. Thus, like hooks, I would stress respect, love, and commitment to emancipatory struggles as necessary corollaries (or complements) to postmodern dispersion, deconstruction, and difference.[6]

In hooks's own words: 'The oppressed struggle in language to recover ourselves – to rewrite, to reconcile, to renew. Our words are not without meaning. They are an action – a resistance.'[7] Indeed it seems a pernicious luxury to perceive language, art, and selfhood as sites of meaninglessness. Those who have been denied identity and voice can hardly afford this version of postmodernism. Edelstein defines the aesthetics of 'resistance postmodernism' as 'stylistic and temporal experimentation linked to political and moral vision.'[8] Postmodern aesthetic strategies – too often, in Shields's words, 'deadly and pretentious' – can be invoked instead to convey the material conditions of inequality that underlie feelings of alienation, emptiness, and loss.[9] *The Stone Diaries* thus undergirds postmodern style and content with the more specific story of the thwarted (white, middle-class) female self in twentieth-century North America. Whereas first-generation postmodernism – with its fetishization of nowhereness and the decentred subject – encourages the reader to throw up her hands in dismay at the ubiquitous, inescapable conditions of homelessness and social constructedness, second-generation (embodied, or resistance) postmodernism renders action and change possible by placing the fragmented, alienated narrator in a specific historical moment and cultural location, joining critique with agency, celebrating especially the small moments of resistance in individual lives.[10]

These moments constitute a subtle yet central pattern in *The Stone Diaries*: chinks of light, of consciousness-raising, riddling its postmodern structure. In a dissertation devoted to the writings of Carol Shields, Patricia Joan Morgan describes 'experiences of self-knowledge' in this particular novel as 'brief moments of illumination, like fireworks in a night sky.'[11] With this poetic image, Morgan reinterprets 'ruptures' in the narrative as flashes of insight.[12] In 'Narrative Hunger,' Shields's contribution to this collection, her formulation of (embodied) postmodernism reframes art in a similar way, 'asking why the rub of disunity strikes larger sparks than the reward of accommodation, and how we've come to record what separates us rather than what brings us together' (33). In an analysis of *Swann*, Clara Thomas tells us 'Shields is a cautious advocate of postmodernist ideas,' quoting Shields herself on postmodernism's usefulness to her: 'It gives you permission to let the story go in curious angles. To imagine unimaginable possibilities.'[13] In an era some pundits call 'postfeminist,' I contend that women's remaining inequalities warrant an art form made precisely for this purpose – to imagine unimaginable possibilities – and that a postmodernism of resistance is one such art form.

Mention *Must* Be Made of the Raspberries

In *The Stone Diaries*, Shields turns postmodernism toward the material conditions of women's lives, creating a lived postmodernism, an in-the-body postmodernism, which manifests itself stylistically in what I am calling a *tactile aesthetics*, where imagery, narrative commentary, and collaboration with the reader converge to create community and groundedness in the lives of characters (and readers) who are at every moment pulled toward dispersion and sensory deprivation. 'There is so much that lies out of reach, so much that touches only tangentially on our lives, or confronts us with incomprehensible images,' writes Shields, and she responds to this feeling of disconnection with a poetics of intimacy and sensation, 'shorten[ing] the distance between what is privately felt and universally known, so that we look up from the printed page and say "Ah-hah"' ('Narrative Hunger' 20, 22).

Traditionally female art forms in *The Stone Diaries* – the folk arts of cooking and gardening – reiterate the alchemy of women's imaginations on everyday materials. Daisy's recollection of her mother, Mercy (a recollection that reaches magic realism style beyond Daisy's birth into the past), recognizes the solitary aesthetic pleasures of cooking: 'Like an artist – years later this form of artistry is perfectly clear to me – she stirs and arranges and draws in her brooding lip' (2). For Mercy, 'paradise' meant 'concocting and contriving' in the kitchen (2). Daisy inherits her mother's talent for making art from things of the earth, becoming a renowned gardener and newspaper columnist on the subject, Mrs Green Thumb. In fact, her ability to transform dire earthly conditions into cultivatable soil is pointed out by the narrator as the one activity through which Daisy becomes able to perceive her own impact on the world around her, making gardening both sensual and subversive:

And the raspberries; mention must be made of the raspberries. Does Mrs. Barker Flett understand the miracle she has brought into being in the city of Ottawa on the continent of North America in this difficult northern city in the mean, toxic, withholding middle years of our century? Yes; for once she understands fully. (195–6)

While not ignoring the fact that Daisy is effaced by the patriarchal custom of taking one's husband's name, this passage quietly celebrates the real and worthy work of Daisy's hands. This act of cultivating raspberries – bringing sweetness and nourishment from the withholding ground – is situated specifically in the 'withholding middle years of our century' (in other words, at the beginning of the postmodern era, mid-twentieth century), and the garden becomes Daisy's space of self-actualization, an aperture in the cultural text of femininity where 'the narrative maze opens and permits [Daisy] to pass through' (190).[14] The reader's eye is directed not at the maze but at this aperture, and the raspberries growing along its borders. Shields writes that '"Reality" ... smells better than words, tastes sharper, presses on the skin more compellingly' ('Narrative Hunger' 23–4), but she makes language strive for these vivid impressions, and, to my mind (or, should I say, mouth and nose), she succeeds.

The reading experience becomes increasingly sensual as one stumbles over stones in strange places: 'The little beveled mirror in its oak frame sends back her image, her flattened-down hair and her eyes, hot as stones in her head' (16). With great textual intricacy, Shields positions stones at various sites of sensory reception, on the tips of our tongues, for instance, like a lost phrase. Here is Clarentine Flett's husband reflecting fondly on his wife's idiosyncrasies after she left him: 'He remembers, too, that she had had a kind of pride, a respect for her own labour, refusing, for instance, to pit the prunes that went into her prune pudding, letting those who ate her steamed offerings wrestle with the stones in their own mouths' (98). My tongue moves around these words shaped like prune pits, tart and fibrous. Wrestling with the stones in our mouths strikes me as an evocative metaphor of the work Shields does with postmodernism, infusing language with the real, giving words hard edges to press against the palate. I am surprised when I read her remarks on 'the crippling limitations that language imposes' (24) in 'Narrative Hunger,' for she consistently brings to the page the sharp taste of text.

Throughout *The Stone Diaries*, abstractions take on physical manifestations, such as 'the sweat of memory' (60) on Cuyler

Goodwill's brow, or the belief held by Daisy's children – that 'memory could be poked with a stick, savoured in the mouth like a popsicle, you could never get enough of it' (175). *The Stone Diaries* shares this trait with the movement of magic realism, one subset of postmodern writing in which 'metaphoric language ... is to be taken literally.'[15] By 'literalizing the metaphor,' magic realists like Gabriel García Márquez and Toni Morrison resist postmodernism's evaporation of language. This concretization of the life of the mind carries questions of postmodernism into the body, moving narrative toward embodiment, a technique also shared by contemporary women writers who seek to reunify consciousness with our living, breathing forms. The empiricist philosophy enacted in Shields's tactile aesthetics – 'the vivid tactile memory' (67) – demonstrates the feminist challenge to Western epistemology, a challenge that locates knowledge in the body rather than in the mind.[16] Words become things with edges and flavours, from Daisy's 'rolling it on her tongue. Do-min-i-on' (132) to her laughter, despite depression, over the word 'woe' – 'such a blind little bug of a word' (262) – and her mother Mercy's indulgence in a multi-layered love for a favourite dish: 'Malvern pudding; she loves the words too, and feels them dissolve on her tongue like a sugary wafer, her tongue itself grown waferlike and sweet' (2). This lavishing of affection on the solid presence of words enacts the French feminist theory of *écriture feminine,* writing at the intersection of body and text, joining the aesthetic with the erotic.[17]

The metaphor of stone weighs the novel down and provides the reader with a much needed sense of groundedness to counterbalance postmodernism's often dizzying stories of textuality, interiority, and multiple realities. The characters perceive themselves adrift – lost like the rest of us – but the narrator insists that they, literally, stand on solid ground:

> These good souls, for that's what they are, are borne up by an ancient shelf of limestone ... Yet each of them at this moment feels unanchored, rattling loose in the world between the clout of death and the squirming foolishness of birth. (40)

This passage presents postmodern homelessness as a problem of perception; the good souls of Shields's novel do not know to take comfort in the 'ancient shelf of limestone' beneath their feet, bearing them up with the force of nature's eternal rhythms. The title itself sets this pattern of reality versus (socially constructed) perception by yoking the lightness of diaries with the enduring quality of stone, challenging the association of text (particularly women's personal 'scribblings,' which Daisy herself relegates to 'the province of girlhood') with the ephemeral and disembodied.[18] Stones surface everywhere in this novel – as monuments, parables, and figurative language – repeatedly reminding readers of the solid ground on which we stand. Stone imagery thus represents what is hard – both concrete and difficult – in life: the lived questions of selfhood, relationships, and language in this postmodern era.

In addition to endowing the novel with this concrete presence, Shields's tactile aesthetics creates a sense of communion between reader and text (a point to which I return in detail below). With an abundance of sensory images, Shields counteracts the deprivation of touch common to postmodern life. As conductors of heat and cold, evocative of smooth surfaces and rounded edges, stones engage the reader's sensory perception. They give us something to close our palms around. The limestone tower Cuyler Goodwill builds in memory of his late wife is like a text in Braille, ridged etchings of images and words so vivid one takes the description in through the fingertips. Limestone is particularly evocative as a medium of communion and emblem of embodied postmodernism; underground, limestone remains soft and very much like flesh, suggesting a bone-deep link between humanity and the natural world. This stone pulses. Only when it comes into contact with air does it harden, but in Shields's aesthetic vision, stone remains closely linked with the human body, challenging the reader to hold its fleshy self and its stoney self in her mind at once, suspended in unresolved paradox – familiar terrain in postmodern fiction.[19]

Donna Haraway's theory of 'situated knowledges' provides

an important context in which to understand the political impact of Shields's embodied postmodern aesthetic (both the multiple narration and the sensate quality of words and ideas).[20] She writes:

> I am arguing for a politics and epistemologies of location, positioning, and situating, where partiality and not universality is the condition of being heard to make rational knowledge claims. These are claims on people's lives. I am arguing for a view from a body, always a complex, contradictory, structuring, and structured body, versus the view from above, from nowhere, from simplicity. (589)

In response to the 'epistemological electroshock therapy' (578) of postmodernism's hyper-deconstructive versions, Haraway asserts, 'Feminists have to insist on a better account of the world; it is not enough to show radical historical contingency and modes of construction for everything' (579). And further, 'we need the power of modern critical theories of how meanings and bodies get made, not in order to deny meanings and bodies, but in order to build meanings and bodies that have a chance for life' (580). Feminist postmodernism is, in this view, 'not partiality for its own sake but, rather, for the sake of the connections and unexpected openings situated knowledges make possible' (590). This theory can be aligned fruitfully with the thematization of perspective and the use of multiple narration in *The Stone Diaries*: 'Subjectivity is multidimensional,' writes Haraway, 'so, therefore, is vision. The knowing self is partial in all its guises, never finished, whole, simply there and original: it is always constructed and stitched together imperfectly, and *therefore* able to join with another, to see together without claiming to be another' (586). Pointing to the relationship between vision and power, Haraway asks, 'Who gets to have more than one point of view? Who gets blinded? Who wears blinders?' (587). In this context, Daisy's multiply narrated story appears heroic; such feats as witnessing her own birth, and seeing her parents' lovemaking even before her conception, indicate an enlarged vision rather than a fragmented or disempowered perspective. Instead of 'a story that loses track of its mediations just where someone might be held responsible for something' (579) – Haraway's reference to masculinist scientific claims of objectivity and, by association, postmodernism – what we need is a story that keeps up with the various angles of vision that constitute any given reality.

Freestone Feminism: 'The Choice, Young Citizens of the World, Is Yours'

Salem limestone provides the central metaphor of feminist postmodernism in this novel. Cuyler Goodwill, Daisy's father and a master stonecutter, impresses upon his daughter the narrative of *possibility* embedded in limestone. Cuyler, who developed early acumen for reading 'the signature of the spiritual' in 'the earth's rough minerals' (63), expounds on its significance to Daisy's graduating college class:

> Salem limestone, he tells his captive audience, is that remarkable rarity, a freestone – meaning it can be split equally in either direction, that it has no natural bias. 'And I say to you young women as you go out into the world, think of this miraculous freestone material as the substance of your lives. You are the stone carver. The tools of intelligence are in your hand. You can make of your lives one thing or the other. You can be sweetness or bitterness, lightness or darkness, a force of energy or indolence, a fighter or a laggard. You can fail tragically or soar brilliantly. The choice, young citizens of the world, is yours.' (116)

Pompous though his speech may sound – and redolent with potentially vapid liberal erasures of social construction and power differentials – its message nevertheless influences the initially embarrassed young Daisy in ultimately positive ways. If we interpret *The Stone Diaries* as Daisy *thinking her autobiog-*

raphy, it becomes clear that she approaches the materials of her life as a carver of freestone, living the credo Cuyler instils in her: 'You can make of your lives one thing or the other.'[21] She does precisely this – 'swirls [her life] one way or the other' (182) like a tropical drink or party dress. This assertion of female agency marks a consistent counterpoint in *The Stone Diaries* to the postmodern theme of social forces bearing down upon and breaking up the individual.[22]

The concept of life as carvable stone is accented by the image of Cuyler's tower – a monument built above his dead wife's grave – on which he inscribes an 'elaborate cipher,' 'patterns' which 'seem to evade the eye,' 'a museum of writhing forms' (64). This tower of texts plays on the tensions of storytelling as resisted (in first-generation postmodernism) and as resistance (in feminist postmodernism), sustaining a tension between narrative and rupture. Both encrypted and out in the open, the tower acts as a centrepiece in a novel filled with disappearing texts, on the one hand (Daisy's letters to Barker, her travel diary), and an abundance of texts, on the other (the found poems of newspaper clippings, lists of flower parts, obituaries, guest narratives, a series of addresses, lists of book titles, scholarly articles and public speeches written by characters, and so on). The shaping of stone, the shaping of text, and the shaping of a life converge upon this metaphor, underlining the elements of choice and imagination, will and vision, that still hold the power, despite the draining atmosphere of postmodern despair, to transform a shelf of limestone, a scattering of facts and rumour and newspaper clippings, and a set of constraining roles and tragic circumstances, into a work of art. Self-fulfilment, community, purpose – it's all in the carving, the motions of our hands on the rough material of our lives:

> Daisy learns her father's lesson well; even as a youth she understood that if she was going to hold on to her life at all, she would have to rescue it by a primary act of imagination, supplementing, modifying, summoning up the necessary connections, con-

juring the pastoral or heroic or whatever, even dreaming a
limestone tower into existence, getting the details wrong occasionally, exaggerating or lying outright, inventing letters or conversations of impossible gentility, or casting conjecture in a
pretty light. (77)

The freedom and creativity of this loose hold on reality resonates with bell hooks's 'On Self-Recovery,' where she asserts,
'Language is also a place of struggle' (28). Inventor of reality,
author of her own life, Daisy reflects on 'the tricks of consciousness' and recognizes her ability to counter the official
stories that would erase her: 'She may be crowded out of her
own life – she knows this for a fact and has always known it –
but she possesses, as a compensatory gift, the startling ability
to draft alternate versions' (190). This marvellous compensatory gift has been given short shrift in Shields criticism, and I
hope to rectify this imbalance by emphasizing it here. On
Daisy's visit to see her father-in-law, the narrator captures
Daisy's self-renewing spirit in a palpably joyful description:
'Oh, she is young and strong again. Look at the way she walks
freely out the door and down the narrow stone street of
Stromness, tossing her hair in the fine light' (307). Daisy repeatedly escapes the constraints of her own life history, and
her realization of 'how suddenly merry the world could turn
if you only let it' (134) suggests the (feminist postmodern)
power we all might exercise over our lives if only we would.

Daisy's daughter Joan also perceives and dramatizes the
possibility of willing joy into a story that would exclude it. In
a brief section narrated by Joan as a child, she creates an
image that demonstrates a feminist postmodern aesthetics of
the body, looking to the motions of her limbs to generate joy
where otherwise there would be none:

She has discovered how she can fill up an empty moment should
one occur. When there is nothing else to do she can always walk
down to the corner where Torrington Crescent meets The Drive-
way and there in front of Mrs. Bregman's big brown house she

can roll down the grassy banked hill that runs across the front lawn. No one has said not to do this, no one seems to have thought of it. As it happens, she hardly ever goes down to the corner to roll down the hill, but she likes to keep the possibility in reserve. Or she can skip along the sidewalk in front of her own house. Learning to skip has brought control into her life. Whenever she feels at all sad she switches into this wholly happy gait, sliding, hopping, and sliding again; when doing this, it seems as though her head separates from her body, making her feel dizzy and emptied out of bad thoughts. Does anyone else in the world know this trick, she wonders. Probably not, though her mother sometimes waves at her from the window, waves and smiles ... [Joan] knows herself to be full of power, able to slip out from under any danger. (172–3)

Determined to find pleasure, and enlisting both her imagination and her body to create it, Joan resists the constraints of girlhood on reality, bounding through space with joy. Joan's skipping mirrors in microcosm Shields's narrative style – not disrupting reality by taking great leaps but rendering it more accurately. I call Shields's style *differently coherent* (as opposed to incoherent).[23] In 'Narrative Hunger and the Overflowing Cupboard,' she says as much: 'Since getting inside reality rather than getting reality right is the task of narrative fiction, it is inevitable that our stories will never mirror back to us a perfect image' (35). This allowance for distortion in representing 'reality' permits Shields's women characters and readers to reject existing rules of behaviour, decorum, and identity in favour of living in leaps and bounds. The agency of 'switching into a wholly happy gait' can be seen as a product of postmodernism's fragmented reality; instead of being overwhelmed by endless possible perspectives, one might, like Joan (and Daisy, and Shields, and me), thrill at the array of stories to choose from in everything from filling an empty afternoon to telling one's autobiography to constructing a novel or critical analysis. As early as the first chapter, entitled 'Birth, 1905,' Daisy confides flirtatiously, 'The recounting of a life is a cheat, of course; I admit the truth of this; even our own stories are obscenely distorted' (28). This is no admission of meaninglessness; it is an embrace of playful authority.

The presence of alternatives to history, and to the story one is assigned by the traditionally gendered rules of society, extends the freestone metaphor beyond individual autobiography to the larger task of reimagining cultural history. The power to determine anew the nature of history empowers the woman storyteller. Shields creates a collage of diaries, family genealogies, recipes, addresses, pictures, lists of long-term must-do's, titles in Daisy's library, the committees on which she served, and the groups to which she belonged. This pastiche form emphasizes the constructedness of conventional historical narratives, underlining the seeming arbitrariness and underlying politics of choosing certain documents and landmarks over others as the material around which to structure story. Here history is based on 'women's' life landmarks – births, marriage, love, the development of a particular family – rather than wars, drawings of national borders, or the passing of one world leader to the next, as told within the walls of most high-school and many undergraduate Western Civilization classrooms. This alternative history asserts the struggles of daily life and individual families as equally important, if not more so, than the struggles of a nation or king.

Daisy notes the necessity of appropriating the power of story after the accidental death of her first husband on their honeymoon, because 'men ... were uniquely honored by the stories that erupted in their lives, whereas women were more likely to be smothered by theirs' (121). 'Why?' she asks. 'Why should this be? Why should men be allowed to strut under the privilege of their life adventures, wearing them like a breastful of medals, while women went all gray and silent beneath the weight of theirs?' (121). The contrast Shields establishes here brings to mind an American literary history – specifically alluding, it seems to me, to *The Scarlet Letter* – in which the female self is conscripted into a patriarchal cultural narrative. With the first line of *The Stone Diaries*, Shields both invokes and rebukes a Western cultural history of (masculine) self and journey; not 'Call me Ishmael,' but 'My mother's name was Mercy Stone Goodwill' (1).[24] Daisy's fantastic feat of witnessing and narrating her own birth and her consistent asides that challenge 'official records' and traditional 'history' insist on the many possible modes of story, placing value on alternative, feminine perspectives.[25] In 'abandon[ing] formal plot,'[26] Shields frees herself to explore life structures apart from conventions that enclose every female self in the marriage plot, creating a critical distance from the quest for socially sanctioned reproductively sexual couplehood (the Jane Eyre effect, one might say, with a nod to Osland).

As Daisy grows old, 'fading fast' she jokes, the telling of her story becomes increasingly urgent and less conventionally arranged. History becomes something we do; reality, a process of stringing story together:

> She feels a new tenderness growing for certain moments; they're like beads on string, and the string is wearing out. At the same time she knows that what lies ahead of her must be concluded by the efforts of her imagination and not by the straight-faced recital of a throttled and unlit history. Words are more and more required. And the question arises: what is the story of a life? A chronicle of fact or a skilfully wrought impression? The bringing together of what she fears? Or the adding up of what has been off-handedly revealed, those tiny allotted increments of knowledge? (340)

Shields and Daisy both firmly choose the latter, and so do I. In the shaping of history, as in the shaping of stone, 'the miracle of the sculptor's imagination is required. And freshness of vision' (114). Daisy reaches her freshest vision in old age, letting go the reins of conventional logic once more, surrendering to the seductive tug of imagination on memory:

> The synapses collapse; well, let them. She enlarges on the available material, extends, shrinks, reshapes what's offered; this mixed potion is her life. She swirls it one way or the other,

depending on – who knows what it depends on? – the fulcrum
of desire, or of necessity. (282)

This correlation of collapsed structures of thought with an
expansion of reality marks *The Stone Diaries* as a prime example of resistance postmodernism: in the collection of textual fragments, in the stringing together of story, in the
carving of a freestone reality, Shields cultivates a tentative
sense of agency for Daisy and all women who would be
narrators. In the blurred space where we don't know if we're
looking at 'the fulcrum of desire, or of necessity,' Daisy and
Shields and all her readers slip through a secret door marked
'not-always-already' and discover a bit of space in which to
turn around.

Shields shares this commitment to storytelling as world
(re)building with other women in the canon currently forming of feminist postmodern fiction writers. Paulina Palmer
outlines 'postmodern trends' in contemporary women's
novels, setting up the discrepancies between feminism and
postmodernism in order to show how Margaret Atwood,
Angela Carter, and Jeanette Winterson undo them:

> There is a contradiction, for example, between the representa-
> tion of subjectivity as decentred and the product of culture and
> the unconscious, which typifies postmodernist thought, and the
> belief in individual agency and collective political action, to
> which feminists are committed. A tension also exists between
> the postmodern view of subjectivity and society as in a state of
> constant flux, and a feminist emphasis on working towards
> positive goals and maintaining the gains which we have
> achieved. In addition, there is a tension between the postmodern
> perception that everything is mediated by representation and
> the recognition of the project of affirming the contribution which
> literature can make to politics and investigating the connections
> between the two.[27]

Palmer posits the exploration of agency and self-determina-
tion – both their limits and their possibilities – as a central

theme in this group of novelists, each of whom reveals the constraints on agency not as an abstract problem (e.g., postmodern deferrals of meaning or the empty centre of the self) but as a result of particular 'cultural and social factors.'[28]

Furthermore, the split or multiple narration of *The Stone Diaries*, that, in one reading, illustrates the novel's postmodern fragmentation of self can, in my alternative reading, be politicized as a critique of sexist inequality. Multiple narrators, often 'an "I" (woman as subject) and a name (woman as object),'[29] reflect the reality of women's split consciousness – subject and object – theorized in Simone de Beauvoir's *The Second Sex* and rendered in story by such authors as Erica Jong and Kate Millett. Elsewhere in this collection, Wendy Roy emphasizes the effect of split narration as a critique of sexist inequality, asserting 'Daisy's displacement from the centre of her story is evident each time *I* or *me* is replaced by *she* or *her*, each time Daisy is constructed – or constructs herself – as an other' (122). Without repudiating Roy's argument, indeed holding our two readings together like two sticks sparking bright friction, I propose an added dimension of analysis, since in some sense 'an understanding of Daisy's story requires all these different versions.'[30] Multiple narration in this novel strikes me, not as a force that splits Daisy apart or crowds her out of her own story, but rather as a way of looking at her life from various angles, acknowledging 'a proliferation of possibilities' in the search for personal and cultural meaning.[31]

The Reader's Part; or, *My* Stone Diaries

The Stone Diaries depicts women's storytelling as dialogic ('she needs someone – anyone – to listen'), and critical responses, as Patrocinio Schweickart writes in another context, ought to be dialogic as well.[32] In this section, I contend that the reader completes the circuit of possibility initiated by Daisy's gesture toward autobiography. Gordon Slethaug captures this relationship almost by accident in his discussion of alienation in the novel, when he states: 'The events of everyday life and those special moments of happiness and sadness are important, but there are intimacies and feelings that cannot be wholly shared, except ironically in this case by the reader.'[33] I don't share his condescension to the reader-text relationship, but I do find his pronouncement on Daisy – 'she represents our longing for wholeness' – rings true, and this longing on my part as a reader drives the arrangement of my own article around the intimacies rather than the alienations of this text, reading for 'what brings us together' rather than 'what separates us' ('Narrative Hunger' 33). Indeed, I am dwelling on the thread of joy that runs throughout this novel, the merriment and the laughter. Daisy and her two sets of friends – those of her youth and those of her old age – 'love a good laugh; there is something filigreed and droll about the way they're always on the cusp of laughter' (318). And there is something in this description that invites me to join in their mirth.

For several weeks in the spring of 1999, I engaged in heated debate with the students in my women's life-writing course over how to read Daisy's imaginative acts of transforming reality. We wanted to know: was Daisy demonstrating agency by drafting alternative stories of her life, recreating reality itself? Or was she copping out, deluding herself, escaping reality? We gathered textual evidence to support both perspectives – heroic author of her own life, or cowardly escapist – and the class tugged back and forth over the final interpretation. How are we to read Daisy in this moment of old age, senility, imagination: 'She enlarges on the available material, extends, shrinks, reshapes what's offered; this mixed potion is her life. She swirls it one way or the other, depending on – who knows what it depends on? – the fulcrum of desire, or of necessity' (282)? The debate led me to ask myself, Why am I so committed to reading Daisy in a positive light? My fear was that, like the Daisy of my students' interpretation, perhaps I was deluding myself, escaping the reality of the text, twisting meaning, wilfully misreading the words and world before me.

Certain moments in the novel admittedly undermine my optimistic reading. For instance, while Alice, Daisy's oldest daughter, takes control of her personality as a young woman, determining to become kind and discovering through altering her life that her life is alterable (233), she later expresses ambivalence toward this fact: 'The pattern of her life is unfolding, a long itinerary of revision and accommodation. She's making it up as she goes along. This is not how she imagined her middle years, but this is the way it will be' (342). Perhaps it is serenity I hear in this passage, but to the degree that it might be resignation, Alice's tone tempers her earlier act of personal transformation. Likewise, Daisy's reflection on sensation as overwhelming complicates my reading: 'All this: the thought of pancakes, the hot bite of chives, the hidden throats of flowers, the sun, the sound of her own name – she is suddenly dizzy with the press of sensation, afraid she will die of it' (338). Shields's tactile aesthetics, an aesthetics of intimacy, boxes Daisy in with its 'press of sensation.' The positive reading, the one that leaves these blemishes out, is the act of my own transformative imagination, which collects the pieces I need while suppressing those that foil feminist pleasure and agency.[34] In this sense, I am recollecting Daisy's life story, joining the novel's many narrators to apply my own slant, telling the story I need to hear.[35] What Mellor calls 'the conspiratorial relationship between the anonymous "I"-narrator and the reader' gives me permission to chime in with my own version of events like just another of Daisy's intimate girlfriends.[36] I am glad when I read Shields's affirmation of the reader's part in the meaning-making process: 'What I have learned ... in my later books is that I can trust the reader, that I can step off in mid-air, so to speak, and take the reader along.'[37] She *expects* us to select among possible readings, to participate in the collaborative project of this autobiography and of reality in general.

The novel itself contains enough moments to support my positive reading that the contradictory strains need not overwhelm. The sad sounds of Daisy's death – 'I'm still here, oh, oh' (352) – do not drown out the myriad voices of choice and joy that precede and pervade the chapters of her life. And perhaps even these deathbed cries are not entirely sad after all. As Morgan writes, 'Daisy's words show a woman who has enjoyed her life, as ordinary as it might appear to others, and is loath to leave it.' She elaborates: 'Critics who have embraced this idea of Daisy as disappearing because she has not captured the gaze of the outside world, appear to affirm the idea that subjectivity is constructed through the gaze of the other.'[38] Maybe the truth is this: Daisy is let down plenty by her life – who isn't? – but these disappointments are not the point. The point of life is one's response to disappointment, one's resiliency, perspective, equanimity. In this, Daisy provides a powerful role model. The ability to draft alternative versions of one's life is key to experiencing joy and fulfilment in a world that seems designed to thwart it. Daisy's struggle is familiar and motivational for her readers in our long swim toward the breathable surface of our lives – as women, as storyers, bearers of social change brought up from the depths of our own autobiographical bodies. *The Stone Diaries* thus represents twentieth-century women's embodied postmodern struggles to know each other and ourselves, and although Shields may not offer unqualifiably happier answers than first-generation postmodernism, she poses questions in fresh ways, whip-stitching the link between the personal and the political, developing ways of managing this life, reconnecting mind and body, sense and sensation, past and present, me and you.

Here is what I ended up telling my class: while there are reasons to read Daisy negatively – that she does not take a more assertive or radical approach to the trajectory of her life as a woman, for instance, or that all the transformations she effects occur in her mind and in authorial revolutions of style that do not affect her relationships or status in the 'real' world – these reasons do not outweigh for me the validity of choosing one's own story and asserting continuity among one's imaginative choices and the quality of life lived. This is the power of embodied postmodernism – to use the potentially terrifying concept of many realities and many selves in a positive project of reconceptualization. Shields thematizes the limits of language and consciousness, but instead of letting that become a distraction from life or a dead end for literature, she seems to say, 'Okay, given these constraints, let's figure out what we *can* do, indeed, how we might shape these elements of life to make them the most useful, to make them what we need.' Like Daisy, 'she enlarges on the available material.' 'Some postmodernists think there is no point beyond the language game,' Shields comments, 'but I think there can be.'[39] *The Stone Diaries* bears out this belief with its undercurrent of joy and critique. *This* must be the postmodernism Edelstein imagines when she 'stress[es] respect, love, and commitment to emancipatory struggles as necessary corollaries (or complements) to postmodern dispersion, deconstruction, and difference.'[40] Speaking of her dissertation, Shields explains her choice of topics as based on emotional fulfilment: 'I thought, "If I'm going to do this, it had better be an act of love."'[41] Her emphasis in *The Stone Diaries* on women's imaginations as agents of personal and social transformation suggests she approaches the postmodern novel in the same way – not as an apolitical renunciation of reality, but as an act of love.

Conclusion

> I like endings that veer off in strange directions, rising rather than falling, or endings that make sudden leaps into the future or the past, bringing about a different quality of oxygen altogether.
>
> CAROL SHIELDS[42]

As I was in the final phases of revising this article, the twin towers of the World Trade Center in New York City were reduced to rubble, and in the aftermath of this attack I am acutely aware that postmodernism's postures – one where we stand gape-mouthed at disintegration, another where we rebuild a world – have material consequences outside the text. This embattled author-ity marks the creative intersection of postmodernism and feminism, where language impacts culture, shapes our relationship to history, nation, self, other. For the fact is, things don't just fall apart; someone takes them apart, for particular political reasons and desired effects. Who is behind the action, we persist, and who is underneath it? Through these more specific naming practices, one might unveil 'postmodernism' as a complex of social, economic, and cultural forces and morés. As the United States wages war in Afghanistan within a haze of evasive rhetoric (pitting 'good' against 'evil'), feminists must, in Haraway's words, 'insist on a better account of the world,' an incisive account of the things falling apart and the patriarchal, imperialist forces responsible. Destruction is far too easy as long as the Other remains an idea, with no face or name or story, no moral complexity to consider.

In contrast, Shields explores the possibility of a socially responsible postmodern aesthetic. The split narration and multiplicity of textual realities in *The Stone Diaries* could be said to enact our lack of peace and our concomitant struggle for it; these techniques locate otherwise abstract 'metaphors of loss, rejection, abandonment' in a particular time and place, dramatized by concrete situations: an unfulfilling marriage, a lifelong mourning of one's lost mother, a fun job as garden columnist hijacked by a greedy colleague. Once postmodern angst is unveiled in this way to reveal the flesh and blood details of a person's life, it becomes manageable, changeable, and the individual once again has access to agency in the pursuit of her own joy and vision.

In the previous essay, Chiara Briganti touches on my interpretive claim that the limestone tower Cuyler builds is a narrative of proliferating possibilities with a gentle reminder: 'one cannot ignore that before the end of the novel the tower is reduced to rubble' (194). With the World Trade Center in mind, I want to distinguish the power to act on one's world from the power that would thwart such action. That the tower in *The Stone Diaries* disintegrates is no reason to see it as a failed monument. We learn that not only do the natural forces of erosion – wind, water, time – wear away at the limestone's engraved surface and solidity; people, too, have their hand in pulling the piece of art apart. Teenagers and tourists pocket the monument rock by hand-carved rock. The tower doesn't actually disintegrate; rather, it is dismantled. This assigning of responsibility is part of the embodied postmodernism enacted in the novel, an insistence on connecting act and actor, hand and will. With the meaningless abyss on one side and the press of overdetermined social scripts (as wife and mother) on the other, Daisy, likewise, does not simply fall apart. Pulled in many directions, she inhabits the necessary roles even as she chooses her own name, story, history. In this transformative resistance, *The Stone Diaries*, in all its partiality and glorious indecision, suggests that women have the capacity to narrate ourselves into a particular way of being in the world, absorbing our surroundings through touch, taste, and personal testimony, then enlarging on the available materials.

Notes

1 Harvey De Roo, 'A Little like Flying: An Interview with Carol Shields,' *West Coast Review* 23.3 (Winter 1988): 41.
2 Carol Shields, *The Stone Diaries* (New York: Penguin, 1995), 23. All further quotations will be from this edition.
3 Marilyn Edelstein, 'Resisting Postmodernism; or, "A Postmodernism of Resistance": bell hooks and the Theory Debates,' in *Other Sisterhoods: Literary Theory and U.S. Women of Color*, ed. Sandra Kumamoto Stanley (Athens: U of Georgia P, 1998), 106.
4 Patricia Waugh, 'Stalemates? Feminists, Postmodernists and Unfinished Issues in Modern Aesthetics,' in *The Politics of Pleasure: Aesthetics and Cultural Theory*, ed. Stephan Regan (Buckingham: Open U, 1992), 178, 191.
5 Edelstein, 102.

6 Edelstein, 106.
7 'On Self-Recovery,' in *Talking Back: Thinking Feminist, Thinking Black* (Boston: South End P, 1989), 28.
8 Edelstein, 103.
9 Eleanor Wachtel, 'Interview with Carol Shields,' *Room of One's Own: The Carol Shields Issue* 13.1/2 (1989): 48.
10 Paula Geyh and her co-editors of *Postmodern American Fiction* (New York: Norton, 1998) differentiate between first- and second-generation postmodernism and affirm a more carefully deployed connection between aesthetics and politics (xix). The second generation includes such authors as Toni Morrison, Isabel Allende, and Jeanette Winterson, to name only a few. José David Saldívar makes a similar distinction between phases of postmodernism; his delineation of a 'fourth phase or "crack"' corresponds with Geyh's second-generation postmodernists ('Postmodern Realism,' in *The Columbia History of the American Novel*, ed. Cathy N. Davidson et al. [New York: Columbia UP, 1991], 524). In this article, I am using 'embodied,' 'resistant,' and 'feminist' as interchangeable qualifiers to signify the politicized postmodernism central to my reading of this novel.
11 Patricia Joan Morgan, 'Transgressive Play: Narrative Strategies in the Novels and Short Stories of Carol Shields' (Ph.D. diss., York University, Toronto, 1997), 223–4.
12 The concept of narrative rupture as an interpretive framework for *The Stone Diaries* comes from an article by Simone Vauthier: 'Ruptures in Carol Shields's *The Stone Diaries*,' *Anglophonia: French Journal of English Studies* 1 (1997): 177–92. While Morgan does not set her position up as antithetical to Vauthier's, I see their work as representative of the two directions – glass half-empty, glass half-full – Shields criticism explores.
13 Clara Thomas, 'Reassembling Fragments: Susanna Moodie, Carol Shields, and Mary Swann,' in *Inside the Poem: Essays and Poems in Honour of Donald Stephens*, ed. W.H. New (Toronto: Oxford UP, 1992), 198.
14 For more on the concept of narrative mazes, see Dee Goertz's article on *Larry's Party* in this volume.

15 Lori Chamberlain, 'Magicking the Real: Paradoxes of Postmodern Writing,' in *Postmodern Fiction: A Bio-Bibliographic Guide*, ed. Larry McCaffrey (New York: Greenwood, 1986), 11.

16 Chiara Briganti, in her essay in this collection, addresses the feminist uses of the body in autobiography, writing, "what is genuinely postmodern in this autobiography is the reclaiming of the maternal body' (185). Her discussion of Shields's 'erotic apprehension of language' as a form of *écriture feminine* relates as well to my concept of tactile aesthetics, which I take to be a feminist postmodern strategy of representation. Also in this volume, Wendy Roy's treatment of the autobiographical body, via Sidonie Smith, resonates with the point I am making here; I second her motion that 'Daisy Goodwill's fictional autobiography helps to take back and honour the repressed female body' (131).

17 I am not alone in interpreting contemporary women's literature in English in the context of French feminism; Paulina Palmer has applied the work of Luce Irigaray to Margaret Atwood, Angela Carter, and Jeanette Winterson, and her article (see note 27 below) certainly underlies my own association of *The Stone Diaries* with continental feminism. Indeed, the tactile quality of Shields's novel can be seen to represent an Americanized version of 'writing the body.' This thread of my argument comes partly from reading Nicole Markotic's essay 'Freedom's Just Another Word / for Nothin' Left to Lose / Desire Constructing Desire Constructing in Gail Scott's *Heroine*,' *Tessera* 16 (1994): 84–96. She could be speaking of Daisy Goodwill when she writes, 'Dreaming herself up as heroine, the narrator slips through the cracks of plot to reclaim her sense of language as poetry, to declare herself a writer of her own text, to give herself permission to follow wherever the poetics of narration meander' (87). My reading of the rocks and raspberries through which Shields persistently binds language to the *real* (that which we take in through the senses) shores up more evidence for Markotic's claim: 'The feminine aesthetic, then, demands the sensual and the erotic to metamorphose "women" as signifier into "woman" as signified' (94).

18 Here my reading differs from Gordon E. Slethaug's in '"The Coded Dots of Life": Carol Shields's Diaries and Stones,' *Canadian Literature* 156 (1998): 59–81. Slethaug writes, 'On the surface, stones have a solidity that does not characterize diaries which are never "cast in stone," either figuratively or realistically, and which are always personal and provisional, often not meant for public dissemination and not necessarily standing for, or representing, public positions. But, the use of stone and diary together is deliberately ambiguous, standing in certain respects for the appearance of solidity and general continuity but only in relation to contingency and randomness' (71). I propose instead that Shields uses stones and diaries to challenge the conventional traits of both, blurring the line between what is meant to endure and what is not. Indeed, recent scholarship on women's diaries suggests that they are often written with an imagined audience in mind, and are, therefore, not necessarily as provisional or private as Slethaug indicates.

19 I learned this geological fact in a personal correspondence with Ted Eden, one of the editors of this volume, who heard Shields speak on the subject at Hanover College in Indiana in 1996.

20 Donna Haraway, 'Situated Knowledges: The Science Question in Feminism and the Privilege of Partial Perspective,' *Feminist Studies* 14.3 (1988): 575–99. All further references to this article will be made parenthetically.

21 I take this idea of Daisy 'thinking' her autobiography from Vauthier, who footnotes an interview with Shields conducted by Joan Thomas which indicates that 'Daisy is "thinking" her autobiography' (186).

22 Here I take a different tack in reading representations of social construction in this novel from previous Shields criticism. In particular, Winifred M. Mellor's analysis replicates Foucault's inescapable structure of power; she asserts, 'The manipulation of narrative technique in the text draws attention to the way women are silenced by the restrictive imposition of the modes of certain genres' ('"The Simple Container of Our Existence": Narrative Ambiguity in Carol Shields's *The Stone Diaries*,' *Studies in Canadian Literature* 20.2 [1995]: 97). While I do not

completely disagree with her point, I wish to move the focus from the paralysing power structure to women's resistances. Thus I emphasize the transformative power of women's imagination, represented in part by Shields's narrative technique and genre-blending, as a positive and resistant response to the social conditions that would silence women.

23 On this point, I am indebted to Bonnie Zimmerman's discussion of feminist fiction and postmodernism, in particular, her reformation of 'magical or experimental realism' as 'expanded realism' – 'because it enlarges the reader's notion of what is real, and to whom' ('Feminist Fiction and the Postmodern Challenge,' in McCaffrey, ed., *Postmodern Fiction*, 181).

24 Scholars writing of another contemporary woman novelist, Marilyne Robinson, have made this point about her well-known novel *Housekeeping*, which begins with the words 'My name is Ruth.'

25 I agree with Morgan's interpretation of the passage in which Daisy narrates her own birth: 'No one knows a "true story" and Daisy has the power to shape this story without fear of contradiction or interference' (254). Daisy's 'reality' thus belongs to her alone, and she is thereby empowered as the storyteller, or author, of her own life.

26 Wachtel, 48.

27 Paulina Palmer, 'Postmodern Trends in Contemporary Fiction: Margaret Atwood, Angela Carter, Jeanette Winterson,' in *Postmodern Subjects / Postmodern Texts*, ed. Jane Dowson and Steven Earnshaw (Amsterdam: Rodopi, 1995), 182.

28 Palmer, 183.

29 Zimmerman, 177–8.

30 Morgan, 274.

31 Edelstein, 106.

32 Patrocinio Schweickart, 'Reading Ourselves: Toward a Feminist Theory of Reading,' in *Feminisms: An Anthology of Literary Theory and Criticism*, ed. Robin Warhol and Diane Price Herndl (New Brunswick, NJ: Rutgers UP, 1997), 609.

33 Slethaug, 70.

34 This move to foreground readerly agency mirrors ground-

breaking work in the field of cultural studies, where critics have argued for the political force of pleasure and the ability of 'marginal' audiences to cultivate this pleasure within otherwise oppressive mainstream texts. This critical lens has not yet been applied wholesale in the world of literary theory, but it illuminates the dynamic between reader and text in *The Stone Diaries*. For an introduction to this perspective, see the articles collected in *Feminism and Cultural Studies*, ed. Morag Shiach (London: Oxford UP, 1999), particularly Jacqueline Bobo's '*The Color Purple*: Black Women As Cultural Readers,' 275–96.

35 In her interpretation of the photograph sequence, Vauthier writes of her 'part as a reader in the construction of the meaning of *The Stone Diaries*' as she recognizes 'the extent of [her] freedom' to accept or reject various parts of the narrative as 'true' (189): 'Although it exposes and disrupts the structures which used to foster the mimetic illusion that narrative reflects reality, and although it disconnects the narrative from stable referents, *The Stone Diaries* ... engages the reader in creative interplay that still has relevance to our construction of reality and to human concerns' (191).

36 I like this image Mellor provides, but I take issue with her reading of Daisy as 'a mute hollow structure' (99). Such characterization seems to me to conspire with the forces in the novel that work against Daisy's selfhood.

37 Wachtel, 48.

38 Morgan, 238, 242.

39 Wachtel, 44.

40 Edelstein, 106.

41 Wachtel, 24.

42 Shields, quoted in Wachtel, 48.

Treading the Maze of *Larry's Party*

DEE GOERTZ

'Who was it said that symbols are the fleas of literature?'

CAROL SHIELDS[1]

Near the end of *Larry's Party*, characteristically out of chronological order, we read a Dear John letter sent to Larry by his soon-to-be ex-wife, 'bossy, pedagogical Beth.'[2] She slathers her rejection of Larry with the kind of flowery figure of speech that gives literary language a bad name:

> Darling Larry,
> All this will be easier for you if you think of life as a book each of us must write alone, and how, within that book there are many chapters ... Your spiritual signature, sweet Larry, has illuminated mine, and I like to think that our combined epigraph has sent shooting stars, sexually as well as intellectually, across the synapse of our stitched together leaves ... (296)

Larry gets out his figurative red pen and gives this literary attempt a 'C-minus. And that was being generous' (297). We are not surprised, having already flunked the letter not only for bad writing but also for pompousness. Shields invites us to laugh at Beth's ham-handed use of this extended metaphor; Beth is clearly more interested in hearing her own voice than in comforting Larry. She uses figurative language simply to dress up a kiss-off, to give her motives the appearance of depth and nobility. The laughableness of this letter makes it clear that Shields herself is quite aware of the dangers of overusing a figure of speech to impose meaning, yet some reviewers have mistaken Shields's use of the maze in this novel as the same kind of unreflecting rhetoric that Beth indulges in.[3] Possibly the sheer abundance of maze references in this novel annoys some; the maze functions not only as a symbol in the novel, but also as image, metaphor, and structural device. Yet Shields uses the maze in a complex and self-reflexive way. As a postmodernist, she uses literary figures ironically, even self-mockingly. Her maze symbolism in *Larry's Party* exposes its own arbitrariness and, by extension, the arbitrariness and limitations of language itself.

However, as Lisa Johnson has argued in this volume, Shields is a second-generation postmodernist, one who allows for agency and presence. Ultimately, the maze as a symbol does convey a meaning; it underscores the main theme of the novel – that the human quest for meaning and pattern in the universe is a quest for connectedness. To find meaning, people must push beyond symbols and reach out to each other. Rereading Beth's letter, then, we notice a second mistake: she characterizes life and book writing as solitary pursuits, whereas everything about *Larry's Party* insists on the necessity of human connection, in the writing and reading of books as well as in life. All of the characteristics of the novel that Shields lists in 'Narrative Hunger and the Overflowing Cupboard' point to the novel's ability to connect to its readers and help them connect to others.[4]

One of her earliest works, *The Box Garden*, shows that Shields was thinking about the issue of symbolism and its viability in the postmodern era even at the beginning of her career. Her poet-narrator, Charleen Forrest, reviles symbolism as a 'grandiose cheat' and an 'impertinence.'[5] But who would blame her, after she has been abandoned by an increasingly mad husband who is 'very big on symbols' (94)? Yet Shields has placed her in a novel whose title includes the word 'garden' and whose first named character is 'Brother Adam,' a juxtaposition that any alert reader with a Judeo-Christian background would notice. Charleen herself, though claiming to 'resist' the 'compulsion,' the 'affliction,' of seeing the world in symbolic terms (37), cannot avoid interpreting the box garden she receives mysteriously in the mail from Brother Adam along symbolic lines: 'they might be supernatural, seeds sprouted from a fairy tale, empowered with magic properties ... their failure to germinate would spell betrayal or, worse, it would summarize my fatal inability to sustain any sort of action' (85). (Note that she uses the word 'summarize' here to avoid saying 'symbolize.') Shields relentlessly thrusts symbols before us even as her narrator rails against being so naïve and 'hopelessly, cheerlessly optimistic' (37) as to accept them.

Like Charleen, Shields herself is ambivalent toward symbolism and handles it with irony. When an interviewer praised *The Stone Diaries* by remarking, 'You do wonderful things with stones and flowers,' Shields replied:

> Actually I worried about this. Who was it said that symbols are the fleas of literature? I hate imposed symbolism. So what I tried to do when I realized there was a double spine to the book, the stones and the flowers, was to exchange the weight of them as often as I could, to create some disorder in that there wasn't *male: stone* and *female: flower* working against each other.[6]

Critics have noticed this fluidity of symbolic meaning in *The Stone Diaries*: Gordon Slethaug points out, for example, that stones are associated with both stability and impermanence.[7] Leona Gom discusses in her brief but perceptive essay 'Stones and Flowers' the multiple meanings of these symbols in human culture, as well as in *The Stone Diaries*: 'Christians put flowers on graves. Jews put stones. Stones or flowers: it doesn't matter. We give them our own meanings.'[8] Moreover, Shields sometimes treats symbolism satirically. Faye Hammill asserts that Charleen's dismissal of symbolism is part of Shields's satire on the Canadian myth of identity: in *The Box Garden*, 'the "manufacture" of myth in Canada is presented as a narcissistic and faintly ludicrous process.'[9] Hammill also quotes Leon Surette on the awkwardness of creating myth in the realistic novel: 'An interesting twist to the formation of the Canadian canon in fiction is a consequence of the unsuitability of the bourgeois realistic novel to the task of forging an indigenous culture. Symbolic, allegorical, and mythopoeic or romance forms of prose fiction are much more suitable to the task.'[10] Shields, her characters, and her critics alike are unsure of the value or appropriateness of symbolism in contemporary realistic fiction. When asked about symbols in *The Box Garden* at a college lecture, Shields laughed and said, 'I just stuck those in at the end.'[11]

On the one hand, then, Shields insists on the arbitrariness of symbols and keeps the fleas jumping. It's important to remember, though, Shields's comment on meaning in postmodern fiction: 'Some postmodernists think there is no point beyond the language game, but I think there can be.'[12] Clearly, our treading of Larry's blind maze of a life in *Larry's Party* does not leave us despairing of the meaningless of existence. As Briganti, Johnson, and Barbour argue in this section of this volume, Shields invites us to reach beyond the limitations of language, not to wallow in despair, by forming human bonds and experiencing fully this human life. Moreover, Shields seeks in her writing 'those ... transcendental moments when you suddenly feel everything makes sense and you perceive the pattern in the universe ... I'm very interested in looking for those and recording them and finding language to record them.'[13] Through her extensive use of the maze in this novel, Shields dramatizes the search for the transcendental moment that reveals the pattern in the universe. Simone Vauthier's praise of *Various Miracles* in this context applies equally well to *Larry's Party*: 'it wonderfully restores trust in a life which is less determined and less chaotic than may appear, where improvization therefore has a place, and it restores faith in language, too, since it allows us to talk, however obliquely, of mystery.'[14]

What Shields is interested in is the human need to seek our place in the universe through symbols, even as our postmodern epistemology would deny that they have any meaning. In *Larry's Party*, Shields uses maze symbolism both ironically and sincerely on two overlapping levels: as a game that the reader and author play together, and as a quest for meaning that the characters engage in. On the first level, Shields entices the reader to enact the search for meaning through symbolism by salting the narrative with verbal and visual images of the maze, an image that human beings have invested with symbolic meaning for thousands of years.[15] The reader is lured into seeking patterns and deeper meanings that may or may not be in the text. Beyond the overt references to mazes, the reader senses that Shields also uses the maze as a narrative structure to show that the author's quest to tell the story is another quest for meaning, itself an exercise in symbol making. The complex path of the story line, maze-like in its dead ends and doublings back, illustrates the author's search for pattern and meaning. On the second level, the characters, particularly Larry, actively and consciously interpret the symbolism of the maze. Larry's growing preoccupation with mazes sparks his intellectual and spiritual growth, and his search inspires his friends, wives, and clients to seek meaning in the intricate gardens he designs. By the end, Larry recognizes that the goal in his life maze is his relationship with his first wife and son, but that to reach the goal he has had to abandon himself wilfully to uncertainty and ignorance – the blind turnings of the maze.

On both levels, the maze becomes a symbol not only for Larry's life journey but also for memory as it doubles back to previous experience like a unicursal maze.[16] Memory does not repeat experience but traces a parallel path in order to find meaning in experience. The writing process, with its endless revisions, follows a labyrinthine path in quest of the perfect expression of its subject. However, this novel leaves the quest for meaning open-ended. Readers cannot be sure whether the patterns they find in the novel are accidental or designed, meaningful or frivolous: the characters' search is undermined by the narrator's irony; and the author's looping back and restarting the narrative time and again suggests that there is no one truth. Linda Hutcheon's description of the postmodern enterprise applies to Shields's use of the maze in *Larry's Party*: 'It is not that truth and reference have ceased to exist ... ; it is that they have ceased to be unproblematic issues.'[17] Shields uses the maze both ironically, as a symbol that exposes its own limitations, and sincerely, as a symbol that may convey a useful meaning – whether arbitrary or not. Alan Wilde's concept of 'generative irony,' which creates 'tentatively and provisionally, anironic enclaves of value in the face of – but not in place of – a meaningless universe,'[18] helps describe Shields's approach to symbolism in this novel.

Larry's Party As Flea Circus

The game begins with the epigraph of the novel. It is excerpted from a poem (quoted fully in W.H. Matthews's *Mazes and Labyrinths*, one of Shields's chief sources of maze lore) about the maze at Hampton Court, the location of Larry's transformative experience with mazes: 'What is this mighty labyrinth – the earth, / But a wild maze the moment of our birth?'[19] This seems at first no more than a straightforward announcement that the image of the maze is going to be used as a metaphor for life in the novel. But Matthews's commentary on this poem suggests that Shields may be using it satirically. Matthews wryly points out that this somewhat gloomy philosophizing supports the criticism that the English cannot enjoy their pleasures straight.[20] After all, the maze at Hampton Court, like most post-Renaissance mazes, was designed primarily as a diversion. The subtext of the epigraph, then, is the tension between frivolity and seriousness, play and meaningfulness, game and life – a tension that runs through the novel, especially in its handling of the maze motif.

The game continues as the title page of each chapter keeps the idea of the maze constantly in the readers' minds with reproductions of maze designs from one of two books – Matthews's book, mentioned above, and Aidan Meehan's *Celtic Design Maze Patterns*.[21] The placement of these maze designs encourages the reader to think of them as illustrations, as sources of illumination for the chapters that follow. As such, they resemble Ashley's knot illustrations at the beginning of each chapter in Annie Proulx's *The Shipping News*.[22] The mazes of *Larry's Party* also have an effect similar to that of the photographs in *The Stone Diaries*; they suggest a link between the real world and the text, a link that might not actually exist when one compares 'illustration' and text, as a number of critics have noted, including Briganti and Johnson in this volume. For interested readers, Shields has made it relatively easy to find the source of the designs: she mentions the title of the Matthews book in the text as one of the books that Larry has read (81), and the Meehan book is credited on the copyright page, though Shields slips in a red herring in the text in the form of a slightly altered version of the title, *Celtic Mazes and Labyrinths*, a book that Dorrie gives to Larry (91).

But once the reader tracks down the source of the designs (see the Appendix for identifications), their significance is not self-evident in most cases. The first thing one looks for is some sort of overall pattern or link among the designs, but one finds more differences than similarities. The only commonality seems to be that they are all line drawings that are easily reproduced. These designs fall into both categories of mazes: unicursal and multicursal. They come in a variety of shapes: circle, square, rectangle, trapezoid, hexagon, and even more complex shapes. In age they date from c. 2000 B.C.E. to the 1980s, though they are all from the European tradition. Most are designs on paper, only, not diagrams of actual hedge mazes, as the reader might first expect, though there are drawings of two pavement labyrinths found in churches, a labyrinth made out of stones that form a path, and the maze at Hampton Court. This last, of course, plays a major role not only in the chapter illustrated by that design, but also in the novel as a whole. This is the only maze design illustrated that actually figures significantly in the plot.

The value of the other designs as illustrations of the text is dubious. At most, the other designs appear as brief allusions, and then only in five cases. In chapter 11, 'Larry's Search for the Wonderful and the Good, 1992,' Larry visits the pavement labyrinth in Chartres Cathedral, which is pictured at the beginning of that chapter. Near the end of that chapter, the narrator reports that 'the richly enigmatic Scandinavian mazes lay ahead of them; Finland alone had over a hundred stone-lined labyrinths' (226). One of these latter is used as an illustration, but not until the last chapter, where it doesn't seem to fit. The other three cases have either humorous or ironic connections to the text. In 'Larry Inc., 1988,' which is dated five years after Dorrie has bulldozed Larry's home-grown maze, we learn that Larry has lifted the design for that maze from a design by Serlio in a book he got from the library. And, indeed, 'Larry's Words,' where we get our first glimpse of Larry's maze, is illustrated by a design by Serlio. However, the description given of Larry's multicursal maze on page 148 does not match Serlio's unicursal design reproduced on page 79. What seems like a clue is really a red herring. In 'Larry So Far,' we learn that Ryan has given Larry a tie for his birthday 'which Larry knows has been selected, paid for, wrapped and mailed by his ex, Dorrie,' and which has a pattern 'based on the ancient Shandwick maze' (172). The next chapter, 'Larry's Kid,' is fronted by a design identified in Meehan as a 'Shandwick panel,' but the link between the illustration and the text is muddled both by the distance between the allusion and the illustration and by the fact that Dorrie picked out the tie, not Ryan. One last correspondence is based on a pun. Twice in 'Larry's Threads,' the word 'thread' is used, not as an outdated metonym for clothes, but as an actual thread used by someone to find his way. This chapter is fronted by a crude petroglyph identified as a 'Cretan style maze' by Meehan, which brings to mind the myth of Theseus who solved the

Cretan maze aided by a thread given him by Ariadne.[23] The reader hoping to find significance in the designs chosen to illustrate the chapters runs into dead ends or jokes. If the maze designs have meaning individually or as a group, it does not seem to be as illustrations of the text, except in the most general way.[24] The gaps between the maze designs and the content of the chapters they illustrate resemble what Simone Vauthier calls 'ruptures' in *The Stone Diaries*.[25]

The design that is given the most prominence in the book is the one at the beginning of 'Larry's Living Tissues, 1996'; it's not only a chapter header, it is also embossed in two places on the hardcover edition. The design is credited to Aidan Meehan, who calls it 'Maze from Figure with Serpent through Waist.' Meehan derives this Cretan-style maze from an ancient petroglyph, 'Horned figure with snake passing through its waist,' which is pictured in its original form at the beginning of 'Larry Inc., 1988.' Why is this particular design chosen to be placed twice on the cover, once under Carol Shields's initials? Perhaps she chose it because it's so organic looking, a bit like a brain, a good choice for a chapter about living tissues and especially one about a coma. Or perhaps it is because of the significance attached to it by Meehan. He uses it to illustrate a link between ancient Alpine mazes and the maze design found on Cretan coins purporting to be the famous labyrinth at Knossos designed by Daedalus. One of these is pictured at the beginning of 'Larry's Penis, 1986.' Shields's choice of Meehan's contemporary distillation of those mazes re-emphasizes the continuity of human culture over four thousand years. This design is the most generic of all unicursal mazes. Its relation to the standard representation of the ur-maze in Western culture, Daedalus's maze in Crete, again suggests the connectedness of human beings over time and space. However, this is all speculation. Except for the connection between the Hampton Court maze design and the chapter in which Larry has his first significant experience with the Hampton Court maze, all of the connections between maze designs and text are tenuous, possibly signifying a great deal and possibly merely teasing the reader.

In addition to the images of and references to mazes, Shields has structured the book like a maze on the level of plot, as the last line of the text, an excerpt from a nineteenth-century poem, suggests. Larry falls in love with Dorrie in chapter 1, gets divorced, marries Beth, gets divorced again, and reunites with Dorrie in the final chapter: as the last line of the text reads, 'and where you start from, there you end.'[26] The novel begins with Larry rushing to meet Dorrie and realizing he is in love with her. But he recognizes that this love, which is legalized in the next chapter, is 'deficient': 'he kept finding it and losing it again. And now, here in this garden maze, getting lost, and then found, seemed the whole point, that and the moment of willed abandonment, the unexpected rapture of being blindly led' (35–6). Shields mirrors Larry's on-again, off-again love for Dorrie in the action of exploring a maze, heightening by the juxtaposition the quality of 'willed abandonment' in love.

Dorrie and their son Ryan represent the centre of Larry's maze, the goal, the reward for having submitted to the contrived confusion. Larry creates this symbol but doesn't recognize its significance, though the reader senses it. He has built a hedge maze surrounding the home that he and Dorrie and Ryan live in, with the path ending at the side door. Significantly, the planned fountain at the end of the path is never installed; it is home itself that is the goal. Years later, Larry remembers walking through the maze with toddler Ryan and wonders why he didn't recognize the happiness of that moment (148).

At that point in his life, mazes separate Larry from the two human beings he cares about most: his wife and son. The build-up to the darkest moment in the novel makes clear that this is Larry's mistake. All through the chapter 'Larry's Words,' as Larry's intellect blooms, and he sees his maze from the god-like perspective of his neighbour's window, he is aware of, but avoids dealing with, his wife's growing bitterness over his 'maze craze': 'He loves the Latin roll of the words in his mouth – *Leguminosae* – and he loves himself for being a man capable of remembering these rare words, for being alert, for paying attention, particularly since he has not always in his life paid sufficient attention' (93). As the passage suggests, Larry has a kind of latent knowledge that he might be headed down the wrong path, that his focus on mazes and words might not be the only path to his life's goal: 'It strikes Larry that language may not have evolved to the point where it represents the world fully' (95). And, indeed, the sight of the 'ruin of his front yard' (96) after Dorrie had his maze backhoed almost obliterates Larry's intellectual advances: 'Larry himself, stunned, battered, and opening his mouth at last, giving way not to speech, but to language's smashed, broken syllables and attenuated vowel sounds: the piercing cries and howls of a man injured beyond words' (97). This is the point of greatest emotional intensity in the novel, and it conveys Shields's theme that symbols can take us only so far. Playing the maze game, as author and reader have been doing along with Larry, may divert and even challenge, but ultimately does not satisfy as an end in itself.

As this example shows, the plot of *Larry's Party* doubles back upon itself like a maze; Larry and the reader must move away from the centre of the maze in order to find it. But on the level of the narrative itself, the threads of the telling loop back on themselves so that we return to the same topics over and over again. In some cases, Shields introduces the topic as if we had never heard of it before and fills in crucial details that we would have expected to have been given the first time. Dorrie, Beth, and Charlotte are introduced each time they appear in the novel as if for the first time.

But a more significant example of this doubling back of the narrative is Larry's first maze. Shields mentions it first on page 71, and we are given a certain number of details about it – how big the lot is, how Larry got interested in mazes (which itself is a looping back to his tour of the Hampton Court maze first described on page 34), how he has protected the young hedges for the winter. We get another glimpse of it in the next chapter when Larry looks at it through Lucy Warkenten's window (86). The maze is backhoed on page 97, and we expect that will be the last of it, except for brief allusions. However, on page 147, we are reintroduced to 'his first maze, which was a crude experiment in his own backyard in Winnipeg.' But this time, Shields gives us a wealth of details that were omitted the first time around, for example, the type of shrubs used, the design he borrowed for it, the inadequate 'second-hand gasoline-powered hedge-trimmer' he used to shape it (148). The most important detail is the image of father and son together: 'Ryan, already bathed for the night and in his pyjamas, toddled by Larry's side, running his free hand across the top of the growing hedges, singing as he went and learning by heart, even at the age of three or four, the secrets of the various turnings' (148).

The continual return to Larry's first maze is typical of Shields's technique in this novel, and this kind of technical experiment is one of the reasons she is such a provocative writer. She gently shakes our sense of what it is to read a novel; she plays the postmodern game of never letting us forget that we are reading. At times this novel reads like a series of short stories. She challenges the convention that the reader readily remembers all of the previous details, because, after all, the reader doesn't. The looping back to the past mimics the author's process of writing and revising; it also reinforces the sense that a life is not lived linearly. In the example of Larry's first maze, this point becomes very important. If Larry had fully recognized the goodness of what he had, he might have been able to better communicate it to Dorrie and might not have had to go through the trauma of divorce and separation from his child. But, as the narrator points out, 'it may be that Larry has romanticized this particular memory' (148). After all, Dorrie was barely speaking to him at this point in their marriage. It was a moment of pure happiness only in retrospect, not that this kind of happiness is any less important or real for that. Shields's technique shows us that memory does not allow us to lead our lives in straight lines: the past circles back to us. We constantly reinterpret it and adjust our forward courses. So, in addition to foregrounding the act of reading, the maze-like narrative line reinforces the overtly stated theme: the maze is 'not unlike this life we spend, / And where you start from, there you end' (339).

'Only (Dis)connect': The Characters' Quest for Meaning

While the overt symbolism and maze-like structure of the novel tend to foreground the arbitrariness of symbols, the outcome of Larry's quest suggests that it is possible to find meaning. Since readers identify with the protagonist, they share in Larry's search for meaning established in the first chapter. Although the image of the maze is not used overtly until the second chapter, alert readers, who have already been primed to look for mazes by the epigraph of the novel and the design on the title page of the first chapter, will recognize its related theme in the interplay between accident and design established in chapter 1. Mazes illustrate this duality perfectly because, as Penelope Doob explains, 'they presume a double perspective: maze-treaders, whose vision ahead and behind is severely constricted and fragmented, suffer confusion, whereas maze-viewers who see the pattern whole, from above or in a diagram, are dazzled by its complex artistry. What you see depends on where you stand.'[27] In the first chapter, Larry ponders the relationship between accident and design, and wonders whether one or the other governs his life. The chapter ends with an image of Larry joyously walking into the unknown, yet much of the chapter emphasizes his admiration for design. The novel as a whole also promotes this dual attitude – embracing chance and simultaneously seeking and promoting design – as the sanest and most productive way to confront one's life. In the quest for connection, one will some-times have to settle for disconnection. Paradoxically, the interplay of accident and design that mazes convey suggests that seekers must accept that they might be imposing meaning on empty symbols.

'By mistake Larry Weller took someone else's Harris tweed jacket instead of his own, and it wasn't till he jammed his hand in the pocket that he knew something was wrong' (3). This sentence, the first in the novel, juxtaposes the idea of a mistake with the idea of exquisite design embodied in the Harris tweed jacket. Larry deeply appreciates its fine craft, as he explores the 'texture, the seams,' 'the tweedy warp and woof' (3) of this higher-class version of his own 'classic' (6). In focusing on the weave of the jacket, Shields subtly reminds the reader of the design and interweaving of the text in our hands, the word 'text' sharing the same root as 'texture.' The words 'accident' and 'design' coming together in a sentence a few pages later underscore that this duality governs Larry's life: 'It was an accident how Larry got into floral design' (7). Even a small detail and its metaphoric elaboration juxtapose accident and design: Shields devotes a whole paragraph to Larry's precise application of cinnamon to the foam on his cappuccino, which he absurdly compares in his mind to a recent dust storm in Winnipeg that 'coated every ledge and leaf and petunia petal with this beautiful, evenly distributed layer of powdery dust' (9). Meticulous design on the human scale is likened to natural accident on a grand scale.

The occurrences of the word 'mistake' accumulate near the end of the chapter, with Larry and Dorrie's accidental meeting, his anxiety over the 'mistake' of taking the wrong jacket, and the 'mistake' of a patient Larry once met who had no arms and legs. Larry's solution to grabbing the wrong jacket is to make another mistake by throwing it in the garbage, since he can't seem to puzzle through a more ethically and socially apt solution. However, this 'mistake' strongly promotes the idea of embracing chance. Shields gives us the first glimpse of a maze in the text proper through her description of Larry's world-view:

> A mistake that led to another mistake that led to another. People made mistakes all the time, so many mistakes that they aren't mistakes anymore, they're just positive and negative charges shooting back and forth and moving you along. Like good luck and bad luck. Like a tunnel you're walking through, with all your pores wide open. When it turns, you turn too. (12)

The turning tunnel is a unicursal maze – a complex path where the only choices demanded (or allowed) are those of beginning and continuing the journey.

The end of the chapter affirms the value of making this journey 'with all your pores wide open.' Even though Larry has just thrown away someone else's expensive jacket when he could have simply called the coffee shop and explained, he accepts his compounding of mistakes and suddenly becomes more alert, more alive, with the wind puffing up his sleeves like Superman and deflating him in the next second. It's not the choices that matter in this situation so much as Larry's awareness of the journey. The last glimpse we have of Larry is 'walking straight toward the next thing that was going to happen to him' (13). Shields highlights this image, placing it as she does at the end of this introductory chapter and alluding to it twice much later in the novel. Larry, as well as the reader, ruminates on the significance of this moment. He recalls it twenty years later, a moment of 'inviting the rest of his life to come at him, to take him in its embrace' (260). Still later Larry gives this moment even more positive value. Soon after Larry realizes that he still loves Dorrie, and that she still loves him, he remembers the moment as prophesying good luck:

> Walking alone on a Winnipeg street, twenty-six years old, he'd seen, perhaps for the first time, the kind of man he could be. He'd felt the force of the wind, and impulsively he'd whipped off his tweed jacket, offering himself up to the moment he'd just discovered, letting it sweep him forward on its beguiling currents. Love was waiting for him. Transformation. Goodness. Work. Understanding ... And children, too, if he were lucky, but

he was going to be lucky, that question was no longer in doubt. The wind that blew against his exposed body informed him of his good fortune. All he had to do was stand still and allow it to happen. (331)

Comparing this memory to the initial experience exposes all sorts of interesting discrepancies; his memory has reshaped the moment, warped it into the embracing of a conscious course of action which Larry did not know at the time that he was taking. Depending on one's perspective, a life's journey is either a continual blind groping or a series of fated turnings – just as is the journey through a maze.

Thus, at the beginning of the novel, Larry is primed for his life's journey through mazes, but his real intellectual development as a symbol reader begins with his honeymoon visit to the maze at Hampton Court, which he retrospectively views through the maze of memory as a 'transformative' experience (217). He comes home and builds his own maze and thereby begins a successful career, but also, ironically, begins to end the honeymoon. As a maze-maker, Larry joins other Shields characters as a creator: in vocation or avocation, her characters include poets, gardeners, a biographer, a quilt maker, and a stone sculptor. Larry not only does creative work himself but appreciates it in all its forms: his father's custom upholstering, his neighbour's bookbinding, and his co-worker's husband's clock repair. Shields's long-held respect for the inherent value of work comes through strongly here, as Hammill has discussed elsewhere in this volume. More importantly for my purposes, Shields shows work as a way to create order and pattern in the world: to create meaning. Even Larry's first career, begun accidentally, gives him the satisfaction of creating order and finding himself part of a larger pattern: his work with flowers makes him feel 'plugged into the planet. He's part of the action, part of the world's work, a cog in the great turning wheel of desire and intention' (77).

Larry's experience in Hampton Court, however, accelerates his intellectual growth, his interest in pondering the big questions of life. What he learns from the maze is to seek the still moment of clarity between the 'departures and arrivals' of his life (37). He revels in the 'willed abandonment,' the 'surrender ... to the maze's cunning, this closed, expensive contrivance ... Someone older than himself paced inside his body, someone stronger too ... Looking back he would remember a brief moment when time felt mute and motionless' (36). As in the first chapter, Larry surrenders to the pull of the journey, but here he also feels the connection to humanity that he felt as a florist. Trusting that there is a pattern to the maze, though as the maze walker he cannot initially see it, he gains a strength not entirely his own. By engaging in the human quest for meaning, whether or not that meaning is constructed by the quester or exists independently, Larry finds his connection to the universe, though to do so, he must paradoxically both seek design and embrace chance.

Ironically, as Larry grows intellectually, as he gets more involved in what a later chapter calls the 'Search for the Wonderful and Good,' he loses his connection to the people who are most important in his life. As Larry discovers his life's interest and vocation in the Hampton Court maze, Dorrie begins to turn away from him. Likewise, when he wins a Guggenheim Fellowship to research mazes around the world, Beth pulls away from him. Shields shows that his over-reliance on symbols as a source of meaning diverts him from the real source of meaning – human relationships. Larry's failure is an old irony, handed down from the Daedalus myth, that first maze-maker, the inventor of the labyrinth. Daedalus's skills never reward him in his personal life. His invention of the labyrinth leads to his imprisonment with his son, Icarus. His brilliant invention of wings to save himself and his son leads to Icarus's death. Although Larry never consciously identifies himself with this myth, Shields drops a jokey hint that there may be a connection. Larry's love of mazes separates him from his son, as Daedalus ultimately loses his son. Like Icarus, Larry's son soars for a time as a track star nicknamed 'Flyin' Ryan,' only to be cast down as 'Lyin' Ryan' when he is discovered to be taking steroids. But to what extent is Shields identifying Larry with Daedalus? Is she duplicating a Joycean transubstantiation of Ulysses into Bloom, of Daedalus into Larry – enacting the myth of the eternal return?[28] Her slight and light-hearted connections between the two suggest only an ironic identification, yet throughout the novel, she shows in different ways that human beings are connected to each other through time and space.

Larry's and his friends' ruminations about mazes intensify in the final chapter – the party of *Larry's Party* – which dramatizes the human need for connectedness while it foregrounds the motif of the maze. Not only is the content of this chapter largely about mazes, but the organizing structure, the party, is also treated as a type of maze that lacks only the spatial element. Shields hints at the similarity between parties and mazes by including handwritten notes and drawings in the chapter. In one way, these illustrations function similarly to the photograph on the frontispiece (as well as the numerous photos in *The Stone Diaries*): they enhance the novel's verisimilitude. More importantly, the visual association between the illustrations in the party chapter and the maze designs creates a link between mazes and parties. Moreover, in form the party is depicted much like a maze. Charlotte, with Larry's passive assent, obsesses over plans to keep some measure of control over the action of the party, hence her drawing up of a menu, a map to Larry's house, and a seating chart – in other words, she designs the party as a maze-maker would design a maze. However, mazes and parties (and books, for that matter) are collaborative projects between the maker and the participants; at one point, Larry quotes someone as having said that 'mazes are machines with people as moving parts' (218). So, in a maze, or a book, or a party, once a participant gets involved, there's no predicting what will happen. As soon as a very pregnant Beth arrives at his doorstep, Larry, like Daedalus, is thrown clueless into his own maze: 'Just five minutes into his party and he was already lost' (306).

As the conversation meanders, personalities clash and connections dissolve and reform. No one knows what will happen next, neither character nor reader. The lack of attribution to lines of dialogue in this chapter intensifies the sense of confusion in the reader, not least in the passage in which the characters discuss mazes. The conversation winds among unidentified speakers from the genesis and opening of the McCord maze, to the symbolism of mazes in general, to thumbprints and blood pressure, and by the end of three pages of this, we see underneath the explicit subject the renewed feeling between Dorrie and Larry and the budding romance between Samuel and Charlotte. The conversation is full of wrong turns, blind alleys, and hidden goals. In the middle of it, though, the characters become symbol-readers and articulate some of the main themes of the novel:

> 'The way we see it, at the center of the maze there's an encounter with one's self. Center demands a reversal, a new beginning, a sense of–'
> '– of rebirth. In the turns of the maze, one is isolated and then comes alive again.'
> 'Which speaks to the contemporary human torment of being alternately lost and found.'
> 'You can see that Garth's become a convert.' (313)

With the last comment, we can be reasonably sure that the speakers have been Garth and Marcia McCord, the commissioners of the maze. At this moment, they are speaking in a kind of harmonious call and response, but a few pages later, after more wine, they will bicker embarrassingly:

> 'Will you shut up, Garth, for God's sake. You don't know what you're talking about.'
> 'Lighten up, Marcia.' (321)

By the next morning, though, Garth reports, 'Marcia and I had a great time. Just great' (338). If the labyrinth is defined as a complex path (81), the conversation at the party and the human relationships it reveals certainly qualify as metaphorical labyrinths.

Likewise, the conversation about mazes leads to unexpected goals, unexpected sympathies and unions. Dorrie comments that the point of a maze is 'controlled chaos and contrived panic' (313). Someone (Larry, as the reader guesses and later confirms) says, 'That's exactly right, Dorrie. Wonderful. But how – ?' Dorrie's remark reinforces Larry's and the reader's understanding that she has changed since she bulldozed Larry's first maze fourteen years and two hundred pages earlier. Another unattributed line – 'What are you two whispering about?' (Charlotte, we guess) – signifies that, amid the swirling talk of the dinner, Larry and Dorrie have reestablished intimacy. Perhaps as a response to this, Charlotte turns toward Samuel to explain Larry's and her complicated romantic pasts, and this turning leads to another establishment of intimacy – and an after-party rendezvous between Charlotte and Samuel. The chaos and panic of human relationships has been controlled and contrived through the gentle confines and design of the party. Significantly, the last symbolic maze in the novel – the party itself – has as its acknowledged goal bringing people together.

One could complain about the contrivance of the happy ending here, reminiscent of old-fashioned Hollywood romantic comedies with happy couples lined up at the end for group weddings. But *Larry's Party* affirms the novelist's right to contrive an elaborate maze / game 'To tire the feet, perplex the mind, / Yet pleasure heart and head,' as the poem that concludes the book asserts. Moreover, the maze symbol conveys Shields's theme that symbols may be a dead end in themselves but are a useful thread. Language may not '[represent] the world fully,' as Larry discovers, any more than a maze represents life fully. ('The map is not the territory,' as Wittgenstein has shown us.) Yet language and other symbols are the ways we approach the goal: connection with others. In exploring the human need to join with others, Shields fills in one of the gaps left in contemporary fiction, which, she asserts, focuses mostly on conflict: 'The notion of conflict in fictional narrative may also need reassessment ... How well or how poorly can we connect with another human consciousness? 'Only connect,' E.M. Forster said, but did he mean in life or in literature?' ('Narrative Hunger' 33). Comically, one of the characters at Larry's party misquotes Forster as saying, 'Only disconnect' (315). And the novel affirms that, as the maze treader stumbles through, connection and disconnection alternate. At this party, though, as well as at Larry's high-school reunion earlier in the novel, the reward for submitting to the confusion of the maze is a transcendent moment of union:

> Laughter flows, and Larry, only moderately drunk, feels blessed. If only they could go on like this forever, seated at this floating table with its covering of love. Friends, friends. Isn't this what he's longed for all his life, to be in the brimming midst of friends? (117)

And so we are rewarded for submitting to the maze of *Larry's Party*. Maze, party, book – all, in Carol Shields's hands, connect us one to another over time and space.

Appendix: Identification of Maze Designs in *Larry's Party*

Each chapter number and title is followed by the identification of the maze design and its source in either W.H. Matthews, *Mazes and Labyrinths: Their History and Development* or Aidan Meehan, *Celtic Design Maze Patterns*.

1. Fifteen Minutes in the Life of Larry Weller, 1977
   [Book of] Mac Durnan, [Ireland], unit (Meehan 146)
2. Larry's Love, 1978
   Maze at Hampton Court (Matthews 129)
3. Larry's Folks, 1980
   Maze by G.A. Boeckler, 1664 (Matthews 122)

4. Larry's Work, 1981
   Maze by G.A. Boeckler, 1664 (Matthews 122)
5. Larry's Words, 1983
   Maze design by J. Serlio (16th century) (Matthews 113)
6. Larry's Friends, 1984
   Pavement labyrinth in parish church, St Quentin (Matthews 60)
7. Larry's Penis, 1986
   Coin from Knossos, Crete, c. 300 B.C. (Meehan 74)
8. Larry Inc., 1988
   Horned figure with snake passing through its waist (Meehan 83)
9. Larry So Far, 1990
   Diagonal grid panel, St Gall, Switzerland (Meehan 116)
10. Larry's Kid, 1991
    Panel, Shandwick, Scotland (Meehan 136)
11. Larry's Search for the Wonderful and the Good, 1992
    Pavement labyrinth in Chartres Cathedral (Matthews 58)
12. Larry's Threads, 1993–4
    'Cretan style' maze, Camonica Valley, Alps (Meehan 75)
13. Men Called Larry, 1995
    Path-line reversal illustration (Meehan 78)
14. Larry's Living Tissues, 1996
    Maze from figure with serpent through waist (Meehan 84)
15. Larry's Party, 1997
    Stone labyrinth on coast of Finland (Matthews 148)

Notes

1 Quoted in Joan Thomas, 'The Golden Book: An Interview with Carol Shields,' *Prairie Fire* 14.4 (Winter 1993–4): 60.
2 Carol Shields, *Larry's Party* (New York: Viking Penguin, 1997), 297. All subsequent references to this work will be made parenthetically in the text.
3 Reviewers tend either to love or hate the mazes. Maggie O'Farrell ('Lost in a Maze,' *New Statesman*, 12 Sept. 1997, p. 46) and Candice Rodd (review of *Larry's Party*, *Times Literary Sup-*

plement, 22 Aug. 1997, p. 22) are particularly scornful, while Michiko Kakutani finds the maze symbolism 'an artful strategy' ('Br'er Rabbit, Ordinary in Nearly Every Way,' *New York Times*, 26 Aug. 1997, p. C13).

4 Carol Shields, 'Narrative Hunger and the Overflowing Cupboard,' 22 (in this volume).

5 Carol Shields, *The Box Garden* (1977; rpt. New York: Penguin, 1996), 37, 60. All subsequent references to this work will be made parenthetically in the text.

6 Quoted in Thomas, 60.

7 Gordon E. Slethaug, '"The Coded Dots of Life": Carol Shields's Diaries and Stones,' *Canadian Literature* 156 (Spring 1998): 72-3.

8 Leona Gom, 'Stones and Flowers,' *Prairie Fire* 16.1 (Spring 1995): 27.

9 Faye Hammill, 'Carol Shields's "Native Genre" and the Figure of the Canadian Author,' *Journal of Commonwealth Literature* 31.2 (1996): 94.

10 Quoted in Hammill, 94.

11 Shields made this comment at an informal talk with freshman writing students at Hanover College, Sept. 1996.

12 Eleanor Wachtel, 'Interview with Carol Shields,' *Room of One's Own* 13.1/2 (1989): 44.

13 Wachtel, 39.

14 Simone Vauthier, '"They Say Miracles Are Past" but They Are Wrong,' *Prairie Fire* 14.4 (Winter 1993–4): 101.

15 Jill Purce lists some of the symbolic meanings of the image of the labyrinth, which is 'at once the cosmos, the world, the individual life, the temple, the town, man, the womb – or intestines – of the Mother (earth), the convolutions of the brain, the consciousness, the heart, the pilgrimage, the journey, and the Way' (*The Mystic Spiral: Journey of the Soul* [New York: Thames and Hudson, 1980], 29).

16 As the name suggests, a unicursal maze has only one possible path; a multicursal maze has many, most of them dead ends.

17 Linda Hutcheon, *A Poetics of Postmodernism: History, Theory, Fiction* (New York: Routledge, 1988), 223.

18 Alan Wilde, *Horizons of Assent: Modernism, Postmodernism, and the Ironic Imagination* (Baltimore: Johns Hopkins UP, 1981), 148.

19 W.H. Matthews, *Mazes and Labyrinths: Their History and Development* (1922; rpt. New York: Dover, 1970). This unattributed poem is quoted fully on page 199.

20 Matthews, 60.

21 Aidan Meehan, *Celtic Design Maze Patterns* (New York: Thames and Hudson, 1993).

22 E. Annie Proulx, *The Shipping News* (New York: Scribner, 1993); Clifford W. Ashley, *The Ashley Book of Knots* (New York: Doubleday, 1944).

23 Ariadne's thread has been a major motif in ongoing debates in the academy over deconstructionist criticism. See J. Hillis Miller, 'Ariadne's Thread: Repetition and the Narrative Line,' *Critical Inquiry* 3 (1976): 57–77; also Paul Bové, 'Variations on Authority: Some Deconstructive Transformations of the New Criticism,' and Donald Pease, 'J. Hillis Miller: The Other Victorian at Yale,' both in *The Yale Critics: Deconstruction in America*, ed. Jonathan Arac, Wlad Godzich, and Wallace Martin (Minneapolis: U of Minnesota P, 1983). See Terry Eagleton, *The Function of Criticism* (London: Routledge, 1984) for an entertaining commentary on the self-importance and self-interestedness of deconstructionist scholars. Thanks to Ted Eden for pointing out these references.

24 In a radio interview, Shields said that she 'wanted to design each chapter as a little maze in itself' (*Bookclub*, Radio 4, 5 March 2000). So, the maze illustrations have a general significance in that way, though specific meanings are more elusive. I am indebted to Faye Hammill for sending me her transcription of this interview.

25 Simone Vauthier, 'Ruptures in Carol Shields's *The Stone Diaries*,' *Anglophonia: French Journal of English Studies* 1 (1997): 177–92.

26 William Bradfield, 'St. Ann's Well,' in *Pictures of the Past* (London: Longman Green, Longman, Roberts, and Green, 1864), 172. The excerpt in *Larry's Party* is identified as 'Bradfield, Sentan's Wells, 1854.'

27 Penelope Reed Doob, *The Idea of the Labyrinth from Classical Antiquity through the Middle Ages* (Ithaca: Cornell UP, 1990), 1.

28 Here I am borrowing the language Mary McCarthy uses to describe Joyce's achievement in *Ulysses*: 'Mr. Bloom is not a symbol of Ulysses, but Ulysses-Bloom together, one and indivisible, symbolize or rather demonstrate eternal recurrence ... The point is consubstantiation' ('Settling the Colonel's Hash,' *Harper's Magazine* 208 [Feb. 1954]: 72).

The Swann Who Laid the Golden Egg: A Cautionary Tale of Deconstructionist Cannibalism in *Swann*

KATHY BARBOUR

A Circuitous Introduction to My Essay on a Novel That Is about a Book of Poetry That Was Falsified Once It Left the Poet's Hands and Was Appropriated by a Professor, a Biographer, a Librarian, a Publisher, a Gaggle of Scholars, and Other Thieves, All Fictitious Characters in a Film about a Symposium in a Section of a Novel by a REAL AUTHOR, Who Has Written a Chapter on Narrative for This Book of Essays, Written by REAL PEOPLE – of Whom I Am One – on Her Fiction in Response to a Call for Papers, Solicited by Letter

'Let's fuck and fuck and fuck forever,' says Dorrie to Larry in the early pages of *Larry's Party*.[1]

Refreshing, isn't it? To hear one clear, abrasive, generative word you know the meaning of, a word still capable of squirting juice. You grow alert, excited, ashamed, nervous, especially in this context – a scholarly work – especially after you've swirled around in the maelstrom of this 'Circuitous Introduction ...'

'Fuck.' What a relief!

Larry's not relieved:

'Do you have to say that? ... Can't you just say "making love"?'
'You say "fuck,"' she said to Larry. 'You say it all the time.'

'No, I don't.'
'Come off it. You're always saying "fuck this" and "fuck that."'
'Maybe. Maybe I do. But I don't say it literally.'
'What?' She looked baffled.
'Not *literally*.'
'There you go again,' she said, 'with those college words.' (10)

And this is how the trouble starts. Dorrie's use of 'fuck' – the one use of this word to which meaning adheres like sticky peach jam, even though the word itself is forever removed from the act and is a more or less arbitrary symbol, anyway, of differentiation from 'folk' or 'flock' or 'fudge' – is still the more meaning-full application, referring to two humans physically conjoined in passion. Larry's euphemism 'making love' is longer but softer, less useful as a tool conveying mutual understanding, intercourse. 'Reading for the later Barthes is not cognition but erotic play,' says lucid Terry Eagleton, unmurking poststructuralism in *Literary Theory: An Introduction*.[2] Larry's language perversion is akin to the cultural perversion of a man calling out, 'What a pair of hooters!' at the sight of an exotic dancer's silicone-injected breasts, yet blushing to see a mother nursing her baby in public.

Jonathan Culler, in *On Deconstruction: Theory and Criticism after Structuralism*, tells us:

[S]ome critics of deconstruction have argued that we should accept ... relative determinacy as the nature of meaning. Meaning is what we understand; and instead of exposing its lack of foundation or decisive authority we should simply say, with Wittgenstein, 'this language game is played' ... A Derridean would agree that the language game is played but might go on to point out that one can never be quite certain who is playing, or playing 'seriously,' what the rules are, or which game is being played.[3]

A Derridean would be describing the Swannians, who might do better to accept relative meaning so they could spend more time physically conjoined in passion.

The Naked and the Dead

> The woman who interviewed me was lanky and menacing, wore a fur vest and was dangerously framed by lengths of iodine-glazed hair. To quell her I talked about the surrealism of scholarship. The pretensions. The false systems. The arcane lingo. The macho domination. The garrison mentality. The inbred arrogance.
>
> She leaned across and patted me on the knee and said, 'You're not coming from arrogance, sweetie; you're coming from naked need.'
>
> Ping! My brain shuddered purple. I was revealed, uncloaked ...[4]

Speaking is Sarah Maloney, Ph.D., twenty-eight, one of the four major characters in large part responsible for the 'Swann industry' (299) that has sprouted from the corpse of Mary Swann, provincial poet, uneducated farm wife, and mother, about whom next to nothing is known. Swann's life would be distinguished only by its ordinariness but for two exceptional facts: her manner of death and her luminous poetry. (She is called by some 'the Emily Dickinson of Upper Canada' [129], less because of her reclusiveness than because her poems, so simple-seeming on the surface, seethe with complexity and teem with deep life.) In 1965, at age fifty, Swann was shot, hacked to pieces, and stuffed into the over-large, upthrust silver silo by her husband, Angus, hours after bringing a paper bag full of some 125 poems written on scraps of paper to a local small publisher, Frederic Cruzzi, who printed 250 copies in 1966 under the dolorous title *Swann's Songs*. By around 1980, the time of the novel's action, only twenty copies remain, and those are rapidly disappearing under mysterious circumstances. Someone seems to be stealing them. These thefts are literal, of course, but inescapably metaphorical – and allusive – as is the hacking 'Death of the Author.' Postmodern themes of disappearing text, disembodiment, and – especially – historical silencing of women rise *not* like invisible gassy abstractions, but rather in bloody flesh and marrowed words. Little pieces of Swann, the holy-ghost artist at whose altar the Swannians kneel, are being subsumed like communion wafers. Swann's publisher, Frederic Cruzzi, her biographer, Morton Jimroy, her museum founder and friend, Rose Hindmarch, and her scholarly unearther, Sarah Maloney, have all come to Swann 'from naked need' at critically low points in their lives. Having consumed her poetry and battened on the transubstantiation, they each depart the altar thinking *they* are responsible for Mary's renewal, not the other way around. Boy, has Swann ever been 'disseminated.'

Her Necktie Modest ... Assertive, Single

'In a sense I invented Mary Swann and am responsible for her,' writes Sarah, then immediately edits herself: 'No, too literary that. Better just say I discovered Mary Swann' (30). A page later: 'In truth, no one really discovers anyone; it's the stickiest kind of arrogance even to think in such terms. Mary Swann discovered herself ...' (31). But Sarah's worthy attempts to rein in hubris and correct herself also lead to confusion in thought, language, and behaviour. Indecision and self-consciousness dog her every step: 'Oh yes, the indomitable Sarah, slain by indecision' (16), she had mocked herself two years earlier as, overwrought, she had fled a marriage suitor, then married him anyway, then soon divorced him. Sarah is given to such pronouncements as 'I'll never require make-up. At least not for another ten years' (12), and, of her current boyfriend, Sam Brown, 'I adore Brownie. But with reservations' (15), and 'But can he be trusted? ... No. Yes. Possibly' (15). Sarah is Prufrock in a frock.

The unexpected fame Sarah received when her graduate thesis, *The Female Prism*, rose to the non-fiction best-seller list (20) has bankrolled not only her fine clothes (which she's 'sick of' by page 51) but her house: 'I live in someone else's whimsy, a Hansel and Gretel house' (19), a 'fantasy house' (37). She sees herself as a fictional character in 'the quirky narrative I like to think of as the story of my life' (20). She says, 'It happens fairly often, this sensation of being a captive of fiction, a sheepish player in my own *roman à clef*. My dwarfish house is the setting' (37). Is this *The Female Prism* or *The Female Prison*? Sarah can't get no satisfaction.

Say 'Amen' and Pass the Radishes

God is dead, peace is dead, the sixties are dead, John Lennon and Simone de Beauvoir are dead, the women's movement is dozing – checking its inventory – so what's left?

The quotidian is what's left. Mary Swann understood that, if nothing else. (21)

Sarah Maloney supplies the answer to her own question. Dailiness is left. In a paper she's writing for the Swann symposium, Sarah seizes on Mary's 'queer little poem on ... thinning a row of radishes ... [as] an emblem for ...' (54–5) and then stops herself: 'Wait a minute ... Radishes to ultimate truth? – that's the leap of a refined aesthete. How did Mary Swann, untaught country woman, know how to make that kind of murky metaphorical connection[?] Who taught her what was possible?' (55).

There are several funnies going on here. Postmodernists will laugh at the notion of 'ultimate truth.' Garden-variety readers will chuckle over those loopy literary types finding symbolism in a radish. Zany scholars, sucking grass blades of irony between their teeth, will laugh at Sarah's supposed respect for Mary's quotidian existence, but will guffaw at her actual let-down when she reads the journal that fed the plain/brilliant poetry and 'linked object with word, experience with language' (54). Here is Sarah's reaction:

Profound disappointment is what I felt when opening that notebook for the first time. What I wanted was elucidation and grace and a glimpse of the woman Mary Swann as she drifted in and out of her poems. What I got was 'Creek down today,' or 'Green beans up,' or 'cash low,' or 'wind rising.' (49)

Shifting their grass blades, the scholars will laugh even harder when they learn that Sarah, who is self-appointed high priestess of Swanniology – referring to her as 'my Mary Swann' (15, 18, 28) – and who zealously guards Swann from the devouring male critics ('These guys are greedy. They would eat her up, inch by inch. Scavengers. Brutes' [32]) has *thrown away* one of the two holy relics Rose Hindmarch has given her, the *Spratt's New Improved Rhyming Dictionary for Practising Poets* (145), and *lost* the other, Swann's journal! (Only it isn't really lost; it's been stolen by the boyfriend, Brownie, Sarah thinks she adores.) So embarrassed and baffled is Sarah by her idol Mary's flesh feet that she has effectually stolen from the scholarly world a piece of the trust she should have cherished, and has selfishly sat on the other relic for three or four years (276). Sarah has begun gnawing on Mary's actuality. It is love at first bite.

But wait – it gets funnier! Scholars of all -isms and just plain readers can come together in back-slapping merriment savouring the final irony: this emblematic poem about radishes with its 'two magnificent, and thus far neglected, final lines' (54), Mary Swann's 'credo for her life as a survivor' (54), has a stench about it – literally, metaphorically. Into the bag of 125 poems on scrap paper that Swann has tendered into the hands of publisher Frederic Cruzzi, Cruzzi's wife, Hildë, has innocently thrown fish guts. 'Thinning Radishes' was written in 'washable blue' ink (221) in handwriting that was 'scarcely legible' (215) to begin with. Half of the bag o' poems were seriously damaged, and Frederic and Hildë have painstakingly tried to reassemble the ponds of blue ink out of which 'one or two letters swam into comprehension' (222) through guesswork and then invention! In a drop-jaw ironic juxtaposition, Shields has Swann chopped to pieces by her husband that very night. Mary and her poems are reduced to rot – dispersed – within that same twenty-four-hour period.

Now, postmodernists – chewing on straw, not grass blades – are switching their stems nervously from one side of their mouths to the other. Is Carol Shields affirming Derrida, Barthes, and de Boys in every single nuance of this scene, giving meta-phorical life to the intellectual concept that something in the nature of writing itself is inherently unstable, eluding fixed meaning like quicksilver minnows darting in washable-blue ponds? Or is Shields goofing on their pretensions of declaring reader and writer co-equal in the creative process? This either/or question itself reveals that Shields – like Maloney – can 'post-mod along with the best of them' (53). Whatever, half of Swann is fishy.

Switching metaphors from wet to dry as we are switching moods, the sands of irony are not yet done shifting under our feet.

Just as Mary Swann's life and a goodly portion of her *oeuvre* were blotted out that 1965 night, so now, over fifteen years later, are all remnants of the artist and her work being stolen. Shields, having fun with literary pretension, has turned her high-brow novel into a 'thriller' (231) presented in film-form flimflam, with subtext focusing on 'the more subtle thefts and acts of cannibalism that tempt and mystify the main characters' (231). So much for literary snobs who sniff, 'Oh, I never read genre fiction!' Sam Brown, Sarah Maloney's adorable 'Brownie,' has been stealing the twenty remaining copies of *Swann's Songs*; the two extant photos of her (one of which Morton Jimroy, Swann's biographer, first lifted from the Swann museum Rose Hindmarch founded); Swann's Parker 51 fountain pen (stolen first by Jimroy from the poet's daughter); her journal (which Sarah received from humble, munificent Rose – 'It would only be wasted on me. What does someone like me know about real poetry?' [45] – and then stole from the world of scholarship); the notes and papers of the Swannians; and, finally, Brownie, by buying Mary Swann's farm, owns her death. (Frederic Cruzzi has told Sarah he thinks Morton 'the body snatcher' [75] Jimroy wants it all, too: 'Mrs. Swann's life. Every minute of it he could have. And ... her death. Or some clue to it' [277].) So once again we have literal and figurative levels of meaning commenting on each other, and can even note that Brownie bought the farm where Mary 'bought the farm.' Irony begets more irony when we learn that bookish Sarah dotes on a man who 'hasn't read a book in ten years, he tells me. Another reason I love him' (53). Sam Brown is a dealer in rare books, seeing them only as commodities, once telling Sarah that he would 'cheat his own granny to make a buck' (15). In cornering the increasingly hot market for cold Swann, however, Brownie needs an 'inside man.' Irony has grandchildren: his accomplice, we are nudged to believe, is none other than Willard 'swine incarnate' (31) Lang, eminent scholar and convenor of the Swann symposium (309–10)! Sigh! All the fine young – and middle-aged and old – cannibals.

Excellent Frederic Cruzzi, though, Swann's publisher and, at eighty, retired journalist, hard-boiled old newspaperman that he is, dealer in 'objective' writing who holds scholars in rather low regard, does not share the Swannians' mania for original text, apparently. In a letter to Sarah Maloney dated November 26, he says,

> I may have rather less reverence than you for the holiness of working papers. If you are familiar with ... the oral tradition of most of the world's literature, you will know that this cherishing of original manuscripts is a relatively new phenomenon ... A manuscript is, after all, only a crude representation of that step between creative thought and artefact, and might just as usefully be employed as kindling for a fire or in the wrapping of fishbones. (192)

Before postmodernists jump up and down claiming Cruzzi for 'their side' (of course, postmodernists are really trying to abolish 'sides' entirely), remember that he might simply be defending his dirty little secret. (And he is temporarily crestfallen when his own four remaining copies of Swann's Songs are stolen from his house on Christmas Eve.) In an October 15 letter, he has told Willard Lang, '[T]he glory of Mary Swann's work lies in its innocence, the fact that it does not invite scholarly meddling or whimsical interpretation' (186). Is this assertion sincerely felt or guiltily self-serving? It might be both.

But I had promised you a change of mood when we went from water to sand, Reader. Here it comes.

Various Miracles: The Fishes and the Loaths

On the first page of the Cruzzi section of *Swann*, the narrative voice states:

> The world claps its hands for the intellectual nomad ... We love these wanderers for their brilliance, their adaptive colouring, their many tongues and tricks of courage; but chiefly we love them for the innocence and joy with which they burrow into the very world so many of us have given up on.
>
> Retired newspaper editor Frederic Cruzzi ... is such a one ... (175)

Compare this joyful burrowing into the world to the dour 'God is dead, peace is dead, the sixties are dead ...' (21) scenario, and you would probably rather bend an elbow with the burrowers. (That Cruzzi is an atheist is beside the point.) In addition to his newspaper background, the octogenarian Cruzzi is described as a 'traveller, atheist, lover of women and poetry, tender son of gentle parents, scholar, immigrant, gardener, socialist, husband, and father – he is also a man who can be said to have been lucky in friendship. His friendships, he sometimes thinks, are all he has to forestall the pursuing chaos of old age' (176). Cruzzi occupies even more roles than Rose Hindmarch, whom we learn, in her introduction, 'wears a number of hats' (123). We are further told: 'In his life Frederic Cruzzi has had two loves: the written word and his wife Hildë. The two loves are compatible but differently ordered, occupying separate berths in his brain and defying explanation or description, something that bothers him not at all' (205). He refuses to deconstruct his loves. He frequently returns to Eastern poetry, such as this verse by the Persian poet Rashid, to connect to 'ancient rhythms' and to reaffirm the 'brief transports' of love (209–10):

On your shoulder a bird alights
Singing, singing a song without words,
A song without meaning or wisdom or words,
A song without asking or giving or words,
Without kindness or judgement or flattering words.
On your shoulder a bird alights
Singing against your loud silence. (209)

An unusual choice for a lover of 'the written word,' no? Perhaps we shall make something of this observation later. But for now, back to Cruzzi's other love, his wife.

On the bitter-cold evening when Mary Swann has just departed his house after depositing her heap of artistic treasure in his lap, he is ecstatic and cannot wait to share this boon with his wife and publishing partner, Hildë. She returns from ice fishing with the fateful string of whitefish, and Cruzzi's happiness is ready 'to burst' out of his skin (217). As Hildë leans before the fireplace to stoke up the flames, Cruzzi suddenly realizes Mary Swann's paper bag of poems is missing. His surging joy and his appreciation for the beloved mate – without whom, he'd been thinking a few seconds earlier, his life would be an unimaginable void (219) – instantly freezes and shatters: 'He addressed her coldly as though she were a stranger. "There was a bag there," he said' (220). The ice splinters thaw, only to reform in moments as daggers when, smiling, she steps toward him, saying, 'Oh, that ... I put it in the kitchen' (220). When he finds Mary's poems mingled with the ooze of fish innards, he strikes his wife to the floor, where she lies bleeding. She forgives him, of course – he is instantly sorry, begging her forgiveness – but his unprecedented violence haunts him in dreams the rest of his life.

So once again the ironies come clamouring: Cruzzi's love of words has momentarily killed his love of woman, and his brutish act is a baby blood brother to Angus Swann's murder of Mary, taking place that same night. Further, whereas we had all chortled at Cruzzi's statement to Sarah – 'A manuscript ... might just as usefully be employed as kindling for a fire or in the wrapping of fishbones' (192) – we now shudder at Cruzzi's exact echo of the *two* ways he had thought his wife had destroyed Mary's poems. On Christmas Day, when Cruzzi discovers the night-before theft of his remaining *Swann's Songs*, the narrative tells us he felt 'pierced with ... the knowledge that a long-delayed act of reprisal had taken place. It was unbearable; some menacing reversal had occurred, leaving him with nothing but his old fraudulent skin hanging loose on his bones' (228). A 'reprisal' for striking his wife over the poems, or a reprisal for having published 'fraudulent' poems? Both, I should think.

Cruzzi, who has sunk too much into himself since Hildë's death a year earlier – cutting off his phone service, loath to leave home, wanting chiefly the company of only his books (184, 185) – is comforted by his friends. Two of them are worth highlighting – both women, one celibate, one sensual – for their wise insights into the relative value of books, insights that directly echo those expressed by Carol Shields in 'Narrative Hunger and the Overflowing Cupboard.' Sister Mary Francis (formerly Mimi Russell), not yet fifty, 'not yet out of a long childhood' (179), is in love with English literature, where she 'sniffs a kind of godly oxygen that binds one human being to the next and shortens the distance we must travel to discover that our most private perceptions are universally felt' (179). Cruzzi believes she is right. And yet, once in a while,

walking ... in shadowed woodland ... or hearing perhaps a particular phrase of music, or approaching a wave of sexual ecstasy, Cruzzi has felt a force so resistant to the power of syntax, description, or definition, so savage and primitive in its form, that he has been tempted to shed his long years of language and howl monosyllables of delight and outrage.

Outrage because these are moments of humility, of dressing down, of rebuke to those, like Cruzzi, who perceive reality through print ... (206)

One such moment has, it seems, been provided old Cruzzi by Pauline Ouilette, widow of a long-time friend, a woman whose 'passion for perfume, pedicures, and expensive underwear

gives an impression of frivolity that is false' (179). Pauline 'is
fully conscious of her powers, appreciates the importance of
good food, knows that books, particularly fiction, form a
valuable core of experience ... ' (179). Since Hildë's death,
Pauline has tried to lure Frederic out of his lonely grief. They
have even, apparently, become lovers. Her insights, the experienced woman's, coupled with those of Sister Mary Francis,
the innocent 'child,' seem to me to embody the truest wisdom
in *Swann*. Pauline writes, 'What I know is that words are
rather pathetic at times and that what we need most is to
reach past them and touch each other' (193). Sister Mary
Francis speaks to the touch of spirit, Pauline to the touch of
flesh; each has a finger in intellect, but both advocate reaching
out.

Sister Mary Francis is a 'child' in the same positive sense as
the intellectual nomads, such as Cruzzi was earlier described
as being, whom we love 'for the innocence and joy with
which they burrow into the very world so many of us have
given up on' (175). Rose Hindmarch is another of these innocent and joyful 'children.' Though openly patronized by the
Swann scholars and marching behind them in intellect and
worldliness, she nonetheless marches far ahead of them in her
goodwill, being blinded to their limitations by her innocence
and delight to be included in their lofty cohort. Yet in her
naïveté, Rose is a bearer of perhaps the most important truth
Shields would convey to bookish types, particularly postmodern scholars: goodwill and the open desire to embrace
meaning, to embrace community, to embrace our jaded planet
in this fagged-out century is what is lacking, is what stinks, is
what makes fishy our veneration for intellectual approaches
to words. Recall how Carol Shields comments directly not
only on postmodernism, but on the old realism, too, in her
opening essay to this volume:

If postmodernism has proved a synthetic discourse, unanimated
by personal concerns, it has at least given writers a breath of
that precious oxygen of permission and, more important, time

to see in what ways the old realism – the mirror of the world – has failed us ...

Realistic fiction passed too quickly through the territory of the quotidian and dismissed as though they didn't exist those currents of sensation that leak around the boundaries of vocabulary. The realistic tradition stressed the divisiveness of human society and shrugged at that rich, potent, endlessly replenished cement that binds us together. ('Narrative Hunger' 34)

Shields *values* postmodernism's 'precious oxygen of permission,' but she *laments* the lack of personal concern, the lack of depiction of everyday realities and people, and the overemphasis on divisiveness of both postmodernism and realism. Just as the concept of 'goodwill' resonates throughout Shields's novel *The Stone Diaries*, so does it resonate in *Swann*. Shields, certainly an intellectual herself, seems to be pleading with contemporary intellectuals to remember how important is the desire to more fully inhabit the primal winds and woods of this planet, the invisible eddies of other people's hidden lives as we feel along the cryptic encodings of words to detect 'those currents of sensation' leaking out. Shields might ask us to say, like Sarah Maloney, 'I want my sweetness back, my girlhood sugar. Not forever, but for awhile' (*Swann* 65).

Sweet and Sour Pork and No Spring Chicken

When Morton Jimroy had travelled to Kingston, Ontario, to consult with Frederic Cruzzi, Cruzzi had arranged a dinner for him with the lively, amiable Sister Mary Francis, also a biographer, to 'talk shop.' Cruzzi's observation: 'never had such sweetness met such sourness' (180). Jimroy, himself, knows he's a pickle: 'He is aware, he alone probably in all the world, of the membrane of sweetness that encases his heart. Well, sweetness perhaps is putting it too strongly' (89). Jimroy thinks of Rose Hindmarch as the 'moist, repulsive Rose' (110) and 'mooney, cheese-faced' Rose (116).

Rose has a kind word for everyone and is proud to claim Jimroy as friend, even 'good friend' (132). Of course, Rose has also told the world she was Mary Swann's 'good friend,' although she 'had been a virtual stranger' (152); Rose – the least culpable of the Swannian cannibals – is ashamed: 'Forgive me the sin of untruthfulness' (152). Rose marches behind the other Swanners (in their estimation and her own) because she's not a true scholar. Her favourite novels are spy stories. She's just an 'ordinary person.' But then so was Mary Swann 'ordinary.' Shields makes wise old Cruzzi her spokesman for questioning the very concept of ordinariness when he mildly reproves Sarah for being disappointed in Swann's lacklustre journal: 'Ordinary? ... Whatever that word means' (276).

Yet Rose, alacritous and compassionate, can read people like a book. When Jimroy visits her in Nadeau, Ontario, to bleed her of her insights into Mary Swann's real life, Rose sees through his superficial charm to his greedy motive; and she sees even further into him than that: 'there was something else, a green shoot that matched her own unfolded greenness' (151). He is fifty-one, recently divorced (on the grounds of 'sarcasm,' his neighbours secretly joke), a misanthrope, a misogynist, and sexually impotent. On his one – and only – sexual attempt with his big-hearted wife, Audrey, he'd failed. Her response, genuine, was 'Never mind, love' (103) – although perhaps she, too, was relieved (104). Rose is a fifty-year-old virgin. She has shared her bed only once, when her downstairs neighbour, Jean, has sought refuge from a fight with her husband, who struck her. Ironically, the non-sexual bed-sharing, the mere physical proximity and warmth of another human body, has been for each of these intimacy-starved souls, Jimroy and Rose, the happiest moment of their lives (104, 136). When, during the Christmas season, Jimroy contemplates, baffled but benignant, all the 'reaching out for affection' of lovers, husbands, wives, and even the most wayward children, he thinks, 'What a wonder it was, the bond that joined human beings. An act of faith, really, faith over reason. Over bodily substance' (117). In moments of lamentation, he chants, 'My wound is that I have no wound' (103), and one is reminded of Henry James's 'The Beast in the Jungle.'

Rose is no beast. She's a butterfly in blue thread and a light fraud. On the iron bed in the Mary Swann Memorial Room that Rose established and furnished is a lovely handmade quilt composed of squares signed by the local women who made it. Their signatures – 'in simple chain stitch' (120) – show them all to be yoked to husbands whose names they use as though they had no identities of their own: 'Mrs. Frank Sears, Mrs. Homer Hart, Mrs. Joseph H. Fletcher, and so on' (130). Near the centre of the quilt is the single embroidered butterfly, with the signature and womanly identity: 'Rose Hindmarch' (130). That the Mary Swann Room is supposedly furnished with Swann's own things is another of Rose's white lies: Rose has bought many of the accoutrements at antique shops. She prefers, however, to think of this powder-winged fraud not as duplicity or deception (163), but as an exercise of imagination, believing the 'charm of falsehood is not that it distorts reality, but that it creates reality afresh' (163). Rose has narrative hunger, a need to create through embroidering, a need to transcend the bare quotidian in brief flights. In this urge, she echoes Daisy Goodwill in *The Stone Diaries*: 'She [Daisy] understood that if she was going to hold on to her life at all, she would have to rescue it by a primary act of imagination, supplementing, modifying, ... conjuring, ... exaggerating or lying outright ...'[5]

Morton Jimroy is harsher on fraudulence (being the greater fraud), particularly when he is seized with doubt about the validity of art; more particularly, when he becomes intensely aware that the two great poets, John Starman and Ezra Pound, of whom he has written biographies, were personal brutes; most particularly, when he realizes that he has spent his energies writing appendices, annotations, and footnotes on the poets' footnotes (25)! 'It seemed to me at that moment that not a single man on earth had ever spoken the truth. We were all, every last one of us, liars and poseurs' (26). In another of

Shields's witty yokings of literal and abstract meanings, Morton 'Mr. Marginalia' Jimroy is experiencing marginal-ization – the role historically assigned to female lives – and he is distressed to be relegated to the sidelines as a mere com-mentator. He covets the starring role as Creator, yet paradoxi-cally detests Starman and Pound for being personal beasts and misogynists (Jimroy's own sins) while glorifying their godlike imaginative powers – which he then must do dirt on, the celebrated poets becoming 'liars and poseurs.' Jimroy fails to understand that a man may wear many hats. As may a woman.

'Rose Helen Hindmarch wears a number of hats' (123) be-gins her section of the novel. She is Nadeau's librarian and town clerk and Swann Museum curator – really, the town's pre-eminent citizen. But there are 'moments when she experi-ences an appalling sensation of loss, the naggy suspicion that beneath the hats is nothing but chilly space or the small scratch-ing sounds of someone who wants only to please others' (126).

And yet there are chilly spaces and there are light-filled spaces. When Rose, the atheist, sits in church, she directs her prayers not toward 'Our Father' but toward the pine pulpit railing 'topped with a pretty moulding of carved leaves ... she can see light shining between the leaves, and it is to these lighted spaces that she addresses her prayers, or rather her questions' (146). When still a young woman, Rose had lost her religious faith, quite painlessly, on hearing a philosophical debate on radio, one debater asking, 'Who can really believe there's a God up there sitting at a giant switchboard listening to everyone's prayers?' (124), at which Rose had laughed aloud, yet she still has the transcendent urge, the lust for light.

Quixote, Meet Quotidian

Morton Jimroy, educating Rose, speaks of the several levels on which serious poetry functions, telling her that in Mary Swann's work, 'The spiritual impulse shines like a light on every detail of weather or habit or natural object. The quest for the spiritual. The lust for the spiritual' (147). But Mary Swann wasn't a church-goer. Jimroy asks Rose why she thought Swann stayed away from church 'so religiously,' pleased with his pun. Rose replies, with a woman's understanding, 'She probably didn't have the right clothes' (147). In another conversation, Jimroy explains the exalted meaning of Mary Swann's 'Blood' poem (the poem most severely damaged by fish ooze – the Cruzzis have guessed it began either 'Blood pronounces my name' or 'Blood renounces my name' [223]) to Rose, whom we later learn is secretly losing half of hers to menopausal flooding caused by undiagnosed fibroids; she fears she's dying. Jimroy effuses: 'What I meant was that great poets write from large universalized perceptions, and Mary Swann's blood poem seems to me to be her central spiritual statement ...The blood, you see, is a symbol. It stands for a continuum of belief, a metaphysical covenant with an inexplicable universe' (150). Rose realizes Jimroy is a world authority in poetry but laments that he is missing the drift of the blood poem. 'Of course he was a man ... and perhaps men have a tendency to overlook what is perfectly obvious to women' (150–1). They are both wrong; they are both right. Another post-mod moment. Not only may each man or each woman wear a number of hats; it seems, in this brave new world, each *poem* may wear a number of hats. Imagine that! (Yes, *do*, I believe Shields would say. Just please *imagine*. If we all come to art from 'naked need' – as have our four principals, Sarah, Morton, Frederic, and Rose – we may at least decorate ourselves, as Walt Whitman did, wearing our hats as we like.)

Ironically, Morton Jimroy – the gherkin, the stinkpot, the sweet 'n sour chauvinist pig – is given some of the most moving lines about the role of literary art in the whole novel, perhaps because he is in the greatest emotional need, trapped deepest in his 'little twisted wordy world' (106) and 'awful quagmire heart' (122):

When he thought of the revolution of planets, the emergence of species, the balance of mathematics, he could not see that any of these was more amazing than the impertinent human wish to reach into the sea of common language and extract from it the rich dark beautiful words that could be arranged in such a way that the unsayable might be said. Poetry was the prism that refracted all of life. It was Jimroy's belief that the best and worst of human experiences were frozen inside these wondrous little toys called poems. (86)

Jimroy's reference to 'common' language – of common every-day life and of common shared experience – is significant. Reaching *into* language, retreating, if that dark grope is at the expense of experiential human life and communication, is not enough. Our retreat should be undertaken into the primal reaches of bodies and rhythms, winds, woods, and actual seas, from which we haul our gleaming catch, words; not first into words from which we form phantasms. That is the lesson Cruzzi intuited from his walks in the woods by the lake; from his enchantment with Eastern poetry and birdsong – a 'song without meaning or wisdom or words' (209); from his re-discovered sexuality with Pauline; from the 'Lost Things' waiting out of sight that cannot be recovered unless the deconstructers put down their paper pieces and, uniting their voices, reconstruct a whole thing of unknowable, evanescent beauty and primal rhythm.

Both Sarah Gamble and Chiara Briganti, in this volume, observe Shields's fascination with the dark voids in human experience that *cannot* be illuminated by words. Gamble says, 'There are points where Shields deliberately leaves blank spots within the text, indicative of experiences or concepts incapa-ble of ever being contained within a conventional narrative framework' (45). Briganti concurs, finding it fitting that the poem 'Lost Things' should end the novel *Swann*, sealing 'Mary Swann's irrecoverability' and thus revealing 'a desire to re-gress to a state of pre-existence' (182). I agree with these points wholeheartedly, yet I still maintain – as does Gamble, as does Briganti, and as does Shields – that the real *desire* to understand other humans, their language, and the mysterious world around us is one hope we have for throwing some light on these unlit lodes, to mine them partially. As Gamble observes of the now-cooperative scholars in *Swann*'s ending, 'Indeed, in this novel it is the "ceremonial act of reconstitution" which forms what is probably the only truly creative achievement in the novel' (55). Another hope, besides goodwill or desire to understand, is a determination to hold on to tangible experience of the world through our bodies and through concrete language – Briganti's point, and also Shields's point in creating Mary Swann. As Sarah Gamble explains Shields's creation of Mary Swann:

> But that, surely, is the point – Mary Swann is no romantic genius, but a woman who used words like tools to describe an existence which, until its bloody and dramatic ending, was essentially representative of the absolutely ordinary. What the critics cannot grasp is that her spare, elliptic poetry is sufficient unto itself: it is not intended to be metaphorical or allusive or deeply meaningful, but a direct expression of concrete experience. (56)

Frederic Cruzzi's intellect, then – *all* intellect – is only fingernail, a hard horn overlay and dead paring, useless unless suffused with the blood of the quick and graced with a half-moon glow. Pauline Ouilette's sensual human reach past words transfuses the crusty old Cruzzi; Sister Mary Francis's 'godly oxygen' of universal longing restores his glow. And we find that the path to the extraordinary does lead through the ordinary, after all. Just as all roads lead to Rome in the classical world, so do all roads lead to Nadeau in the fagged-out present. There awaits the quotidian; there await non-intellectual Rose with her hungry imagination starved for colour and Mary Swann, spinning gold from straw and Mother Goose nursery rhymes (93, 261). But perception is everything.

No, Nadeau Is Not *Exactly* the Centre of the World

Early in the symposium scene, when the swanning and preen-
ing scholars are still being divisive and bitchy, one of them
turns to the other and, disparaging Mary Swann's lack of
feminist message and lack of sophistication, huffs, '[W]ell,
when you consider that Nadeau, Ontario, is not exactly the
centre of the world – ' (251). It is my favourite moment of slip-
on-a-banana-peel humour in the whole novel when pretentious figurative and publican literal meanings collide in
falling-down irony in a chapter titled 'Some Words of Orientation' (126). We discover that, were we to put our finger on a
map, Nadeau would be located *almost* at the geographical
centre of North America, but just 'an inch or two to the right
(and one-quarter of an inch downwards)' (126). Significantly,
Rose Hindmarch's butterfly quilt square is described the same
way: 'near the centre of the quilt, just an inch or so to the
right – yes, there!' (130). Nadeau is, at least, a place where
women, at least, know how to sew things of beauty together
cooperatively, not tear them asunder in useless scraps. And
Nadeau is deceptively banal – to the untrained senses of the
outsider. Take the Nadeau Legion, for example, on an average
weekend night:

> [Y]ou will be unable in a single visit to take in the *sense* of the
> Nadeau Legion. The faces floating before you and the brief
> scraps of conversation you overhear will be dissociated from
> any meaningful context, just as though you were observing a
> single scene plucked at random from an extremely long and
> complex play. For every ounce of recognition provoked, there
> would be an answering tax of bafflement; a glimpse of 'life in
> Nadeau on a Saturday night' conceals more than it reveals.
> Although you listen intently (and perhaps take notes), the scene
> before you never rounds itself out into the fullness of meaning.
> Too much is taken for granted by the speakers ... and the allu-
> sions tossed up are patchy and fleeting and embedded in long,
> shared histories. (140)

The last part of that quotation could be describing the inner workings of a long, happy marriage as well as a long-linked community – perhaps seen as boring to outsiders (a point Shields makes in her opening essay: 'What can be done with folks so narratively unpromising?' [33]). In fact, Frederic Cruzzi describes his vintage love for Hildë in precisely those terms (207–8). But for our purposes, we can understand the above passage as a metaphor for all that is wrong-headed in scholarship – perhaps scholarship of the Derridean school most of all. While seeming to affirm the postmodern premise that language is inherently incapable of conveying essential meaning, Shields is actually undercutting that assertion as too brittle – a fingernail paring. Shared meaning *can* be felt, understood non-verbally, through a gradual build-up of shared experience, and through goodwill and willing perception. The above-quoted passage additionally provides an explanation of Shields's method in the madness of *Swann*'s final section, the symposium, presented as a screenplay of a film in which actors who are described externally – 'Silver Cufflinks,' 'Wimpy Grin' – speak fragments of lines that overlap and collide in splinters of meaning and squabbling. These scholars do *not* have goodwill or a shared sense of building up understandings. They must be robbed of their words on paper and of their mouthfuls of the dead flesh of Mary Swann before they can reassemble in right heart and recreate the living, rhythmic beauty that had originally pulled them all out of the narrow constraints of self into the communal literary conference. The scene, describing Mary Swann and all the Swannians as fictional, further reminds us, the readers, that although narrative hunger – our own – is real, fiction is not life.

Make Hash, Not War

Throughout 'Narrative Hunger and the Overflowing Cupboard,' Shields, like a good housewife, stews over how much nourishing story fare we throw out because it seems somehow unliterary, trivial, or inauthentic. She also chafes against formal constraints, rules 'about unity of time and space, about conflict, rising action and the nature of story conclusions' (28). While lamenting that postmodern fiction is 'unanimated by personal concerns,' she lauds the 'precious oxygen of permission' (34) postmodernism brings writers as they break out of mimetic fiction's hall of mirrors. A revolutionary, Shields invites the rabble, the deviants, into the Palace at Versailles, welcoming narrative experimentation in both substance and style. She notes with glee that women writers, in particular, are dismantling the 'rigidities of genre' (35), are storming the barricades to freedom of expression historically erected and, um, manned by men. Women, clacking metaphorical knitting needles, strewing quilt pieces, carrying pots full of peas, potatoes, and soup bones, aim to warm and feed a world in narrative want. 'Give us leftovers,' these formerly marginalized word-cooks chant, 'and we'll make hash!' In fact, Shields seems to relish the challenge of inventive cooking-up, her novels *Swann* and *The Stone Diaries* being her richest stylistic farragos. She throws poems, letters, journal entries, formal invitations, newspaper clippings, announcements, and other written odds and ends into her fictional pot, even tossing in a few pinches of miracle, so that desiccated words and verities and even cultures gain new savour.

In *Swann*, for example, Shields manipulates chapter headings, point of view, and written correspondence so that structure reinforces meaning, style remarries sense, and readers at least crawl into bed with writers, whether or not they form a true union.

The chapter headings in Sarah's, Morton's, Rose's, and Frederic's sections sit like so many mismatched chairs around the same table. Sarah's chapters are numbered, Morton's have *no* headings, Rose's and Frederic's are introduced by titles. This technique invites – no, screams for – literary interpretation. But beyond differentiating the characters, *is* there a deeper significance to these mismatched chapter headings? Possibly not! Shields seems to be giving scholarly readers a lesson: 'Quit insisting on meaning, on order, on consistency.

Real life isn't like that, so why should fiction be? Forget what the characters' sections are *called* and plunge into the characters' motley lives, their mixed bags of foible and fineness.' But even while so chiding us, Shields is reaffirming the link between form and content, reaffirming the need to pay close attention to detail, and this good-natured toleration of paradox unreconciled illustrates Shields's postmodern sensibility.

Next, let's move on to two interdependent techniques: Shields's manipulation of point of view and written correspondence in *Swann*. In the opening section of the novel, the storytelling voice is first located *inside* the character. Sarah's account is in the first-person 'I.' Morton's, then Rose's, and then Frederic's stories follow in succession, all told in third-person, limited omniscient, as though the subjective self has been breached after Sarah, and readers are getting more objectivity on each character. And yet splinters of first-person point of view are lodged in each character's narrative, since all four principals maintain a web of written correspondence and we read their 'I' responses to letters, noting how they choose to present themselves to different people, whether charming or curmudgeonly. Each character is acutely conscious of his or her projected persona. As Sarah notes, 'Pick up a pen and a second self squirms out' (24). The characters also fret about their mis-steps, their false faces, and they sniff out falsity in their correspondents. And even though Morton's, Rose's, and Frederic's narratives are presented in third person, there are two intriguing developments after the Morton section. First, the written communications Rose and Frederic receive are not just personal letters. When Rose goes to the post office to pick up her mail, we are told 'there were three items for her today – not unusual, not at all ... her telephone bill ... a postcard ... ' and a 'large square beige envelope' (131), which we learn is the invitation to the Swann symposium. In Frederic's section, we read his replies not just to personal letters, but to invitations to speak, responses to his editorials, dinner invitations, a mysterious rare book dealer's query, and so forth (183–95).

Shields seems to emphasize a broader engagement with the world beyond self and scholarship that the many-hatted Rose and, especially, the multi-dimensional Cruzzi enjoy. No doubt Sarah and Jimroy receive phone bills and invitations of all sorts, but we don't hear as much about them.

The second – and related – intriguing development after the third-person Morton Jimroy section is that in Rose's and Frederic's third-person narratives, *we* creep in through the fourth wall. In these two sections, the narrative voice makes reference to the readers as though we are, simultaneously, Rose's or Frederic's neighbours, as well as intimates of the voice telling the story, with whom we share the telling. A neat post-mod feint: so we *are* both readers and readers-as-writers! An example would be: 'And why doesn't Rose confide any of this to you? You've known her for years, all your life in fact. Perhaps she detects lack of interest on your part ... ' (131). In Cruzzi's chapter: 'We love these wanderers for their brilliance' (175). Now that we have become complicit with the narrative voice, however, we still have the question of who is relating 'Frederic Cruzzi: His (Unwritten) One-Sentence Autobiography' (182–3). Cruzzi is disgusted by the 'cosy cherishing of self' and the 'inevitable lack of perspective' (181) that he feels are implicit in autobiography and so refuses to write his, though urged to do so. So have we penetrated Cruzzi's actual consciousness to 'hear' his innermost thoughts, or is some all-knowing boogey-narrator relating them? This blurring between subject and object seems, as an aesthetic strategy, both to keep paradox alive and blooming two-headed and yet to gather reader, writer, and character into one vase.

In the novel's fifth section, 'The Swann Symposium,' the illusion of an objective/dramatic voice letting the actors say and do for themselves is presented. The 'author' is 'disappeared'; we have, instead, the 'director,' who 'hopes to remain unobtrusive throughout, allowing dialogue and visual effects (and not private passions) to carry the weight of the narrative' (231). Yet, of course, this is a disingenuous ruse, as, for example, the following 'Director's Note' illustrates: 'Another sort of director, distrustful of his or her audience, might employ a flashback at this point' (259). The 'unobtrusive director,' while claiming to deflect attention from her/himself, is in fact calling attention to her/himself as a shaping force.

Inescapable, though, is the cooperative merging of individuated voices at the end of 'The Swann Symposium' as each of the formerly squabbling scholars, now robbed of their – and Mary Swann's – materials, contributes to the oral reconstruction of Swann's poem, bringing forth scraps from memory much in the manner of the Nadeau ladies at a quilting bee cooperating to bring forth something of beauty, and enjoying the social opportunity as they do so. These now-harmonious scholars, their faces 'subtly transformed' (311), are seen joined in 'a ceremonial act of reconstruction, *perhaps* [my emphasis] even an act of creation. There need be no suggestion that any one of them will become less selfish, less consumed with thoughts of tenure and academic glory, but each of them has, for the moment at least, transcended personal concerns' (311).

But the scholars don't have the last word in *Swann*. Shields opens and closes the novel with Mary Swann poems, the last one being 'Lost Things,' the poem the Swannians are labouring to piece together as we leave them. It seems appropriate to me that poetry – that genre in which meaning depends least on cognition, most on suggestion and sensual apprehension – brackets the novel, being given first word and last and thus re-embodying the eclipsed presence of Mary Swann, the author, the creator. Significantly, the last word of the narrative (312) gives echo to the last word of the poem 'Lost Things' and of the novel *Swann* – 'shame' – so that we hear 'shame ... shame,' because Carol Shields has told us a cautionary tale.

Learning How to Take Your Lumps

The outgrowth of the novel *Swann* – and of Shields's other works – is, of course, this essay and all of the other scholarly essays preserved here inside Carol Shields's 'Overflowing Cupboard.' Have we scholars earned the right to partake of

Shields's creative bounty, sitting 'round the table with her in our mismatched chairs, engaged in spirited but convivial dinner conversation, yet still mindful we are guests at Carol's Party? Or should our *Carol Shields, Narrative Hunger, and the Possibilities of Fiction* be retitled *Scholarly Cannibalism: The Shields Symposium*, featuring an assemblage of rude guests who interrupt each other, bicker, and backbite as we not only gobble Shields's cooking but, in ignoring our hostess, dispatch her, too? Or shall we all – author, scholars, readers – declare this a carry-in feast, with each of us contributing a dish for the table, Shields being only one of a number of cooks? The answer to that question – as to the questions 'What is the proper fare to assuage narrative hunger?' and 'What etiquette pertains to its presentation?' – Shields has given in her opening essay: 'Your response will depend on the culture you live in, the era into which you are born, on the width or narrowness of your aesthetic or moral responses' (26). Spoken like a true postmodernist.

For my own part, the outgrowth of studying the novel *Swann* and the other essays in this book is an ingrowth, a sort of *memento mori* I carry around in my mind's gut. Just as the minor characters Pauline Ouilette and Sister Mary Francis seemed to me to embody the novel's truest wisdoms – that the role of literature in life is to bind people closer together and to supplement, but not supplant, real life through imaginative projection – so does an unrealized character seem to have the last word, though unspoken, on the postmodern dilemma. Tellingly, this 'character' is dead and cannot speak for itself. It is the miraculous lump Sarah Maloney's mother has been delivered of. Sarah tells us:

[T]he lump from my mother's side this morning was not, as they had feared, the pulpy sponge of cancer but a compacted little bundle of bone and hair, which, they told me, was a fossilized foetus, my mother's twin sibling who somehow, in the months before her own birth, became absorbed in her body ... This fleshy mystery drives all other thoughts from my head. (56)

The significance of this lump certainly begs for our under-standing. Does it speak of stunted life possibilities, particu-larly for women born in less liberated times? Does it implore us to crawl out of mental abstraction and synthetic malaise and re-enter the fleshy, daily miracle of bodily existence? Does it warn us, metaphorically and literally, of the dangers of self-absorption? Probably all three of these surmises, and more, hold true. But the effect this 'little carved monkey of human matter' (56) has on *Sarah* interests me most keenly. First, it drives political, scholarly, and even romantic woes from Sarah's head: 'All these recent events, these *things*, seem suddenly trivial and rawly hatched in the light of what has happened: my mother's strange deliverance' (57). Note the final emphasis of that quotation is double: Sarah's concern and love for her mother regain primacy, *and* all other worldly cares pale in the face of pure wonder! Second, the little petri-fied person causes Sarah to speculate upon how this strange deliverance will affect her mother – 'There's no telling how my mother will react' (57) – and in speculating, Sarah begins to make up little stories, imagining her mother's sense of separa-tion and loss, her possible disgust, then even her laughter:

> She may bestow on her little nugget a pet name, Bertie or Sweet Pea, and make a fully rounded story out of it, her very own medical adventure, suitable for the ears of her canasta cronies, more interesting ... now that it's out and sitting in a jar of formaldehyde. (57)

Notice how Sarah's imagined stories give rise to projections of her mother's stories, as though the satisfaction of narrative hunger is not so much an end as a means, a procreative and transformative urge. Notice also how the death Sarah's mother has been carrying in her centre is not an emptiness (the dolorous plaint of postmodernists), not an absence, but a tangible presence that, once brought out and storied about with others, becomes humanized and intensely interesting, even entertaining.

Shields doesn't leave Sarah – or her mother – laughing in this scene, however. Sarah's final projection is darker toned: 'Or she may grieve. Lord, *I* would grieve. I *am* grieving. Just thinking of this colourless little bean of human matter sharing my mother's blood and warmth all those years brings a patch of tears into my throat' (57–8). Sarah cries for a lost human being and for her own loneliness.

Shields, through this wee homunculus, this unborn Bertie or Sweet Pea, shoves us back into our own inescapable lumps. We are at once trapped inside our flesh and pregnant with it. Lest we become self-absorbed, we must deliver ourselves of ourselves and imagine our lives into being with others around conference, canasta, and dinner tables.

Notes

1 Carol Shields, *Larry's Party* (New York: Viking, 1997), 10. All subsequent references are to this edition and will be made parenthetically.

2 Terry Eagleton, *Literary Theory: An Introduction* (Minneapolis: U of Minnesota P, 1983), 10.

3 Jonathan Culler, *On Deconstruction: Theory and Criticism after Structuralism* (Ithaca: Cornell UP, 1986), 130–1.

4 Carol Shields, *Swann* (New York: Penguin, 1990), 21. All subsequent references are to this edition and will be made parenthetically.

5 Carol Shields, *The Stone Diaries* (New York: Penguin, 1995), 76–7. All subsequent references are to this edition and will be made parenthetically.

SECTION FOUR

Annotated Bibliography

FAYE HAMMILL

Carol Shields: An Annotated Bibliography

FAYE HAMMILL

Section I of this bibliography lists Carol Shields's published fiction, drama, poetry, and criticism. Her works are classified according to genre, and listed chronologically within each category. The publication details are those of the first editions, and information about literary prizes is also given. A summary of contents is given for her critical writing only, since her imaginative work is discussed elsewhere in this volume.

Section II of the bibliography lists all the critical articles on Shields's work (excluding book reviews) that have appeared in English- or French-language books and journals. A summary of contents is given for each item listed. This section also includes selected theses, interviews, and profiles. Within these categories, items are listed alphabetically under the name of the author.

Section III gives details of films concerning Shields or her novels.

I. Works by Carol Shields

A. Novels

Small Ceremonies. Toronto: McGraw-Hill Ryerson, 1976.
The Box Garden. Toronto: McGraw-Hill Ryerson, 1977.
Happenstance. Toronto: McGraw-Hill Ryerson, 1980.

A Fairly Conventional Woman. Toronto: Macmillan, 1982.

> *Happenstance* and *A Fairly Conventional Woman* were published in one volume (London: HarperCollins-Flamingo, 1994), under the title *Happenstance.* The two sections are renamed *Happenstance: The Husband's Story* and *Happenstance: The Wife's Story.*

Swann: A Mystery. Toronto: Stoddart, 1987.

> This was the first book by Shields to appear in Britain, and was published as *Mary Swann* (London: Fourth Estate, 1990). The 1993 Stoddart edition is titled *Swann: A Literary Mystery.* The most recent edition (Toronto: Random House, 1995) is titled *Swann,* which was Shields's preferred title. Winner of the Arthur Ellis Award for Best Canadian Mystery (1988) and shortlisted for the Governor General's Award of Canada.

A Celibate Season. Co-written with Blanche Howard. Regina: Coteau, 1991.

> Howard adapted *A Celibate Season* into a play, which was a finalist in the Canadian National Theatre Playwriting Competition in 1989 and was produced in 1990.

The Republic of Love. Toronto: Random House, 1992.

> Runner-up in the 1992 UK Guardian Fiction Prize.

The Stone Diaries. Toronto: Random House, 1993.

> Winner of the Governor General's Award (1993) and nominated for the Booker Prize (1993). This novel also won the Canadian Booksellers Association Prize (1994) and the McNally Robinson Award for the Manitoba Book of the Year (1994); and in the United States, the Pulitzer Prize (1995) and the National Book Critics' Circle Award (1995).

Larry's Party. Toronto: Random House, 1997.

> Winner of the 1998 Orange Prize for women's fiction. The opening chapter of this novel is a version of a short story, 'By Mistake,' published in *Prairie Fire* 16.1 (Spring 1995): 13–21.

Unless. Toronto: Random House, 2002.

B. Poetry Collections

Others: Poems. Ottawa: Borealis P, 1972.

> Seven of the fifty poems in this collection were written for a

CBC competition for young writers, which Shields won in 1965.

Intersect: Poems. Ottawa: Borealis P, 1974.

Coming to Canada. Ottawa: Carleton UP, 1992. Rev. ed. 1995.
The poems of the title sequence are supplemented in the 1995 edition by selections from *Others* and *Intersect*, plus thirty-three new poems.

C. Short Story Collections

Various Miracles. Toronto: Stoddart, 1985.
There is some variation between the North American and British versions. The Canadian edition contains the following stories: 'Mrs Turner Cutting the Grass,' 'Various Miracles,' 'Home,' 'Dolls, Dolls, Dolls, Dolls,' 'Poaching,' 'Scenes,' 'Accidents,' 'Others,' 'The Journal,' 'Love So Fleeting, Love So Fine,' 'The Metaphor Is Dead – Pass It On,' 'Taking the Train,' and 'Sailors Lost at Sea.' Several of the stories were first published in journals and magazines. 'Mrs Turner Cutting the Grass' won the National Magazine Award in 1985.

The Orange Fish. Toronto: Random House, 1989.
This was selected by the *Christian Science Monitor* as one of the two best books of short fiction of the year. It contains the following stories: 'The Orange Fish,' 'Chemistry,' 'Hazel,' 'Today Is the Day,' 'Hinterland,' 'Block Out,' 'Collision,' 'Good Manners,' 'Times of Sickness and Health,' 'Family Secrets,' 'Fuel for the Fire,' and 'Milk Bread Beer Ice.' Several of these were first published in journals and magazines. 'Today Is the Day' was first published as 'Close Observation' in the *West Coast Review*. This book has not been published in the UK, but seven of the stories are included in the British edition of *Various Miracles* (Fourth Estate, 1994).

Dressing Up for the Carnival. Toronto: Random House, 2000; London: Fourth Estate, 2000.
Contains: 'Dressing Up for the Carnival,' 'A Scarf,' 'Weather,' 'Flatties,' 'Dying for Love,' 'Ilk,' 'Stop!,' 'Mirrors,' 'The Harp,' 'Our Men and Women,' 'Keys,' 'Absence,' 'Windows,'

'Reportage,' 'Edith-Esther,' 'New Music,' 'Soup du Jour,' 'Invention,' 'Death of an Artist,' 'The Next Best Kiss,' 'Eros,' 'Dressing Down.' Several of these were first published in magazines, newspapers, anthologies, or individual limited editions, with the earliest being 'Reportage' in 1988. 'Dying for Love' has already been published in two journals and one anthology.

D. Plays and Screenplays

'Women Waiting.' Radio drama broadcast on CBC in 1983.
Departures and Arrivals. Winnipeg: Blizzard Publishing, 1990.
The Republic of Love. 1993.
　　Screenplay written by Shields for a Winnipeg producer. The film was still in production in 2001.
Thirteen Hands. Winnipeg: Blizzard Publishing, 1993.
　　Premiered in Toronto in 1995.
Fashion, Power, Guilt and the Charity of Families. Co-written with Catherine Shields. Winnipeg: Blizzard Publishing, 1995.
　　Premiered in Winnipeg in 1995. Shields's daughter also collaborated on her two previous plays, but here the arrangement is formalized. An extract from the play appears in *Prairie Fire* 16.1 (Spring 1995).
Anniversary. Co-written with David Williamson. Winnipeg: Blizzard Publishing, 1998.
Sisters by Chance. Broadcast on CBC Radio, 3 October 1999.

E. Criticism and Non-fiction

Note: This section excludes book reviews by Shields.

Susanna Moodie: Voice and Vision. Ottawa: Borealis P, 1977.
　　The published version of Shields's master's thesis (University of Ottawa, 1975). She argues that Moodie has suffered at the hands of thematic critics (especially Atwood) who have turned her into a shorthand symbol for a supposed Canadian national character. Shields's reading of Moodie

emphasizes her 'unique vision' and discusses her fascination with her own personality and her singular attitudes to gender and class. She believes that Moodie's character gives unity to her books about Canada. An excerpt from this book appears as 'Mrs Moodie and Sexual Reversal' in the Canadian Critical Edition of *Roughing It in the Bush* (Ottawa: Tecumseh, 1997).

'Dorothy Livesay, Miriam Waddington, Beth Harvor, Audrey Thomas, Gwen Pharis Ringwood, Elizabeth Brewster and Margaret Atwood. "My Craft and Sullen Art": The Writers Speak.' *Atlantis: A Women's Studies Journal* 4.1 (Fall 1978): 144–63.

Shields's contribution to this article is only two pages, but it is worth reading for its comments on other Canadian women writers: Frances Brooke, Susanna Moodie, Sara Jeannette Duncan, and Alice Munro. Shields says she cannot believe in the 'attractive myth of the feminine voice,' but she does delineate her concept of feminine subject matter.

Response to the Applebaum-Herbert Report. *Room of One's Own* 4.4 (March/April 1983): 8–12.

Shields's synthesis of comments from various Manitoba writers about arts funding and cultural agencies, copyright regulations, and translation fees in Canada.

Afterword to *Life in the Clearings versus the Bush*, by Susanna Moodie. Toronto: McClelland & Stewart, 1989.

This essay shows some marked developments from Shields's evaluation of Moodie in her master's thesis. The Moodie she portrays in the Afterword is a woman whose 'contradictions are her chief delight' and whose 'acts of re-imagination rise from an unconscious strategy of survival.' Shields here focuses on the disjunctive and ambivalent nature of Moodie's texts.

'The Same Ticking Clock.' In *Language in Her Eye: Views on Writing and Gender by Canadian Women Writing in English*, edited by Libby Scheier, Sarah Sheard, and Eleanor Wachtel, 256–9. Toronto: Coach House P, 1990.

A meditation on the human need to escape the limitations of the self through the stories of others. Shields argues that writers need not be confined to the experiences and places which they know at first-hand, but can 'leave [their] own skins' and explore alternative perspectives. She concentrates particularly on writing from the point of view of the opposite sex.

'Thinking Back through Our Mothers: Tradition in Canadian Women's Writing.' In *Re(dis)covering Our Foremothers: Nineteenth-Century Canadian Women Writers*, edited by Lorraine McMullen, 9–13. Ottawa: U of Ottawa P, 1990.

This is one of three short essays on the same topic (the others are by Clara Thomas and Donna E Smyth). Shields remembers the books belonging to her mother which she read as a child: *Anne of Green Gables, A Girl of the Limberlost, Helen's Babies,* and *Beautiful Joe.* She mentions the childhood reading of other Canadian women writers and posits a feminine reading tradition which embraces popular fiction.

'Jane Austen Images of the Body: No Fingers, No Toes.' *Persuasions: Journal of the Jane Austen Society of North America* 13 (16 Dec. 1991): 132–7.

The transcript of a talk, this entertaining piece notes the scarcity of references to the body in Austen's novels. Shields picks out those body parts which *are* mentioned frequently (eyes, hearts, hands), observing that those belong more to the eighteenth-century rational system than to anatomy. She traces the attitudes toward the human body which prevailed in different centuries, concluding that Austen believed the body to be without consequence unless yoked to reason.

'Leaving the Brick House Behind: Margaret Laurence and the Loop of Memory.' *RANAM: Recherches Anglaises et Nord-Américaines* 24 (1991): 75–7.

A short exploration of the symbolism of the Brick House, Margaret Laurence's girlhood home, which later featured in her book *A Bird in the House.* Shields discusses, in particular, the implications of a brick house in the Prairie provinces and Laurence's heroine's changing perceptions of the house where she grows up.

'Arriving Late: Starting Over.' In *How Stories Mean*, edited by John Metcalf and J.R. (Tim) Struthers, 244–51. Erin, ON: Porcupine's Quill, 1993.

An interesting account of her experiences as a writer of short stories, in which Shields focuses particularly on the composition of *Various Miracles*. She discusses her disruption of the linear narrative, and her rejection of some of the conventions of fiction writing. She also comments on her inclusion of domestic and everyday subject matter.

'Others.' Part of the 'Women: Summer Madness' series. *The Guardian* (25 Aug. 1997). G2T, p. 4.

A detailed statement from Shields about her fascination with other people's lives. Shields explains how her curiosity about the ordinary habits of others has shaped her writing, but also discusses the importance of privacy and the pitfalls of inquisitiveness.

'On the Burdens of Being a Writer.' In *Twenty-Two Provocative Canadians: In the Spirit of Bob Edwards*, edited by Kerry Longpré and Margaret Dickson, 26–31. Calgary: Bayeux Arts, 1999.

A brief but interesting essay on the practical and psychological experience of authorship.

Jane Austen: A Life. London: Weidenfeld and Nicholson, 2001.

A concise, readable, and elegant biography, intended for readers seeking an introduction to Austen's life. It will also appeal to admirers of Shields because it sheds light on her relationship to Austen, and offers a subtle exploration of the pleasures and problems of biographical research.

Dropped Threads: What We Aren't Told. Ed. Carol Shields and Marjorie May. Toronto: Vintage, 2001.

A collection of thirty-four essays and short stories by Canadian women, with an afterword by Shields.

II. Works about Carol Shields

Several of the following pieces are contained in two special journal issues devoted to Shields: *Room of One's Own* 13.1/2 (1989) and *Prairie Fire* 16.1 (Spring 1995).

A. Reminiscences, Creative Responses, Profiles,
and Selected Interviews

Anderson, Marjorie. Interview with Carol Shields. *Prairie Fire*
16.1 (Spring 1995): 139–50.

Conducted in May 1993, this interview elicits some fascinating comments from Shields. Her responses to nineteenth-
century women writers are particularly interesting: she
describes the affinities she feels with Austen and Charlotte
Brontë, the subtexts she finds in Moodie's work, and the
way the women's movement has affected our reading of
Victorian literature. Other topics covered include genre,
gender, audience, loneliness, and romance.

Cumming, Laura. 'Find Your Own Way.' *The Guardian*
(14 Aug. 1997). G2T, p. 12.

An edited version of a piece that first appeared in the
summer 1997 edition of Waterstones's 'W' magazine. Shields
explains that her first two poetry collections attempted to
capture the 'secluded, unexplored lives' of the people she
encountered in Winnipeg in the 1970s. She also discusses
Larry's Party in these terms.

Denoon, Anne. 'Playing with Convention.' *Books in Canada*
22.9 (Dec. 1993): 8–12.

This interview covers a variety of topics from Shields's
interest in nineteenth-century literature through biography
and parody to nationality. Shields makes some interesting
comments about the gradual alterations which have taken
place in her writing habits and techniques.

De Roo, Harvey. 'A Little like Flying: An Interview with Carol
Shields.' *West Coast Review* 23.3 (Winter 1988): 38–56.

De Roo's interview was conducted by correspondence and
contains some intriguing statements from Shields about the
inadequacies of genre classification, her own early writing
of poetry, the complexities of 'voice' in fiction, her desire to
write about 'the real lives of women,' the importance of
language, and many other topics. One of the best interviews available.

Duncan, Sandy. 'Open Letter to Carol Shields.' *Room of One's Own* 13.1/2 (1989): 77–81.

Duncan feels that she cannot write *about* Shields but must write *to* her, and mentions the 'women's genre' of the letter. She relates several anecdotes about her friendship with Shields, describing their many conversations in the late 1970s about women's writing, families, Vancouver life, and so on.

Giardini, Anne. 'Reading My Mother.' *Prairie Fire* 16.1 (Spring 1995): 6–12.

A sensitive and highly personal essay by one of Shields's daughters, this piece is much more than a reminiscence. Giardini touches on the way some of the experiences and characteristics of the Shields family have been transmuted into fictional material. But she also articulates her own gradual recognition that her mother and the writer Carol Shields 'are in every important way the same,' and that she can get to know her mother more intimately by reading her books.

Herbert, Susanna. 'The Strangeness of Men.' *The Daily Telegraph*, 16 Aug. 1997, A5.

A well-written article based on an interview with Shields at the time of publication of *Larry's Party*. A couple of factual inaccuracies, but some interesting comments from both Shields and Herbert about the male perspective, the 'search for the self,' and the writer's habit of detailed observation of others.

Hollenberg, Donna Krolik. 'An Interview with Carol Shields.' *Contemporary Literature* 39.3 (1998): 339–55.

Includes discussion of *Fashion, Power, Guilt and the Charity of Families, Happenstance, Small Ceremonies* and *The Stone Diaries*. Detailed and useful, especially as some of these texts are not often covered in interviews.

Honigsbaum, Mark. 'Goddess of Small Things: The Guardian Profile.' *The Guardian*, 23 May 1998, 6–7.

An extended profile of Shields written the week she won the Orange Prize for *Larry's Party*, this piece discusses

Shields's life and several of her novels at some length. The author has clearly done his homework, and come up with a wealth of interesting details, including some taken from the *Room of One's Own* and *Prairie Fire* special issues on Shields. He incorporates a number of comments from Don Shields and from Carol Shields's colleagues and editors.

Howard, Blanche. 'Collaborating with Carol.' *Prairie Fire* 16.1 (Spring 1995): 71–8.

An account of her friendship with Shields, their copious correspondence dating back to the 1970s, and their collaboration on *A Celibate Season*. She reveals that she wrote Jocelyn's letters and Shields wrote Charles's, and that they actually sent them to each other, one by one. Howard also describes the long process of getting the novel published and her adaptation of it into a playscript.

Hughes, Lesley. 'The Shields Diaries.' *Chatelaine* (April 1996): 110–15, 138.

A combined interview and biographical article, this piece was written by a journalist friend of Shields. It is best summarized by Helen Buss: 'Hughes constructs Shields for *Chatelaine* as preoccupied with family and husband ... placing the literary accomplishment in the ... category of hobby' ('Abducting Mary and Carol,' 437).

Marshall, Andrew G. 'Eight Hundred Women Heard My Voice.' *The Independent*, 9 Sept. 1997, Tabloid, p. 10.

A continuous statement by Shields rather than a conventional interview, this piece describes her gradual awakening to the women's movement. She identifies the 1983 Women and Words conference in Vancouver as the point at which she acquired faith in the authenticity of women's experience, and its validity as a subject for literature.

McMullen, Lorraine. 'Carol Shields and the University of Ottawa: Some Reminiscences.' *Prairie Fire* 16.1 (Spring 1995): 132–7.

Lorraine McMullen directed Shields's M.A. thesis in the early 1970s, and this piece provides very interesting information about the blossoming of Canadian studies at that time. McMullen describes the symposiums and readings by Canadian poets which Shields attended, and the courses she took, as well as giving her own impression of Shields's personality.

Smith, Giles. '"When I Read Books, I Certainly Don't Read for the Plot": An Interview with Carol Shields.' *The Independent*, 3 July 1995, Supplement, pp. 4–5.

Lots of biographical material and information on Shields's literary reputation in Canada and the UK, and a few choice quotations from Shields about her early career.

Thomas, Joan. 'The Golden Book: An Interview with Carol Shields.' *Prairie Fire* 14.4 (Winter 1993–4): 56–62.

In this interview, Shields discusses the difficulties of writing in the complex (auto)biographical form she chose for *The Stone Diaries*, and the status of the photographs within the text.

– '"... Writing Must Come Out of What Passionately Interests Us. Nothing Else Will Do." An Epistolary Interview with Carol Shields.' *Prairie Fire* 16.1 (Spring 1995): 121–30.

Shields's responses to interview questions are always thoughtful and precise, but this exchange of six letters produces an especially coherent discussion. Shields recalls the social fabric of her Oak Park childhood, and describes the way Daisy in *The Stone Diaries* is confined by 'social strictures' and is unable to define her own needs. She also writes about the inspiration she herself found in having children, and ends by saying that her 'life theme' is the question 'how do we value a human life?'

van Herk, Aritha. 'Extrapolations from *Miracles*.' *Room of One's Own* 13.1/2 (1989): 99–108.

A creative response to Shields's work, best described in Eleanor Wachtel's introduction: 'Aritha van Herk takes off from *Various Miracles* and weaves a story of her own, about Shields and the miracle of words.' Many of the characters from *Various Miracles* resurface in this text, and step outside their respective stories to interact with one another in new ways. The last few paragraphs present an imaginary portrait of Shields herself.

Wachtel, Eleanor. 'Interview with Carol Shields.' *Room of One's Own* 13.1/2 (1989): 5–45.

An extended interview which begins with Shields's childhood and her early reading and writing, and progresses chronologically through her life. There are details on every phase of her education and married life, and comments about each of her books. Shields's engaging personal reminiscences and anecdotes are interspersed with many reflections on education, language, genre, history, gender, ethnicity, socialism, Canadian literature, changing social mores, and other general topics. Wachtel also published a profile of Shields, based on material from the *Room of One's Own* interview: 'Telling It Slant,' *Books in Canada* 18.4 (May 1989): 9–14.

Wilkins, Charles. 'The Deconstruction of Love.' *Room of One's Own* 13.1/2 (1989): 91–8.

Wilkins relates how, inspired by reading 'Home' from *Various Miracles*, he wanted to write to Shields, but after several failed beginnings, he sent her a blank sheet of paper instead. After this, he went to show her a 'short story' of his which was in fact another blank sheet.

B. Criticism: Books

Werlock, Abby. *The Stone Diaries: A Reader's Guide*. London: Continuum, 2001.

The first book-length study of Shields's work. This is a concise (80,000-word) and extremely lucid companion to *The Stone Diaries*, which would be a very useful resource for teaching the novel. It approaches the book from a variety of angles, includes details of the reception of the novel, and also provides a bibliography of further reading.

C. Critical Articles

Bak, Hans. 'Between the Flower and the Stone: The Novel As Biography / The Biography As Novel – Carol Shields's *The Stone Diaries*.' In *European Perspectives on English-Canadian Literature*, edited by Charles Forceville, 11–22. Amsterdam: Free UP, 1995.

A very appreciative assessment, this article explores Shields's manipulation of the conventions of (auto)biography. Bak enumerates the strategies employed in *The Stone Diaries* to force the reader into the position of biographer, reconstructing the life of Daisy Goodwill Flett from undigested raw material such as letters, pictures, and lists. A second line of argument connects the absence of Daisy from her own text with her lifelong habit of self-effacement. Readable and cogent, but tending to veer into paraphrase or character study.

Begley, Adam. 'Raiders of the Lost Archives: The Latest Academic Novels Make Sexy Sleuths out of Text-Hungry Scholars.' *Lingua Franca: The Review of Academic Life* 3.5 (July/August 1993): 36–40.

This article on the portrayal of academics in English, Canadian, American, and Italian literature includes some paragraphs on *Swann*.

Billingham, Susan. 'Fragile Tissue: The Fiction of Carol Shields.' *British Journal of Canadian Studies* 13.2 (1998): 276–87.

Billingham argues that Shields's work is impossible to categorize since it contains realist, modernist, and postmodernist elements. She discusses *Small Ceremonies* and *The Stone Diaries*, concentrating on the exploration of biography and autobiography and the blurring of genre boundaries in those novels, as well as Shields's preoccupation with the 'fragile tissue of connection' between human beings. Shields's use of images of filaments is analysed to particularly good effect.

Buss, Helen. 'Abducting Mary and Carol: Reading Carol

Shields's *Swann* and the Representation of the Writer through Theories of Biographical Recognition.' *English Studies in Canada* 23.4 (Dec. 1997): 427–41.

Drawing on various theories of biographical writing, Buss analyses the way the characters in *Swann* abduct and commodify their subject, Mary Swann. She argues that the novel exposes the appropriative agendas of traditional biography. Buss also discusses a selection of interviews with Shields and biographical articles about her, pointing to 'the abductive processes that effect the biographical construction of the writer Carol Shields.' Accomplished and penetrating.

Giltrow, Janet. 'Strange Attractors.' *West Coast Review* 23.3 (Winter 1988): 58–66.

A perceptive reading of several stories from *The Orange Fish*, this article begins by exploring Shields's vision of the relationship between art and audience. Neatly linking the short stories with some of the novels, Giltrow then expands her discussion to cover point of view and narrative self-consciousness.

Godard, Barbara. 'Sleuthing: Feminists Re/writing the Detective Novel.' *Signature: Journal of Theory and Canadian Literature* 1 (Summer 1989): 45–70.

A survey of selected feminist detective novels is followed by a detailed and innovative reading of *Swann* in terms of this emergent genre. Godard insists on the subversive potential of the new form she identifies, arguing that Shields implicates all her characters in criminal acts of misappropriation and misreading, thereby 'confronting the meaning-making rituals of our society.' The novel is said to parody many detective conventions, particularly in offering Mary Swann's life, and not her death, as the mystery which defies reconstruction. Aside from the rather impenetrable theoretical introduction, this article is striking and persuasive.

Gom, Leona. 'Stone and Flowers.' *Prairie Fire* 16.1 (Spring 1995): 22–7.

This article explores the two principal image patterns which

Shields uses to depict Daisy and the other characters in *The Stone Diaries*. Gom enumerates the subtle and complex connotations which the novel ascribes to stones and flowers / gardens, and analyses the relationship between the two groups of images. Brief but intriguing.

Groening, Laura. 'Still in the Kitchen: The Art of Carol Shields.' *Canadian Forum* (Jan. / Feb. 1991): 14–17.

A brief but interesting article which explores the domestic settings of Shields's fiction.

Hall, Susan Grove. 'The Duality of the Artist / Crafter in Carol Shields's Novels.' *Kentucky Philological Review* 12 (March 1997): 42–7.

This article discusses the artist figure in *The Stone Diaries*, *Happenstance*, and *The Box Garden*, and explores the distinction between art and craft in those novels. A short but useful addition to the small body of work on *Happenstance* and *The Box Garden*.

Hammill, Faye. 'Carol Shields's "Native Genre" and the Figure of the Canadian Author.' *Journal of Commonwealth Literature* 31.2 (1996): 87–100.

A discussion of *Small Ceremonies* and *Swann* in terms of Shields's commentary on Canadian literary institutions and their construction of supposed national traditions. The focus is on the novels' gently ironic perspective on cultural nationalism, 'authenticity,' and the machinations of academic critics and biographers.

– 'Margaret Atwood, Carol Shields and "That Moodie Bitch."' *American Review of Canadian Studies* 29.1 (Autumn 1999): 67–91.

A comparison of Atwood and Shields in terms of their fictional and critical writing on Susanna Moodie. The Shields texts discussed are *Small Ceremonies*, *Susanna Moodie: Voice and Vision*, *Swann*, and the Afterword to Moodie's *Life in the Clearings*.

Howells, Coral Ann. 'In the Subjunctive Mood: Carol Shields's *Dressing Up for the Carnival*.' *Yearbook of English Studies* 31 (2001): 144–54.

This essay explores Shields's feminized postmodern ver-

sion of the Bakhtinian carnivalesque as it is figured in the
first and last stories in this collection, 'Dressing Up for the
Carnival' and 'Dressing Down.' By invoking the subjunctive mood in association with the carnivalesque, Shields
opens up possibilities for shifts of emphasis, quietly subverting generic conventions of the realist short story.

Ings, Katharine Nicholson. 'Illuminating the Moment: Verbal
Tableaux in Carol Shields's Poetry.' *Prairie Fire* 16.1 (Spring
1995): 168–73.

'Visual moments of almost epiphanic clarity' are the subject
of this essay, which is not, however, a formal analysis but a
discussion of the 'moral codes' which Ings believes are built
into Shields's poetry. This is an assured critique, claiming
that the reader must not distance herself from the moral
universe of the poems, or else she will lose the full impact
of the climactic moments. Many of these epiphanies are
connected, it is argued, with the explosion of traditions or
fantasies. A related topic, according to Ings, is Shields's
ironic refusal of political correctness.

Johnson, Brian. 'Necessary Illusions: Foucault's Author Function in Carol Shields's *Swann*.' *Prairie Fire* 16.1 (Spring 1995):
56–70.

This intelligent analysis relates *Swann* to Foucault's idea
that readers impose their personal image of the author onto
a text, thus limiting their readings of it. According to Johnson,
the novel 'raises questions about power and appropriation'
and in effect dramatizes Foucault's theories, beginning with
the Barthesian premise of the dead author. The article offers
a detailed exploration of the way the four Swann 'detec-
tives' construct their different versions of Mary Swann and
appropriate her discourse.

Johnson, Chris. 'Ordinary Pleasures (and Terrors): The Plays
of Carol Shields.' *Prairie Fire* 16.1 (Spring 1995): 161–7.

Few literary critics have discussed Shields's dramatic work,
but Johnson offers a serious consideration of it. He has
much to say about the sophistication of the plays and the
density of the individual scenes, repudiating charges of

flimsiness and sentimentality which have been levelled by some theatre critics and academics. (He does express, however, reservations about certain elements of the plays.) His descriptions of the first productions of *Departures and Arrivals* and *Thirteen Hands* are especially interesting.

Kröller, Eva-Marie. 'Resurrections: Susanna Moodie, Catharine Parr Traill and Emily Carr in Contemporary Canadian Literature.' *Journal of Popular Culture* 15.3 (1981): 39–46.

This article includes a short discussion of *Small Ceremonies*, connecting it to Atwood's *Journals of Susanna Moodie* and other texts which have revisited the Strickland sisters.

Léger, Benoit. 'Traduction littéraire et polyphonie dans "Mrs Turner Cutting the Grass" de Carol Shields.' *Studies in Canadian Literature* 20.1 (1995): 16–28.

Responding to Kent Thompson's article on the multiplicity of voices in two stories from *Various Miracles*, Léger extends the analysis by invoking Bakhtin's concept of the polyphonic text. He concludes that Shields's stories do not employ 'social polyphony,' since she foregrounds voices from privileged sectors of society and uses free indirect style rather than extensive dialogue to render different voices. Her brand of polyphony, it is argued, is on the level of discourse because she draws on a variety of discursive spheres: masculine and feminine; intellectual and popular; specialized and clichéd. Léger goes on to discuss the way translations of Shields's work into French should respond to her narrative plurality, but this second part of the article has not the clarity and detail of the first.

Levenson, Christopher. Introduction to *Coming to Canada*, by Carol Shields. Ottawa: Carleton UP, 1995.

In this accessible and informative introduction, Levenson discusses the thematic and tonal connections between Shields's fiction and her poetry. Almost half the essay focuses on the novels, offering some interesting comments on the development of Shields's style and subject matter over time. In his second section, Levenson quotes liberally from Shields's poetry, tracing her particular blend of wit and understatement. He also explains his reluctance to align her with a specifically Canadian tradition.

Mellor, Winifred M. '"The Simple Container of Our Existence": Narrative Ambiguity in Carol Shields's *The Stone Diaries.' Studies in Canadian Literature* 20.2 (1995): 96–110.

Mellor reads *The Stone Diaries* as a feminist-poststructuralist disruption of the conventions of autobiography. Drawing on a range of theoretical discussions of life writing, she traces the way in which 'the conspiratorial relationship between the anonymous "I"-narrator and the reader' deprives Daisy herself of a voice. A perceptive and valuable article.

Niederhoff, Burkhard. 'How to Do Things with History: Researching Lives in Carol Shields's *Swann* and Margaret Atwood's *Alias Grace.' Journal of Commonwealth Literature* 35.2 (2000): 71–85.

A comparison between the attitudes to research represented in these two novels, and an interesting consideration of the relevance of Hutcheon's term 'historiographic metafiction' to each book. Nothing particularly new on *Swann*; rather better on *Alias Grace* and on the connections between the two texts.

Nodelman, Perry. 'Living in the Republic of Love: Carol Shields's Winnipeg.' *Prairie Fire* 16.1 (Spring 1995): 40–55.

Nodelman entertainingly describes his response as a Winnipeg reader to *The Republic of Love*, and the excitement of reading about one's home town in fiction. He gives details of the actual shops, streets, and cafes which appear in the novel, and also of the small inaccuracies of street names and locations which he concludes are intentional and designed to convey a certain strangeness. His sensitive exploration of the relationship between a real and an imagined city leads into a discussion of the novel's portrayal of love and romance.

Page, Malcolm. '*Small Ceremonies* and the Art of the Novel.' *Journal of Canadian Fiction* 28–9 (1980): 172–8.

One of the earliest critical assessments of Shields. Rather a lot of plot summary, but some useful comments on the different forms of writing (biography, fiction, autobiography) and plagiarism which are explored in the novel. Clear and concise.

Schnitzer, Deborah. 'Tricks: Artful Photographs and Letters in Carol Shields's *The Stone Diaries* and Anita Brookner's *Hotel du Lac.' Prairie Fire* 16.1 (Spring 1995): 28–39.

The (auto)biographical idiosyncrasies in *The Stone Diaries* are here explored in terms of the photographs and the letters to Daisy which are embedded in the text. Schnitzer explains how she repeatedly revised her interpretation of Daisy as she read *The Stone Diaries*, and discusses the sophistication of Shields's use of the unreliable narrator. An excellent analysis of the text's contradictions and paradoxes, and some illuminating comparisons with Brookner.

Slethaug, Gordon E. '"The Coded Dots of Life": Carol Shields's Diaries and Stones.' *Canadian Literature* 156 (Spring 1998): 59–81.

According to Slethaug, 'The diaries and stones announced in the title of Shields's book serve as figures for the main character's self-construction and her construction by others, and for their "chaotic" implications.' His analysis of *The Stone Diaries* is complicated, drawing as it does on Bakhtin, Derrida, and Pierre Bourdieu, but it offers some lucid insights into the subtleties of the novel's narrative voice and the implications of the stone references. He emphasizes the coexistence of pattern and incoherence, continuity and fragmentation, within the novel and within Daisy's life. Some of his arguments echo those of Bak, Mellor, and Schnitzer, though he does not cite their articles.

Smyth, Donna E. 'Shields's Swann.' *Room of One's Own* 13.1/2 (1989): 136–46.

This response to *Swann* is a blend of the critical and the creative, as befits its novelist-academic author. Smyth explores the oppositions between the various characters, and their fluctuations between the 'negative pole of being' and occasional moments of transcendence. She emphasizes the aspects of loss and loneliness which emerge from the novel. Since Smyth also looks at mystery and falsification, her piece forms an interesting dialogue with Clara Thomas's, which appears in the same volume.

Sweeney, Susan Elizabeth. 'Formal Strategies in a Female Narrative Tradition: The Case of *Swann: A Mystery.*' In *Anxious Power: Reading, Writing and Ambivalence in Narrative by Women*, edited by Carol J. Singley, 19–32. Albany: State U of New York P, 1993.

Framing her essay with an exposition of her own feminist aesthetic, Sweeney skilfully analyses those formal aspects of Shields's narrative which reveal 'her anxiety about the production and interpretation of women's writing.' She equates the multiplicity of narrative voices in *Swann* with a peculiarly feminine ambivalence toward authority, and points out that Shields's characters offer a series of 'solipsistic interpretations' of Swann's blood poem, guided by their personal preoccupations. But Sweeney does not herself avoid a solipsistic interpretation of the novel, since her reading is entirely governed by her feminist agenda.

Thomas, Clara. '"A Slight Parodic Edge": *Swann: A Mystery.*' *Room of One's Own* 13.1/2 (1989): 109–22. Rpt. in *Multiple Voices: Recent Canadian Fiction*, edited by Jeanne Delbaere, 104–15. Sydney: Dangeroo P, 1990. Proceedings of the IVth International Symposium of the Brussels Centre for Canadian Studies (1989).

A cogent reading of *Swann* which concentrates on Shields's parodic and intertextual strategies, and her play with genre and characterization. Thomas argues that Jimroy, Rose, and Cruzzi each begin in caricature and develop toward humanity, but that the final film-script section of the novel deconstructs this realism.

– 'Reassembling Fragments: Susanna Moodie, Carol Shields and Mary Swann.' In *Inside the Poem: Essays and Poems in Honour of Donald Stephens*, edited by W.H. New, 196–204. Toronto: Oxford UP, 1992.

Thomas connects Mary Swann with Susanna Moodie via

their fragments of poetry. She offers a brief appreciation of the poems included in *Roughing It in the Bush*, arguing that just as Moodie's text is incomplete without the poetry, so *Swann* would be incomplete without the inserted snatches of Mary Swann's verse. An extended rehearsal of *Swann's* plot leaves Thomas little space for critical commentary or broader comparison between Swann and Moodie.

– 'Stories like Sonnets: "Mrs Turner Cutting the Grass."' *Prairie Fire* 16.1 (Spring 1995): 79–83.

A brief but perceptive analysis of the irony and narrative sophistication of Shields's most admired short story.

– 'Carol Shields's *The Republic of Love* and *The Stone Diaries*: "Swerves of Destiny" and "Rings of Light."' In *'Union in Partition': Essays in Honour of Jeanne Delbaere*, edited by Gilbert Debusscher and Marc Maufort, 153–60. Liège, Belgium: L3– Liège Language and Literature, 1997.

This essay covers Shields's treatment of chance, destiny, deception, and appearance, and is valuable in being one of only two pieces to discuss *The Republic of Love*. Thomas likens Shields's works to Vermeer paintings, and also discusses their relation to fairy tale. The phrase 'swerves of destiny' comes from Marina Warner's *From the Beast to the Blonde*.

Thompson, Kent. 'Reticence in Carol Shields.' *Room of One's Own* 13.1/2 (1989): 69–76.

Thompson was an undergraduate classmate of Shields, and later, as editor of the *Fiddlehead*, he published some of her work. His essay combines an account of their shared educational experiences with comments on *Various Miracles*. He mentions the multiplicity of voices in her fiction, relating this to her enjoyment of radio drama.

Vauthier, Simone. 'On Carol Shields's "Mrs Turner Cutting the Grass."' *Commonwealth: Essays and Studies* 11.2 (Spring 1989): 63–74.

Vauthier argues convincingly that Shields displaces conventional narrative expectations in her short story by defying linearity, causality, and traditional plotting. The article analyses the temporal sequences and shifts in perspective in 'Mrs Turner,' and points out that supposedly important facts, such as Girlie Fergus's teenage pregnancy, are subordinated to everyday details – something which Vauthier believes to be a peculiarly feminine strategy. She also offers an intriguing account of how Shields manipulates the reader's attitude toward Mrs Turner. This essay is reprinted in Vauthier's 1993 book, *Reverberations: Explorations in the Canadian Short Story* (Concord, ON: Anansi, 1993).

– '"They Say Miracles Are Past" but They Are Wrong.' *Prairie Fire* 16.1 (Spring 1995): 84–104.

A dense but penetrating examination of 'the negotiation between continuity and discontinuity' in the story 'Various Miracles.' Vauthier examines the differing narrative structures of the seven 'miracles' described in the story, and the way they frustrate the reader's expectations. She also analyses the meaning of 'miracle,' and its relation to synchronicity and coincidence. Eventually she categorizes Shields as 'a postmodernist of the middle ground.'

– 'Writing about Writing: Carol Shields's "The Journal."' In *Contemporary Women Writing in Canada and Quebec*, edited by Georgiana M.M. Colvile, 331–47. Vol. 3 of Contemporary Women Writing in the Other Americas series. Lewiston, NY, and Lampeter: Edwin Mellen, 1996.

An analysis of the short story 'The Journal' in *Various Miracles*. Vauthier concentrates on the language and narrative strategies of the story, and the juxtaposition of the narrator's account of events with the account recorded in the protagonist's journal. She also considers whether Shields's narrative voice can be described as 'feminine,' and relates the story to current theories of women's autobiography.

– 'Ruptures in Carol Shields's *The Stone Diaries*.' *Anglophonia: French Journal of English Studies* 1 (1997): 177–92.

An analysis of the narrative lacunae in *The Stone Diaries*, which is critically acute, detailed, and sophisticated, but which overlaps to a certain extent with other articles on the same novel.

Wachtel, Eleanor. Introduction. *Room of One's Own* 13.1/2 (1989): 1–5.

In this short introduction to 'The Carol Shields Issue,' Wachtel describes what she perceives as a shift in Shields's style, around 1985, to a more 'whimsical, non-naturalistic ... post-modern' mode than she employed in her earlier work.

Weil, Herb. 'From "Dying for Love" to "Mrs Turner": Narrative Control in Stories by Carol Shields.' In *Contemporary Manitoba Writers: New Critical Studies*, edited by Kenneth James Hughes, 163–76. Winnipeg: Turnstone P, 1990.

An examination of the relationships among narrator, characters, 'implied author,' and readers, this essay raises several important issues but unfortunately does not pursue them very far. The analysis of 'Mrs Turner' recalls Vauthier's without extending it significantly, and the comparison between four stories in terms of their 'effect of autobiographic truth' is interesting but sketchy.

Werlock, Abby H.P. 'Canadian Identity and Women's Voices: The Fiction of Sandra Birdsell and Carol Shields.' In *Canadian Women Writing Fiction*, edited by Mickey Pearlman, 126–41. Jackson: UP of Mississippi, 1993.

Werlock advances the slightly dubious argument that Shields depicts 'fictional women who may be profitably viewed as metaphorical of the Canadian condition,' and also claims unequivocally that Shields is the 'literary daughter' of earlier Canadian women writers. While overemphasizing the national aspect, Werlock nevertheless offers some interesting points about the figurations of women's reading and writing in Shields's texts.

Williams, David. 'Re-imagining a Stone Angel: The Absent Autobiographer of *The Stone Diaries*.' In *O Canada: Essays on Canadian Literature and Culture*, edited by Jørn Carlsen, 126–41. Aarhus, Denmark: Aarhus UP, 1995.

Williams compares the autobiographical forms used in *The Stone Diaries* and Margaret Laurence's *The Stone Angel*, contrasting the tangible presence of Hagar in Laurence's text with the absence of Daisy from Shields's. He argues that

Shields's creation of a postmodern, decentred subject involves an undercutting of Laurence's totalizing metaphor of the stone angel. He also explores the imaginative principle which underlies Daisy's 'autobiography,' and her creative construction of other lives and other points of view.

Williamson, David. 'Seven Steps to Point-Of-View Perfection.' *Prairie Fire* 16.1 (Spring 1995): 105–14.

Taking Shields's first seven solo novels in turn, Williamson fluently discusses her shifts of perspective, her prose style, humour, characterization, and plots. He analyses, in particular, her strategy of 'pairing' – of books, characters, and so on – and the historical and cultural research which underpins some of her work.

D. Selected Theses

Anderson, Marjorie. 'The Affirmative Feminism of Four Women Writers of the Nineteenth and Twentieth Centuries.' Ph.D. diss., University of Manitoba, 1994.

Hammill, Faye. 'Inspiration and Imitation: Responses to Canadian Literary Culture in the Work of Frances Brooke, Susanna Moodie, Sara Jeannette Duncan, L.M. Montgomery, Margaret Atwood and Carol Shields.' Ph.D. diss., University of Birmingham, 1999.

Hansen, Nina. 'Contradiction and Correspondence: Artful Ambiguities in Carol Shields's *The Stone Diaries*.' M.A. thesis, University of Copenhagen, 1997.

Hendriks, Hanneke. 'Love, Marriage and Compromise in Carol Shields's Novels.' Ph.D. diss., Nijimegen University, Holland, 1996.

Kruk, Laurie Ann. 'Voices of the "Concerned Middle": The Short Stories of Six Canadian Women Writers (Edna Alford, Sandra Birdsell, Joan Clark, Elisabeth Harvor, Carol Shields, Janette Turner Hospital).' Ph.D. diss., University of Western Ontario, 1992.

Léger, Benoit. '*Miracles divers* de Carol Shields suivi de traduire la polyphonie.' M.A. thesis, McGill University, 1991.

Magrath, Jane L. 'The Resurrection of the Author: *Possession, Swann* and *Changing Heaven* (A.S. Byatt, Carol Shields, Jane Urquhart).' M.A. thesis, University of Guelph, 1992.

Morgan, Patricia Joan. 'Transgressive Play: Narrative Strategies in the Novels and Short Stories of Carol Shields.' Ph.D. diss., York University, Toronto, 1997.

Roy, Wendy. '"An Assemblage of Dark Voids and Unbridgeable Gaps": Engendering Autobiography in Carol Shields's *The Stone Diaries*.' M.A. thesis, University of Saskatchewan, 1997.

Sydney, Margaret Hill. '"She Must Write Her Self": Feminist Poetics of Reconstruction and Inscription. Six Canadian Women Writing (Daphne Marlatt, Carol Shields, Betsy Warland, Madeleine Monette, Madeleine Ouelette-Michalska, France Theoret).' M.A. thesis, Carleton University, 1998.

III. Films

'Carol Shields.' 1985. A documentary film broadcast on Access Network, Canada.

Swann. 1996. Directed by Anna Benson Gyles; screenplay by David Young; starring Brenda Fricker, Miranda Richardson, Sean Hewitt. Released at the Toronto Film Festival.

The Enduring Enigma of Susanna Moodie. 1997. Directed by Patrick Crowe; produced by Keith Clarkson, Upper Canada Moving Picture Company (Toronto). Shields appears in the film as a talking head to comment on Moodie and read from *Small Ceremonies*.

This bibliography contains all the critical material I was able to trace at the time of writing, and I apologize if there are any omissions. I would like to thank Carol Shields for her patient assistance with factual details, and also Julie Ho, Patrick Crowe, Edna Hajnal, Dee Goertz, and Nina Hansen for help with the references.

Contributors

Kathy Barbour is Associate Professor of creative writing at Hanover College in Indiana. She has published a number of creative essays and poems.

Chiara Briganti is Professor of English and women's studies at Carleton College in Minnesota. She has published widely on nineteenth- and twentieth-century British and Commonwealth literature. She has written a book on father-daughter incest; she is working with a colleague on a book on E.H. Young and the domestic novel; and she is also writing a book on Storm Jameson.

Edward Eden is Associate Professor of English at Hanover College. He has published work on Sarah Orne Jewett, Toni Morrison, and Frederick Douglass.

Melissa Pope Eden is Associate Professor of English at Hanover College, where she teaches women's literature. She has published two interviews with Isabel Allende.

Sarah Gamble is Senior Lecturer in English at the University of Northumbria at Newcastle, UK. She is the author of *Angela Carter: Writing from the Front Line* (1997) and editor of *The Routledge Critical Guide to Feminism and Postfeminism*

(1999). She is currently working on a guide to Angela Carter criticism.

Dee Goertz is Professor of English at Hanover. She has published articles on Angela Carter and James Joyce.

Faye Hammill teaches English and postcolonial literature at Cardiff University in Wales. Her research interests are in Canadian literature, women's writing between the wars, and contemporary fiction. She has previously published two articles on Shields's work, and she has also recently published on Margaret Atwood, Frances Brooke, Stella Gibbons, and Sara Jeannette Duncan.

Lisa Johnson teaches women's literature at Lenoir-Rhyne College in North Carolina. She is the editor and contributing author of *Jane Sexes It Up: True Confessions of Feminist Desire*, and has published articles on representations of women in film and television, as well as in American literature.

Dianne Osland is Senior Lecturer in the Department of English at the University of Newcastle, New South Wales, Australia. She has a particular interest in the narrative strategies of novel and romance. She has published widely on subjects such as Australian writing, medieval romance, Henry Fielding, E.L. Doctorow, and the relationship of Daniel Defoe and John Fowles. She has published recently on eighteenth-century and contemporary fiction, and is currently collaborating on a study of 'designing women' from *Arcadia* to *Jane Eyre*.

Wendy Roy is a postdoctoral fellow at the University of British Columbia, where she is researching women's travel writing in Canada. She has published essays on Canadian writers Margaret Laurence, Carol Shields, and Anna Jameson.

Carol Shields is Chancellor Emeritus at the University of

Winnipeg and Professor Emerita at the University of Manitoba. She is a 1957 graduate of Hanover College and earned an M.A. in English at the University of Ottawa in 1975. Since 1972, she has published over twenty books, including fiction, poetry, drama, and criticism. She is best known for her 1993 novel, *The Stone Diaries*, which was a finalist for the Booker Prize and won the Pulitzer Prize for Fiction in 1995.

Index